Writing
in
Society

Writing

in

Society

Raymond

Williams

VERSO

London · New York

153340

First published 1983
This edition published by Verso 1991
© Raymond Williams 1983
All rights reserved

Verso
UK: 6 Meard Street, London W1V 3HR
USA: 29 West 35th Street, New York, NY 10001-2291

Verso is the imprint of New Left Books

ISBN 0 86091 772 X

Typeset in Times by Comset Graphic Designs
Printed in Great Britain by Biddles Ltd, Guildford

Contents

Acknowledgements

The following sources of original delivery or publication are acknowledged: *Drama in a Dramatised Society*, Inaugural Lecture as Professor of Drama, Cambridge 1974, published by Cambridge University Press; *Form and Meaning: Hippolytus and Phedre*, Cambridge English Faculty Lecture, 1977; *On Dramatic Dialogue and Monologue*, Cambridge seminars and Faculty lectures, 1980-83; an earlier version of sections (ii) and (iii) published in *Teaching the Text*, ed. N. Bryson and S. Kappeler, Routledge and Kegan Paul 1983; *Notes on English Prose, 1780-1950*, revised from Introduction to Volume II of *Pelican Book of English Prose*, 1969; *Hume, Reasoning and Experience* in *The English Mind*, ed. H. S. Davies and G. Watson, Cambridge University Press 1964; *The Fiction of Reform* in Times Literary Supplement, March 25 1977, copyright Times Newspapers Limited; *Forms of English Fiction in 1848*, Essex Conference on the Sociology of Literature, 1977, Proceedings published by University of Essex, 1978; *The Reader in Hard Times*, from British Council *Contrasts* volume, ed. G. Storey; *Cambridge English Past and Present* and *Beyond Cambridge English*, retirement lectures April 25 and 26 1983, printed in shortened version in London Review of Books, July 1983; *Crisis in English Studies*, Cambridge English Faculty lecture March 1981, printed in New Left Review 129, 1981; *Region and Class in the English Novel* in *The Uses of Fiction: Essays on the Modern Novel in Honour of Arnold Kettle,* ed. Douglas Jefferson and Graham Martin, reprinted by permission of Open University Press; *The Ragged-Arsed Philanthropists*, Tressell Memorial Lecture, Hastings 1982; *On First Looking Into 'New Lines'*, unpublished, 1956; *The Tenses of Imagination*, based on lectures at University College of Wales, Aberystwyth 1978.

I am grateful to my wife and to Francis Mulhern for much editorial help.

R.W.

Writing

'And what are you going to write about, dear?'
'My dear aunt, one doesn't write *about* anything, one just *writes*.'

Orwell, recalling this joke from *Punch*, thought it was a 'perfectly justified criticism of current literary cant'. Is it? Between the simple prejudice of *Punch* and the most extreme assertions of 'the autonomy of the writing process' there is a set of problems which are unlikely to be solved by some flat commonsense. In modern industrial societies writing has been in effect naturalized. It is then easy to assume that the process itself is straightforward, once the basic skills have been mastered in childhood. There is then only the question of what to write *about*. Attention is transferred to knowledge, facts, experience, imagination: properties that can be discussed as if on their own. Yet from some other part of the mind there is another set of apparently straightforward questions: about writing well or badly; about being elegant or witty or forceful or jargon-ridden or clumsy or boring. Many people try to resolve the two sets of questions by asserting a regular relation between the properties and the qualities. A clear mind produces clear writing. An adequately informed mind gets its facts across without difficulty. A powerful imagination enlivens writers and moves readers. Commonsense and 'practical criticism' agree on this: that there are discoverable and demonstrable relations between the properties and the qualities.

It is a very simple position, yet it cannot be simply denied. Its first difficulty is its tendency to exclude history. We do not have to read very far to discover how many ways there are of writing well or otherwise. Some of these remain as differences between individuals, but many do not. There are both relatively obvious and relatively subtle differences in the practice of writing in different periods, and these spread across otherwise diverse individuals. In grammar and spelling, in effective vocabularies, in the structure and composition of sentences, there are observable social and historical changes. This is to take only the most visible practical elements. Once we examine also the changing methods of telling a story, of writing a play, or of presenting an argument, it is clear that there is a history of writing in these more general senses: an important history of *forms of composition*. Where does this leave the argument about the relations between the properties and the qualities?

History, also, can be flattened by commonsense. It can be taken for granted that though the methods changed, in these recorded ways, the purposes have been constant, so that there are still regular relations between the properties of individual minds and the qualities of individual pieces of writing. Perhaps there are, but they are unlikely to be seen, in any convincing way, if history is taken to be a set of general and relatively external changes, within which both individual minds and the qualities of writing go on more or less unchanged. What is excluded, in this way of looking at the matter, is the whole series of changing relationships which are evident in the changing practice of writing.

These relationships, adequately seen, are in themselves social and historical relationships, with their direct evidence in forms of writing. It is not first a matter of looking for social and historical evidence that is there *alongside* the writing, in all other kinds of activities. That evidence will eventually enlighten us, and suggest many new questions about the writing, even supply some answers. But between an enclosed kind of study of a body of writing marked off as 'literature' and a reduced kind of study of political, military, economic and generalized social facts marked off as 'history', there is an important and neglected area of evidence and questions: in the practical history of writing and of forms of writing, and in what these can show us of how, in this increasingly important practice, people assumed, developed, extended, realized and changed their relationships. It is with this kind of evidence and this set of questions that the essays collected in this book, from work over twenty years, are primarily concerned.

What ought also to be said, though, is that there is a body of evidence and a set of questions about writing itself, which ought not to be overlooked or hurried through to what could be a set of simply empirical applications. One of the effects of the naturalization of writing, and in the last two centuries the effective naturalization of print, is that the essential history of these major transformations, even in their most general terms, is overlooked or is treated as mere generality. Yet this history, at every stage, interlocks with more local and more demonstrable changes. There really is a world of difference, beyond the more accessible evidence of interests and content, between the writing of Shakespeare for an oral public performance by a number of voices and actions, and the writing of George Eliot for silent print-reading by a temporarily separated individual. What can be grasped in this obvious example is relevant, with many differences of degree, in all forms of writing, once the principle of the conditions of composition as a fact in the process of composition has been understood.

Yet it is more, even, than the conditions of composition: the kinds of 'audience' or 'reader' in mind or addressed; the available forms and conventions; the state of the language itself. Writing, as such, has a history, and has specific properties. I have discussed these more fully elsewhere, especially in my essays in *Contact* (1981) and in the chapter on 'Means of Production' in *Culture* (1981), but some main points can be repeated here.

First, writing is distinct from most other forms of communication in that its basic skills—putting words into a conventional material form and being able to read them—do not come necessarily as parts of the basic process of growing up in a society. A spoken language, in terms of an ability both to speak and to understand, comes as part of the normal process of growing up in a particular society, unless there are some individual physical disabilities. Writing, by contrast, has been from the beginning a systematic skill that has to be taught and learned. Thus the introduction of writing, and all the subsequent stages of its development, are intrinsically new forms of social relationship. There has been great variation in making these skills available, and this has had major effects on the relationships embodied in writing in diverse historical and cultural conditions. Thus we can speak of English literature over an extent of some six centuries but of English literacy, necessarily, in much more problematic ways. It was only at some point in the nineteenth century, very late in the record of English literature, that the majority of English people could write and read. It is impossible that this had no effect on what was written and what was read.

At the same time this does not mean that there was no composition in words, of a generally accessible kind, before this general literacy. From a general literacy we can read back all kinds of writing as 'literature', or invent the retrospective hybrid of 'oral literature'. But this flattens some of the most important facts and relationships. There is the fact that the early reservation of writing to certain classes of clerk and scholar introduced a problem about the status of knowledge and record, in such central matters as history and law, in societies in which effective access was socially differentiated. When writing and reading spread more widely, and when printing came to ensure both more accurate reproduction and more widespread distribution, there were still major variations in access and, as the importance of writing and printing increased, in the possibility of effective contribution. Even today, after more than a century of general literacy, it would be wrong to say that there is effectively equal access to written and printed material or anything like effectively equal opportunities to contribute to it. There are important individual differences in this, but there are also basic social differences.

What is a matter of degree, after the coming of general literacy, is often a matter of kind in the centuries before it. It is never only a question of readers—of the 'reading public'—highly differential as that has been. It is also a question of where the writers and the writing came and come from: what relationships, what shared interests and assumptions, the actual social differentials of writing and reading compose. It is genuinely difficult for someone who has spent a working life with print, and has had access, through it, to writing in societies quite unlike his or her own, to take seriously the idea that the conditions the reader shares with those available writers, through the common property of the texts, are socially specific conditions, which cannot be simply read back as the central truths of all active writing and reading.

This problem bears most heavily in cases of what were originally or primarily 'oral' forms. It is obvious that almost all oral forms we now know of, except those of our own time which are usually placed at some distance from 'writing' and 'literature', have in one way or another been written down, and can thus seem to be absorbed into more typical writing and reading conditions. But this 'solution' is much too simple. It is impossible to read 'dramatic writing' adequately unless we are aware that it is writing for speech in many voices and for action. In its essential composition it is not a text for silent reading, though eventually that specialized and different use may be made of it. I have explored these problems previously, mainly in modern drama though I attempted a more general examination in *Drama in Performance* (1954 and 1968). In two essays in this book I have extended this work, and looked for some new kinds of close analysis, in relation to the dramatic writing of Euripides and Racine, and to the complex functions of dialogue and monologue in Shakespeare.

Yet there can then be recognition of these questions as related only to a specialized form, 'drama', which can be put at some relative distance from 'literature' even while reclaiming its most important examples. The full questions are very much wider than this. In the essays grouped in the second and third parts of this book I examine a range of evidence and questions which cannot be displaced to a separated and specialized form, but are inherent in what are taken to be unambiguously 'literary' forms. I have looked at several kinds of writing with what come through as two main questions. First, about the relations between writing and both speech and the written representation of speech. Second, about the changing relationships, in several kinds of writing, between writers and assumed or intended readers, in conditions that developed from uneven and partial literacy to a more general literacy in which there were persistent inequalities in access to writing and reading. The essays were not written as a connected argument, for there were always more particular works in view, but an effective continuity of interests and themes seems to be evident. Moreover, in the range of the essays, I am glad to be able to emphasize that the development of this kind of work, at its most specialized in the analysis of dialogue and monologue in Shakespeare, ought not to be separated from other more familiar and more general questions. It should, though this always needs to be very precisely done, be eventually connected and reconnected with them.

The lectures grouped in the fourth part of the book may have their own interest as one of the forms of writing for speech. Unusually, in these cases, I lectured from a full text, with some consciousness that I would be speaking it but still with an evident difference from the verbatim lectures, given from a few or no notes, collected in *The English Novel from Dickens to Lawrence* (1971) or represented here by the talks on Tressell and 1848. As it happens, the lectures were given with an exceptional consciousness of particular occasions and audiences, yet the prepared written forms served to connect, obviously, with a more general reading.

In the essays grouped in the fifth part I am concerned with the questions of uneven and privileged access to writing and to print in a fully modern context of relationships between social classes. The discussion of *The Ragged-Trousered Philanthropists* engages these directly, and there is a broader discussion in the analysis of what is meant by 'region' and 'class' in the modern novel. From my own social history I have been very aware of these questions and problems, not only as they bear on analysis and scholarship, but in my own work as a writer. The concluding essay, on 'the tenses of imagination', is a direct reflection on this, in what I see as a general but often only externally examined situation.

It should be said, finally, that the essays and lectures collected in this book have a specific relation to the theoretical work I have published in recent years, notably in *Marxism and Literature* (1977) and *Culture* (1981). In certain key areas, these essays and lectures are the working papers through which the theoretical arguments were directed. At certain points in those arguments I moved, necessarily, beyond forms of writing, in the received sense. I was concerned with a major cultural shift of our own period, in which the relations between writing and speech, between writing and dramatic action, and then, in quite new ways, between writing and the composition of images, were changed or were newly developed in radio, television and film. It was clear that these new relations and forms were important in themselves. But, also, in their increasing centrality, they allowed us to see, in some new ways, the historically specific relations between writing, print and silent reading which had been taken for granted, and at the same time privileged, in the four centuries in which these relations were dominant and were often, specifically in 'literary' studies, assumed to be universal.

There are now many occasions for work before and after this period of the dominant relations of print. Yet within this major period itself the new perspectives allow certain questions that were always necessary but that within the orthodoxies of literary studies had been crowded out or treated as peripheral. What had been seen as the *normal* relations of writing and reading, enclosing a given set of questions, could now be seen as specific and often problematic or even precarious relations, in the uneven distribution of writing and reading, and in the uncertain relations between forms of writing and forms of speech.

These new questions will be decisive in the new cultural period we have already entered, in which print and silent reading are again only one of several cultural forms, only one even of the forms of writing. Yet the writing for print is still there, from the past, and is still, in itself, of major importance. That is why these essays and lectures, mainly concerned with such writing but setting it beside earlier kinds of dramatic writing and considering it, throughout, in its full social relations, seemed worth bringing together, in a particular emphasis.

1

Drama in a Dramatized Society

The problems of drama, in any of its many perspectives, are now serious enough to be genuinely interesting and indeed to provoke quite new kinds of question. Real and nominal continuities can of course be traced, but my own emphasis is on a transformed situation: one that I have tried to indicate in my title. Drama is no longer, for example, coextensive with theatre; many dramatic performances are now in film and television studios. In the theatre itself—national theatre or street theatre—there is an exceptional variety of intention and method. New kinds of text, new kinds of notation, new media and new conventions press actively alongside the texts and conventions that we think we know, but that I find problematic just because these others are there. Dramatic time and sequence in a play of Shakespeare, the intricate rhythms and relationships of chorus and three actors in a Greek tragedy: these, I believe, become active in new ways as we look at a cutting bench or an editing machine, in a film or television studio, or as we see new relations between actor and audience in the improvised theatre of the streets and the basements.

Again, we have never as a society acted so much or watched so many others acting. Watching, of course, carries its own problems. Watching itself has become problematic. For drama was originally occasional, in a literal sense: at the Festival of Dionysus in Athens or in medieval England on the day of Corpus Christi when the waggons were pulled through the streets. The innovating commercial theatres of Elizabethan London moved beyond occasion but still in fixed localities: a capital city, then a tour of provincial cities. There was to be both expansion and contraction. In Restoration London two patent theatres—the monopoly centres of legitimate drama—could hardly be filled. The provincial theatre-building of the eighteenth century, the development of variety theatres and music-halls, the expansion of London's West End theatres in the second half of the nineteenth century: all these qualified occasion but in the light of what was to come were mainly quantitative changes. It is in our own century, in cinema, in radio and in television, that the audience for drama has gone through a qualitative change. I mean not only that *Battleship Potemkin* and *Stagecoach* have been seen by hundreds of millions of people, in many places and over a continuing period, nor only that a play by Ibsen or O'Neill is now seen simultaneously by ten to twenty million people on television. This, though the figures are enormous, is still an understandable extension. It means that for the first time a majority of the population has regular and constant access to drama, beyond occasion or season. But what is really new—so new I think that it is difficult to see its significance—is that it is not just a matter of audiences for particular plays. It is that drama, in quite new ways, is built into the rhythms of everyday life. On television alone it is normal for viewers—the substantial majority of the population—to see anything up to three hours of drama, of course drama of several different kinds, a day. And not just one day; almost every day. This is part of what I mean by a dramatized society. In earlier periods drama was important at a festival, in a season, or as a conscious journey to a theatre; from honouring Dionysus or Christ to taking in a show. What we now have is drama as habitual experience: more in a week, in many cases, than most human beings would previously have seen in a lifetime.

Can this be merely extension: a thing like eating more beef muscle or wearing out more shirts than any ancestor could have conceived as a widespread human habit? It certainly doesn't look like a straight-line extension. To watch simulated action, of several recurrent kinds, not just occasionally but regularly, for longer than eating and for up to half as long as work or sleep; this, in our kind of society, as majority behaviour, is indeed a new form and pressure. It would of course be easy to excise or exorcise this remarkable fact if we could agree, as some propose, that what millions of people are so steadily watching is all or for the most part rubbish. That would be no exorcism: if it were true it would make the fact even more extraordinary. And it is in any case not true. Only dead cultures have scales that are reliable. There are discernible, important and varying proportions of significant and trivial work, but for all that, today, you can find kitsch in a national theatre and an intensely original play in a police series. The critical discriminations are at once important and unassumable in advance. But in one perspective they pale before the generality of the habit itself. What is it, we have to ask, in us and in our contemporaries, that draws us repeatedly to these hundreds and thousands of simulated actions; these plays, these representations, these dramatizations?

It depends where you ask that question from. I ask it from watching and from contributing to the extraordinary process itself. But I can hear—who can not?—some familiar voices: the grave merchants whose apprentices and shopboys slipped away to Bankside; the heads of households whose wives, and the heads of colleges whose students, admitted to read English, would read novels and comedies in the morning. These sober men would know what to say about contemporary California, where you can watch your first movie at six-thirty in the morning and if you really try can see seven or eight more before you watch the late movie in the next recurrent small hours. Fiction; acting; idle dreaming and vicarious spectacle; the simultaneous satisfaction of sloth and appetite; distraction from distraction by distraction. It is a heavy, even a gross catalogue of our errors, but now millions of people are sending the catalogue back, unopened. Till the eyes tire, millions of us watch the shadows of shadows and find them substance; watch scenes, situations, actions, exchanges, crises. The slice of life, once a project of naturalist drama, is now a voluntary, habitual, internal rhythm; the flow of action and acting, of representation and performance, raised to a new convention, that of a basic need.

We cannot know what would have happened if there had been, for example, outside broadcasting facilities at the Globe. In some measure, at least, we must retain the hypothesis of simple extension of access. Yet I would argue that what has happened is much more than this. There are indeed discoverable factors of a probably causal kind. We are all used to saying—and it still means something—that we live in a society which is at once more mobile and more complex, and therefore, in some crucial respects, relatively more unknowable, relatively more opaque than most societies of the past, and yet which is also more insistently pressing, penetrating and even determining. What we try to resolve from the opaque and the unknowable, in one mode by statistics—which give us summaries and breakdowns,

moderately accurate summaries and even more accurate breakdowns, of how we live and what we think—is offered to be resolved
in another mode by one kind of dramatization. Miner and power
worker, minister and general, burglar and terrorist, schizophrenic
and genius; a back-to-back home and a country house; metropolitan
apartment and suburban villa; bed-sitter and hill-farm: images,
types, representations: a relationship beginning, a marriage breaking
down; a crisis of illness or money or dislocation or disturbance. It is
not only that all these are represented. It is that much drama now
sees its function in this experimental, investigative way; finding a
subject, a setting, a situation; and with some emphasis on novelty,
on bringing some of that kind of life into drama.

Of course all societies have had their dark and unknowable areas,
some of them by agreement, some by default. But the clear public
order of much traditional drama has not, for many generations,
been really available to us. It was for this reason that the great
naturalist dramatists, from Ibsen, left the palaces, the forums and
the streets of earlier actions. They created, above all, rooms; enclosed rooms on enclosed stages; rooms in which life was centred but inside which people waited for the knock on the door, the letter or the
message, the shout from the street, to know what would happen to
them; what would come to intersect and to decide their own still intense and immediate lives. There is a direct cultural continuity, it
seems to me, from those enclosed rooms, enclosed and lighted framed rooms, to the rooms in which we watch the framed images of
television: at home, in our own lives, but needing to watch what is
happening, as we say, 'out there': not out there in a particular street
or a specific community but in a complex and otherwise unfocused
and unfocusable national and international life, where our area of
concern and apparent concern is unprecedentedly wide, and where
what happens on another continent can work through to our own
lives in a matter of days and weeks—in the worst image, in hours and
minutes. Yet our lives are still here, still substantially here, with the
people we know, in our own rooms, in the similar rooms of our
friends and neighbours, and they too are watching: not only for
public events, or for distraction, but from a need for images, for representations, of what living is now like, for this kind of person and
that, in this situation and place and that. It is perhaps the full
development of what Wordsworth saw at an early stage, when the

crowd in the street (the new kind of urban crowd, who are physically very close but still absolute strangers) had lost any common and settled idea of man and so needed representations—the images on hoardings, the new kinds of sign—to simulate if not affirm a human identity: what life is and looks like beyond this intense and anxious, but also this pushed and jostled, private world of the head.

That is one way of putting it; the new need, the new exposure—the need and exposure in the same movement—to a flow of images, of constant representations, as distinct from less complex and less mobile cultures in which a representation of meaning, a spectacle of order, is clearly, solidly, rigidly present, at certain fixed points, and is then more actively affirmed on a special occasion, a high day or a festival, the day of the play or the procession. But there is never only need and exposure: each is both made and used. In the simplest sense our society has been dramatized by the inclusion of constant dramatic representation as a daily habit and need. But the real process is more active than that.

Drama is a special kind of use of quite general processes of presentation, representation, signification. The raised place of power—the eminence of the royal platform—was built historically before the raised place of the stage. The presentation of power, in hierarchical groupings, in the moving emphases of procession, preceded the now comparable modes of a represented dramatic state. Gods were made present or made accessible by precise movements, precise words, in a known conventional form. Drama is now so often associated with what are called myth and ritual that the general point is easily made. But the relation cannot be reduced to the usual loose association. Drama is a precise separation of certain common modes for new and specific ends. It is neither ritual which discloses the God, nor myth which requires and sustains repetition. It is specific, active, interactive composition: an action not an act; an open practice that has been deliberately abstracted from temporary practical or magical ends; a complex opening of ritual to public and variable action; a moving beyond myth to dramatic *versions* of myth and history. It was this active variable experimental drama—not the closed world of known signs and meanings—that came through in its own right and in its own power; significantly often in periods of crisis and change, when an order was known and still formally present but when experience was pressing it, testing it, conceiving breaks and alternatives; the dramatic possibility of what might be done within what was known to have been done, and each could be present, and mutually, contradictorily potent, in specific acted forms. We need to see this especially now, when myth and ritual, in their ordinary senses, have been broken up by historical development, when they are little more, in fact, than the nostalgia or the rhetoric of one kind of scholar and thinker, and yet when the basic social processes, of presentation, representation, signification have never been more important. Drama broke from fixed signs, established its permanent distance from myth and ritual and from the hierarchical figures and processions of state; broke for precise historical and cultural reasons into a more complex, more active and more questioning world. There are relativities within its subsequent history, and the break has been made many more times than once. Any system of signs, presenting and representing, can become incorporated into a passive order, and new strange images, of repressed experience, repressed people, have again to break beyond this. The drama of any period, including our own, is an intricate set of practices of which some are incorporated—the known rhythms and movements of a residual but still active system—and some are exploratory—the difficult rhythms and movements of an emergent representation, rearrangement, new identification. Under real pressures these distinct kinds are often intricately and powerfully fused; it is rarely a simple case of the old drama and the new.

But drama, which separated out, did not separate out altogether. Congruous and comparable practices exist in other parts of the society as in the drama, and these are often interactive: the more interactive as the world of fixed signs is less formal. Indeed what we often have now is a new convention of deliberate overlap. Let me give the simplest example. Actors now often move from a part in a play, which we can all specify as dramatic art, to deploy the same or similar skills in the hired but rapturous discovery of a cigar or a facecream. They may be uneasy about it but, as they say, it's better than resting. It's still acting after all; they are no more personally committed to that cigar than to the character of that bluff inspector, for which they were also hired. Somebody wrote it, somebody's directing it: you're still in the profession. Commercials in Britain have conventional signs to tell you they're coming, but the overlap of method, of skill and of actual individuals is a small and less easily read sign of a more general process, in which the breaks are much harder to discern.

Our present society, in ways it is merely painful to reiterate, is sufficiently dramatic in one obvious sense. Actions of a kind and scale that attract dramatic comparisons are being played out in ways that leave us continually uncertain whether we are spectators or participants. The specific vocabulary of the dramatic mode—drama itself, and then tragedy, scenario, situation, actors, performances, roles, images—is continually and conventionally appropriated for these immense actions. It would moreover be easier, one can now often feel, if only actors acted, and only dramatists wrote scenarios. But we are far past that. On what is called the public stage, or in the public eye, improbable but plausible figures continually appear to represent us. Specific men are magnified to temporary universality, and so active and complex is this process that we are often invited to see them rehearsing their roles, or discussing their scenarios. Walter Bagehot once distinguished between a real ruling class and a theatrical ruling show: the window of Windsor, he argued, in his innovating style of approving and elegant cynicism, is needed to be shown, to be paraded, before a people who could never comprehend the more complex realities of power. I watched this morning the televised State opening of Parliament. It is one thing to say that it was pure theatre; it is harder to see, and to say, that beyond its residual pageantry was another more naturalized process which is also in part a cousin of theatre. Monarchs, of course, have always done something like this, or had it done for them. Those who lasted were conscious of their images even if they called them their majesties. Moreover, like many actors, people find roles growing on them: they come to fit the part, as he who would play the King. What is new, really, is not in them but in us.

It is often genuinely difficult to believe in any part of this pervasive dramatization. If we see it in another period or in or from another place, it visibly struts and frets, its machinery starts audibly creaking. In moments of crisis, we sometimes leave this social theatre or, as easily, fall asleep in it. But these are not only roles and scenarios; they are conventions. When you can see a convention, become really conscious of it, it is probably already breaking down. Beyond what many people can see as the theatricality of our image-conscious public world, there is a more serious, more effective, more deeply rooted drama: the dramatization of consciousness itself. 'I speak for Britain' runs the written line of that miming public figure, though since we were let in on the auditions, and saw other actors trying for the part, we may have our reservations; we may even say 'Well I'm here and you don't speak for me'. 'Exactly,' the figure replies, with an unruffled confidence in his role, for now a different consciousness, a more profound dramatization, begins to take effect; 'you speak for yourself, but I speak for Britain.' 'Where is that?', you may think to ask, looking wonderingly around. On a good day from a high place you can see about fifty miles. But you know some places, you remember others; you have memories, definitions and a history.

Yet at some point along that continuum, usually in fact very early, you have—what? Representations; typifications; active images; active parts to play that people are playing, or sometimes refusing to play. The specific conventions of this particular dramatization—a country, a society, a period of history, a crisis of civilization; these conventions are not abstract. They are profoundly worked and reworked in our actual living relationships. They are our ways of seeing and knowing, which every day we put into practice, and while the conventions hold, while the relationships hold, most practice confirms them. One kind of specific autonomy—thisness, hereness—is in part free of them; but this is usually an autonomy of privacy, and the private figure—the character of the self—is already widely offered to be appropriated in one or other of these dramatized forms: producer or consumer, married or single, member or exile or vagrant. Beyond all these there is what we call the irreducible: the still unaccommodated man. But the process has reached in so far that there are now, in practice, conventions of isolation itself. The lonely individual is now a common type: that is an example of what I mean by a dramatic convention, extending from play to consciousness. Within a generation of that naturalist drama which created the closed room—the room in which people lived but had to wait for news from outside—another movement had created another centre: the isolated figure, the stranger, who in Strindberg's *Road to Damascus* was still actively looking for himself and his world, testing and discarding this role and that image, this affirming memory and that confirming situation, with each in turn breaking down until he came back, each time, to the same place. Half a century later two ultimately isolated figures, their world not gone but never created, sat down on the road waiting for what?—call it Godot—to come. Let's go, they said, but they didn't move. A decade later other more radically isolated figures were seen as buried to their neck, and all that was finally audible, within that partial and persuasive convention, was a cry, a breath. Privacy; deprivation. A lost public world; an uncreatable public world.

These images challenge and engage us, for to begin with, at least, they were images of dissent, of conscious dissent from fixed forms. But that other miming, the public dramatization, is so continuous, so insistent, that dissent, alone, has proved quite powerless against it. Dissent, that is, like any modern tragic hero, can die but no more. And critical dissent, a public form you can carry around to lectures or even examinations: it too comes back to the place where it started, and may or may not know it for the first time. A man I knew from France, a man who had learned, none better, the modes of perception that are critical dissent, said to me once, rather happily: 'France, you know, is a bad bourgeois novel.' I could see how far he was right: the modes of dramatization, of fictionalization, which are active as social and cultural conventions, as ways not only of seeing but of organizing reality, are as he said: a bourgeois novel, its human types still fixed but losing some of their conviction; its human actions, its struggles for property and position, for careers and careering relationships, still as limited as ever but still bitterly holding the field, in an interactive public reality and public consciousness. 'Well, yes,' I said politely, 'England's a bad bourgeois novel too. And New York is a bad metropolitan novel. But there's one difficulty, at least I find it a difficulty. You can't send them back to the library. You're stuck with them. You have to read them over and over.' 'But critically', he said, with an engaging alertness. 'Still reading them'. I said.

I think that is where we now are. People have often asked me why, trained in literature and expressly in drama, making an ordinary career in writing and teaching dramatic history and analysis, I turned—*turned*—to what they would call sociology if they were quite sure I wouldn't be offended (some were sure the other way and I'm obliquely grateful to them). I could have said, debating the point, that Ruskin didn't turn from architecture to society; he saw society in architecture—in its styles, its shaping intentions, its structures of power and of feeling, its façades and its interiors and the relations between them; he could then learn to read both architecture and society in new ways. But I would prefer to speak for myself. I learned something from analysing drama which seemed to me effective not only as a way of seeing certain aspects of society but as a way of getting through to some of the fundamental conventions which we group as society itself. These, in their turn, make some of the problems of drama quite newly active. It was by looking both ways, at a stage and a text, and at a society active, enacted, in them, that I thought I saw the significance of the enclosed room—the room on the stage, with its new metaphor of the fourth wall lifted—as at once a dramatic and a social fact.

For the room is there, not as one scenic convention among all the possible others, but because it is an actively shaping environment—the particular structure within which we live—and also, in continuity, in inheritance, in crisis—the solid form, the conventional declaration, of how we are living and what we value. This room on the stage, this enclosed living room, where important things happen and where quite another order of importance arrives as news from a shut-off outside world; this room is a convention, now a habit, of theatre; but it is also, subtly and persistently, a personage, an actor: a set that defines us and can trap us: the alienated object that now represents us in the world. I have watched, fascinated, as that room has broken up; the furniture got rid of, a space cleared; people facing each other across an emptiness, with only the body, the body as object or the body as rhythm, to discover, to play with, to exhaust itself. But more important than this has been a dynamic process when the room is dissolved, for scene is no longer external and yet is still active, and what we see is a projection of observed, remembered and desired images. While Strindberg at the turn of the century was writing a new drama of moving images—a wall papered with faces; aspects of character and appearance dissolving, fragmenting, fusing, haunting; objects changing literally as you look at them; while Strindberg was writing this, beyond the capacity of the theatre of his time, other men, in quite different ways, were discovering means of making images move; finding the technical basis for the motion picture: the new mobility and with it the fade, the dissolve, the cut, the flashback, the voice over, the montage, that are technical forms but also, in new ways, modes of perceiving, of relating, of composing and of finding our way.

Again I heard, as if for the first time, what was still, by habit, called dramatic speech, even dialogue; heard it in Chekhov and noticed a now habitual strangeness: that the voices were no longer speaking to or at each other; were speaking with each other perhaps, with themselves in the presence of others. But there was a new composition, in which a group was speaking, yet a strange negative group; no individual ever quite finishing what he had begun to say, but intersecting, being intersected by the words of others, casual and distracted, words in their turn unfinished: a weaving of voices in which, though still negatively, the group was speaking and yet no single person was ever finally articulate. It is by now so normal a process, in writing dramatic speech, that it can be heard, any night, in a television serial, and this is not just imitation. It is a way of speaking and of listening, a specific rhythm of a particular consciousness; in the end a form of unfinished, transient, anxious relationship, which is there on the stage or in the text but which is also, pervasively, a structure of feeling in a precise contemporary world, in a period of history which has that familiar and complex transience. I don't think I could have understood these dramatic procedures as *methods*— that is to say, as significant general modes—if I had not been looking both ways. I could have seen them, perhaps, as techniques: a professional viewpoint but in my experience not professional enough, for it is where technique and method have either an identity or, as now commonly, a significant fracture, that all the hard questions of this difficult discipline begin.

Form and Meaning:
Hippolytus and *Phèdre*.

In his preface to *Phèdre* Racine wrote:

> ... je me suis très scrupuleusement attaché à suivre la fable.

But what is this fable? As in most cases of later understanding of classical 'fables' or 'myths', there is more than one written source, but in this as in other cases a predominant one, in the *Hippolytus* of Euripides. Racine records that he has taken some elements from Vergil and Plutarch, and that he has read Seneca and other *'Anciens'*. Yet he begins by saying that *Phèdre* is 'a tragedy of which the subject is taken from Euripides'. He adds that he has followed 'a slightly different route for the conduct of the action'.

It is in these terms, having noted the uncertainties of 'fable' and 'subject', that it is useful to make a direct comparison between *Hippolytus* and *Phèdre*, as an unusually interesting example of the structural relations between form and meaning. As a matter of general convenience I shall quote in English, though with reference to the original texts where necessary. The translations used are *Hippolytus*: E.T. Coleridge as amended in *The Complete Greek Drama*, ed. Oates and O'Neill, New York 1938 and *Phaedra*: Robert Lowell, in *The Classic Theatre*, IV, ed. Bentley, New York 1961. The important linguistic problems involved in these or any translations are not in the first instance decisive for the formal analysis proposed.

The key difference in form between *Hippolytus* and *Phèdre*, as more generally between 'classical' and 'neo-classical' drama, is between the use of a chorus and the use of *confidents*. I argued in *Modern Tragedy* that the chorus is the uniquely defining element of classical Greek drama:

The specific and varying relations between chorus and actors are its true dramatic relations... The known history is enacted by the three masked actors, who have separated out from the chorus but, as their sharing of roles and their formal relations with the chorus make clear, not separated out altogether. What the form then embodies is not an isolable metaphysical stance, rooted in individual experience, but a shared and indeed collective experience, at once and indistinguishably metaphysical and social, which is yet capable of great tension and subtlety, as in the dynamic isolation of the *kommos*, or the dramatically shifting yet formally controlling singing of the chorus. It is no accident that as this unique culture changed, the chorus was the crucial element of dramatic form which was weakened and eventually discarded.

This is especially clear in comparison with the neo-classical form. The communal basis of the Greek form, which by the fifth century B.C. had become, in the full sense, drama, by the distinction of two and then three actors is radically different from the aristocratic basis of the neo-classical plays. At some limited practical levels, chorus and *confident* have comparable functions. Information is given by exchanges between either chorus or *confident* and the (principal) actors. In more complex ways, responses to words and acts occur directly within these relations, as a dramatic presentation to the audience. Further, though then the differences become more evident, either the chorus or the *confident* can be an object of address for an actor: the local focus of speech which may, over the range, be directed to specific persons, in a relatively enclosed form of dramatic dialogue, or be directed through the nominal addressee to the audience.

These instrumental similarities have to be noted, but they can disguise a more essential formal shift. The chorus in *Hippolytus* are the women of Troezen. Their relations with the royal household are close and direct, but they are the relations of citizens. What they sing at the end of the play—'on all our citizens hath come this universal sorrow'—is the unity of social and metaphysical experience, embodying and containing the whole action, which is the essential element of the chorus as a form. By contrast the relations in *Phèdre* between principal actors and their *confidents* are simple local relations between masters or mistresses and their *servants*: Phèdre and her nurse Oenone; Hippolyte and his tutor Théramène; '*Madame*' Aricie and Ismène. The formal difference is a difference between social orders. There are no citizens in Racine. The drama is between ruling personages, supported by their servants, rather than within a royal household, in full view of the people of the city.

It is surprising how far this distinction takes us, in a comparison of meanings in the plays. What is remembered from the plays, or more generally from the 'fable' or 'myth', is the guilty love of Phaedra, wife of Theseus, for Hippolytus son of Theseus by an earlier marriage. It can be said that this is a desperate passion which destroys both Phaedra and Hippolytus, but this familiar formulation covers most of the relevant questions. Consider first the action which most clearly imperils Hippolytus: the false, self-protecting accusation by Phaedra that he has attempted to violate her. In Euripides this falsehood is a dying act:

> Yet shall my dying be another's curse, that he may learn not to exult at my misfortunes; but when he comes to share the self-same plague with me, he will take a lesson in wisdom.

The thematic emphasis of wisdom—*sophrosyne*—is important in the whole play, though it can at best only modify the act of falsehood itself: an act which is part of Phaedra's more general loss of control and judgment (ideas which the idea of *sophrosyne* attempts to unite). Racine, within a different social order and system of beliefs, was shocked by the falsehood in an interesting way. As he records in his Preface, he took care to render the action 'a little less odious', and a device was to hand:

> I believed that the calumny had something too low and dark about it to be put in the mouth of a princess who elsewhere has such noble and virtuous feelings. This lowness appeared to me more suitable for a nurse, who could have more servile inclinations, but who nevertheless only undertakes this false accusation to save the life and honour of her mistress. Phaedra agrees only because she is in an agitation of mind which puts her outside herself, and a moment later she reaches the intention of justifying the innocence [of Hippolytus] and declaring the truth.

It is significant enough that the action can be split between princess and servant, preserving virtue to rank. Actions of this kind between master and servant have been very common in post-Renaissance drama. They allow not only for baser actions and feelings among the base, but for what is often, in dramatic terms, an instrumental splitting of the principal character, in which the nominal master is full of

virtue and care and the nominal servant full of calculation and dis-
honour. In its full development this allowed the retention of privileged honour by its displacement to mere agents, as commonly between
lord and steward, ruler and deputy, landlord and bailiff. But in its
earliest stage it allows also for a paradoxical unity in division, where
the servant acts by consent or under actual orders and yet is still the
nominal (and often dramatically the 'real') agent. The social and
ethical flexibility of what is apparently only the device of the *confident* is then significant.

Yet the formal contrast cuts deeper even than this. Racine, in his
world, has shifted the whole dimension of motivation. It is not just a
matter of who tells the convenient lie, but a more general question of
the way in which the sources of any action are seen. In the ethics of
rank Racine may now seem further away from us than Euripides, but
in the matter of motivation he is so much nearer that we may even
miss the distinction, transposing a modern sense to Euripides. For
the second key difference in form between the two kinds of drama is
the dramatic status of the metaphysical dimension, which in
Euripides is explicit.

Hippolytus begins with a prologue by Aphrodite, in which she
gives her reasons for taking vengeance on Hippolytus, who has in-
sulted her by preferring hunting to love. It is by the design of the
goddess that Phaedra conceives her passion for Hippolytus, and that
Theseus comes to know of it and to punish his son. A second goddess, Artemis, who favours Hippolytus, arrives too late to save him
but grants honours to the city. This wholly distinct sense of divine
powers, which saturates Greek culture, is explained by Artemis:

> It was Aphrodite that would have it so, sating the fury of her soul. For
> this is law amongst us gods: none of us will thwart his neighbour's will,
> but ever we stand aloof.

Thus the whole course of human action and passion is seen as essentially determined by the deliberate but then often competitive or conflicting impulses of a diversity of gods. What may then come
through as arbitrary is part of the facts of the world; and within them
human beings, at times most clearly through suffering, have to learn
their relative powerlessness, as 'wisdom'.

In *Phèdre* the gods are not dramatically present. They have been distanced or excluded from the visible action, as in almost all post-medieval drama. Racine maintains a nominal continuity with the 'fable', or with Euripides. Phèdre speaks of

> those gods who have lit the fatal flame in all my blood, those gods who have found a cruel glory in seducing the heart of a weak mortal.

But the decisive metaphysical dimension is not in these formal allusions and references; it is indeed, as a dimension, problematic, in the way that Goldmann, writing of Racine, defined as the consciousness of a 'hidden god'. It is then not at the level of specific motivation, but at a deeper and more uncertain level of the consciousness of observation, judgment and punishment that what remains, dramatically, of the metaphysical is latent. This in turn opens a way for other kinds of motivation and contingency. What can be abstracted from both plays is the idea of an ungovernable sexual passion, in the memorable single figure of Phaedra: a tragic figure since Hippolytus is unobtainable and the passion only destroys. Yet this, which can be taken as a dominant reading from either play, and which offers a simple human continuity over and above both cultural and dramatic conditions, involves a typical displacement. It is at best secondary to discuss whether Euripides 'believed' in the gods as the direct source of human actions and desires. What the play shows is the passion as destructive, beyond moderation and control. It can then not be abstracted from the 'fable' as passion in itself: the tragic love story. The unified social and metaphysical dimension, explicitly controlling and limiting human possibilities of any such kind, encloses what we might now abstract. In Racine, at least explicitly there are no such absolute and unified limits. In a radically different social order, and within the altered status of the metaphysical, he looks for other conditions and contingencies.

He adds four of these to the main 'fable'. First, he has Thésée reported dead in the First Act: an event which in part releases Phèdre from her conventional obligation. Second, even before this false report, the character of Thésée has been powerfully described, by Hippolyte in his relation with Théramène, as that of a tyrant and reckless adulterer:

> So many others, whose names even have escaped him, too trusting souls whom his passion has cheated.

(The Lowell translation must be avoided here; he introduces a quite different and even opposite consciousness—...

> ... that long list
> Of women all refusing to resist...
> ...all deceived
> If their protestations can be believed).

Thus, before Phèdre's passion is acknowledged or declared, her husband is both wicked and (apparently) dead.

It is clear how this already shapes a different situation, in which Phèdre can be more sympathetically or apologetically seen. The action has moved towards a modern sense of individual character and motivation, as distinct from the sense of a general human condition, within the unified laws of an at once metaphysical and social world, which is the basis of action and its dependent characterization in Greek tragedy. The modern sense is further emphasized by Racine's third addition: Phèdre's jealousy of Aricie:

> Hippolytus is not insensible,
> Only insensible to me

Again: 'Aricie has his heart'. Thus the consequence of the passion includes a new and specific feeling: self-pity is added to the more basic suffering:

> Perhaps I am
> The only woman that he could refuse.

Moreover this feeling is made to support a key point in the action. Phèdre says that she was about to tell the truth, and withdraw her accusation of Hippolyte, until she saw that he loved Aricie. It is not the 'low' nurse but the jealous princess who then sustains the lie.

These three additions move the play towards a structure of feeling which is much nearer to us than anything in Euripides. Yet it is not only this, in combination with what he took from the 'fable', that constitutes Racine's play. His fourth addition is at least equally significant, in tracing the relations of his dramatic form to its actual social order. Unlike the other additions, moreover, it is not of a kind which can be assimilated to a twentieth-century structure of human feelings centred on individual characters. For what it involves is a precise set of social relations inherent in a particular aristocratic-monarchic state. The conclusion of the action in Euripides is the giving of divine honour, within its mourning, to the city. The conclusion in Racine is the settling of title by inheritance: Thésée, grieving for his dead son, adopts Aricie as his daughter. Yet the more powerful inclusion of the theme of inheritance and succession comes earlier, at several key points in the action. Once Thésée is reported dead, the manoeuvres and intrigues for the succession to power begin. Oenone advises Phèdre to close with Hippolyte, not only because with her husband's death 'votre flamme devient une flamme ordinaire'—the guilty passion now an everyday matter—but also because if he thinks her hostile he could become the head of 'sedition'. In her approach to declaring her love to Hippolyte she begins with an account of her own exposure and that of her child by Thésée—an apparent heir—who has already 'a thousand enemies'. Hippolyte has of course his own claim to succession, as the elder son of Thésée, but he has already approached Aricie, not with a proposal of love but for a political arrangement, in which he would renounce his own claim and that of his brother for alliance with Aricie, who has an older right and title than Thésée himself. When Aricie is surprised, he confesses his love for her. Aricie accepts both proposals, though 'this empire' of power is less precious to her, she adds, than his love.

This authentic integration of personal love with political manoeuvre and alliance is a central fact of the social order which underlies Racine's dramatic form. The inclusion of the political motives is not a sub-plot, of intrigue, but an element of a new form of unity of action. What in the Greek drama is an integrated city-social and metaphysical world is in the neo-classical drama (and also in that of the dramatic mainstream in the English Renaissance) an integrated world of royal and aristocratic title and succession combining with impulses of love and honour. In Euripides the unlawful passion of Phaedra breaks the laws of one kind of controlling integration; in Racine, by sheer force, it disturbs and destroys another kind of ideal integration. Indeed it is in just this specific contingency of the disturbance of both an ideal and a convenient order by ungovernable personal feeling that post-feudal tragedy finds one of its central themes. The passion is there as disturbing, in what can be taken as a primarily personal or (as it would now be put) generally sexual form, but within this precise social order and dramatic action there are other matters, of this new and different social kind, to be disturbed. Thus the two comparable plays which relate to the 'fable', and which can be loosely assimilated generalized version of either, show themselves in fact to be embedded, in their most basic dramatic forms, in the full and different social orders within which they were written.

One further point should be made. The neo-classical form is at one with the classical in its verbal centrality: a condition which can be most clearly seen by contrast with the alternative dramatic forms which had come through with such power in the English Renaissance. Action, even of the most 'dramatic' kind, is reported and narrated in Racine as in Euripides. The death of Hippolytus, when his horses panic as a monster comes from the sea, is in both plays narrated: in Euripides by a messenger, in Racine by Théramène. The distance of both forms from modern theatrical and cinematic actions is very obvious, but already in English Renaissance drama, though some narrative of this kind was retained, there had been a movement to direct staging of many kinds of action, including some of the most violent and spectacular.

Yet this similarity of the classical and neo-classical forms cannot hide an actual change, of a related though still strictly verbal kind. In Euripides Phaedra and Hippolytus scarcely even meet; the passion is reported by the nurse, offstage, and what is acted is the reaction to it, by Phaedra and Hippolytus in effect separately. This is very different, in a significant element of form, from the major scene (II, v) in which Phèdre goes to Hippolyte and at last confesses and declares her passion.

> . . . connais donc Phèdre et tute sa fureur.

This knowing of feeling, by its direct presentation face to face with another, is a decisive dramatic development. It is in the sustained writing of this addressed feeling that most of the power of Racine's drama is to be found.

It is still speech, rather than the more broken speech-with-action that succeeded it in almost all modern dramatic forms. But there has been a further decisive step in the development of what we now take for granted in drama: direct and decisive exchanges between persons, as distinct from the Greek form which, while including important exchanges, still holds them within the earlier form of narrative, responses and choral song, or, where it does not fully hold them—and to us, accustomed to the later form, the limited exchanges (one-to-one) come through with great power—necessarily places and encloses them, within a unique formal conception. A different form still places and defines these exchanges in Racine, at a number of levels from the reported key actions to the convention of the *confident*, with its own formal indirectness. But the exchanges themselves, person to person, are where the new dramatic power flows, allowing us to see the future outline (or by retrospect the essential impulse of Racine) of a drama which is wholly formed by the relations of person to person, beyond both a metaphysical and a public world.

On Dramatic Dialogue
And Monologue

(particularly in Shakespeare)

Dialogue

Dialogue is an apparently simple term, but the uses of 'dialogue' in drama are very much more complex. The root word is the Greek *diálogos*, meaning conversation or discourse, and this had passed through Latin and French into English, with the usual variations of spelling finally settled in the French form, by the thirteenth century. The general sense has been of talk between two or more persons, though there has been some tendency to use it especially of talk between only two persons, associating the Greek prefix *di* from *dis*, twice or double, with the actual prefix *dia*, from a preposition meaning through or across, and then often, with its variable suffix, a composition of several parts.

The general use of *dialogue* has continued relatively unchanged, though for everyday talk or conversation it now seems very formal and literary. Something of this formality is drawn on for a common contemporary use in certain kinds of politics, where it is a soft alternative, but also sometimes a preliminary, to actual *negotiation*. In this use it carries a strong sense of trying to reach an understanding.

The uses in written composition have also been relatively stable. There is a familiar kind of written argument in which the method is the representation of different positions, and of exchanges between them, through the arranged alternating speech of named persons or elements. This has been common in philosophy and related arguments since Plato. We do not call such dialogues *dramatic*, in any serious way, though there is obviously some overlap between these written arguments and written drama in the method of representing the speech of two or more persons. It can be said that in drama the method is different because it has wider purposes than argument. A play is a whole action rather than only an intellectual exchange. But while this can be agreed, its careless application can push us too far in another direction, in which, supported by the persistent general sense of *conversation* between two or more persons, we find ourselves with an unreasonably restricted idea of dramatic dialogue and its actual variations. This consideration is especially important when we come to look at any pre-realist or pre-naturalist drama.

The prepotence of the conventions of what we know as 'realist' and 'naturalist' drama is especially great in this matter of multivocal speech. Thus it is almost universally assumed, under the influence of these conventions, that dramatic dialogue is a representation of people speaking *to each other*, in the simplest sense. In almost all modern drama the governing convention is that of an audience which simply watches and listens and of actors who speak and behave as if they were not being watched and (over) heard. This is a very specific convention, to which we are all now well used, but it has the effect, when we think about dialogue, that the actors must be speaking to each other, since there is, within the convention, nobody else to speak *to*. This leads to the familiar difficulty of monologue or soliloquy in modern productions of plays which still used those forms, or of comparable writing in modern plays. Indeed, as will be more fully argued below, the post-eighteenth-century sense of *soliloquy*, as a person talking 'to himself', follows from this conventional understanding of *dialogue*. If there is not another actor on the stage, to whom this actor is speaking, he must be talking *to himself*. The idea that an actor alone on the stage can have an *audience* to speak to, directly or otherwise, is beyond the convention in which the audience is technically not noticed, in effect not present.

Yet this enlightening problem can be set aside as a special case, and the idea of dialogue as an exchange of conversation between two or more persons of the drama simply retained. It is that much easier to retain because a large part of dramatic dialogue is indeed of this kind, and in modern drama virtually all dialogue. Yet we have only to look closely at dialogue in most older forms of drama to realize that it serves several other purposes, and in particular some purposes which cannot be reduced to exchange and especially an enclosed exchange. The problem now is to find ways of identifying these purposes, and putting some technical markers on them. I am sure that this is necessary if we are, for example, to read and play Shakespeare adequately. I will first set out, summarily, some preliminary definitions of the more obviously distinctive kinds of dialogue, and go on to illustrate these with some examples from *Troilus and Cressida*. In the later sections of this essay, after some general and particular analysis of monologue and soliloquy, I will return to questions of dialogue, in some more complex examples from *Hamlet* and *King Lear*.

Three general types of dialogue can be distinguished as follows:

D (i): FORMAL EXCHANGE

This typically occurs in certain socially marked situations, in which there is a congruence between the immediate dramatic situation and some more general social institution in which certain kinds of rule-governed formal discourse are practised: a royal court, a public assembly or hearing, a trial in law. The 'set' speeches and their connecting forms are governed by such rules of exchange, though there is often some dramatic variation from the simplest formalities. This type of formal exchange can be extended to less obviously marked situations, in which nevertheless the forms of such discourse are broadly followed, as notably in long, fully developed speeches of argument, report and appeal. In all these cases the audience should be seen as in a *public* relation to the formal exchanges; they are in a full conventional sense among its actual auditors, and the mode of address itself, while at any point it may be directed at a person or persons on the stage. remains essentially public: talking *in* public, on a public occasion. For a simple example see *Henry the Fifth*, I, ii. In *King Lear*, I, i, 36–265 and in *Hamlet*, I, ii, 1–128—characteristically formal occasions at a royal court—there are interesting examples of dramatic flexibility within the dominant mode of formal exchange, in the 'asides' by Cordelia, 61, 75–7, and Hamlet, 65. Yet the general importance of this form of dramatic dialogue, which is certainly something more than the exchange of conversation between individuals, remains evident.

D (ii): ENCLOSED PERSON-TO-PERSON

This has become so much the type of all dialogue in modern drama that it is especially necessary to define its formal characteristics. Its key element is its private character, though this obviously varies in intensity, from the most intimate or secret—its most powerful use—to everyday talk which would not be altered if it were known that it was being (over) heard but which is still governed by modes of direct personal address. As an element within forms which contain other kinds of dialogue, these characteristics are rarely as fully developed as in later forms based wholly on the representation of private talk and conversation. Indeed some early examples, while based on such a relationship, are still very formally written—as in *Romeo and Juliet*, II, ii. There are other and varying Shakespearean examples in *Antony and Cleopatra*, III, iv; *Henry VIII*, V. i; *Merchant of Venice*, II, iii; etc. Such passages are often inset into other more complex modes.

D (iii): INFORMAL EXCHANGE

Between the sharply distinguishable types of formal exchange and enclosed person-to-person speech there is a less easily defined area which further analysis might well subdivide but which needs, meanwhile, to be generally defined. It is different from D (ii) in that two or more persons are represented as speaking *with* rather than *to* each other, and from D (i) in that it is less marked by formal situations and speaking relationships; again speaking *with* rather than *with* and *at*. The mode is then very variable and flexible, and there are frequent shifts within scenes to the more formal D (i) or to inset monologue and the more enclosed speech of D (ii). The numerous examples include *Richard III*, I, iii; *Julius Caesar*, I, iii; *Antony and Cleopatra*, II, ii; etc.

I now turn to examples of each of these three kinds in passages from *Troilus and Cressida*.

D (i): FORMAL EXCHANGE

There is a type example in Act One, Scene Three, when the Greek leaders meet to survey their situation before Troy. The linguistic markers of formally regulated speech are clear. The scene opens with the general address by Agamemnon:

> Princes...

After Agamemnon has spoken, there is Nestor:

> With due observance of thy god-like seat,
> Great Agamemnon, Nestor shall apply
> Thy latest words...

Then Ulysses:

> Agamemnon,
> Thou great commander, nerve and bone of Greece,
> Heart of our numbers, soul and only spirit,
> In whom the tempers and the minds of all
> Should be shut up, hear what Ulysses speaks.
> Besides the applause and approbation
> The which, most mighty for thy place and sway,
> And thou most reverend for thy stretched-out life,
> I give to both your speeches...
> ...yet let it please both,
> Thou great, and wise, to hear Ulysses speak.

This is indeed formal exchange, in regulated order and compliment, with both previous speakers noted and with the characteristic formal request for permission to speak, as regulated by rank. At the same time, in its regulated use of these formal rhetorical modes, it is a dramatic base for extended argument. It is a significant linguistic framework for one of the most formal arguments in all dramatic writing, when Ulysses generalizes from the disorder in the Greek camp—'The specialty of rule hath been neglected'—to the fully extended argument for 'degree':

> ...The heavens themselves, the planets, and this centre
> Observe degree, priority, and place,
> Insisture, course, proportion, season, form,
> Office, and custom, in all line of order...

This whole speech, of fifty-eight lines, is not easily understood as dialogue in its reduced modern sense, yet as formal discourse it is essentially dialogic. After two interjections Ulysses continues, in a further forty-three lines, to analyse the present disorder, and significantly includes a dramatic figure to describe Achilles:

> ...like a strutting player, whose conceit
> Lies in his hamstring, and doth think it rich
> To hear the wooden dialogue and sound
> 'Twixt his stretch'd footing and the scaffoldage—
> Such to-be-pitied and o'er wrested seeming
> He acts thy greatness in: and when he speaks
> 'Tis like a chime a-mending; with terms unsquared...

The formal linguistic base is so settled that it can even be used internally, as here, to define a divergence from it—not only 'strutting'

—the abuse of formality—but lack of control in the 'terms unsquared'.

D (ii): ENCLOSED PERSON-TO-PERSON

The formality of Act One, Scene Three, should remind us that in the most extended forms of drama there can be no categorical distinction, as 'essentially dramatic', between direct personal talk and formal discourse. *Troilus and Cressida* has the full range of both. There is a formally written example of D (ii), showing the influence of the linguistic formalities of oaths, in the exchange between Troilus and Cressida in Act Three, Scene Two: 'As true as Troilus'... 'As false as Cressid'...

This exchange is balanced in speeches of twelve and thirteen lines. There is what was to become the more characteristic form of this type in the extended leavetaking of Troilus and Cressida in Act Four, Scene Four, where the linguistic markers are close to those of private conversation:

> T: Hear me, my love. Be thou but true of heart
> C: I true! how now! What wicked deem is this?
> T: Nay, we must use expostulation kindly,
>   For it is parting from us.

It is not only that this mode permits or encourages interjection (at the opposite end of the range from formal requests to speak), but also that the level has shifted to a more colloquial idiom.

> T.   Wear this sleeve.
> C. And you this glove. When shall I see you?
> T. I will corrupt the Grecian sentinels
>   To give thee nightly visitation.
>   But yet, be true.
> C.   O heavens! 'be true' again!
> T. Hear why I speak it, love...

In this passage, carefully written for this precise situation, the mode of what will later be taken as the necessary form of all dialogue is in effect fully established.

D (iii): INFORMAL EXCHANGE

In Act Four, Scene Five, there is a passage of a quite common kind which is clearly intermediate between the full modes of D (i) and D (ii) when Aeneas comes to the Greek camp to settle the details of the fight between Hector and Achilles. It begins and ends in the relative formalities of rule-governed address, but its centre is different:

Ag: ...Hector bade ask.
Ag: Which way would Hector have it?
Ae: He cares not; he'll obey conditions.
Ac: 'Tis done like Hector; but securely done,
A little proudly, and great deal disprizing
The knight opposed.
Ae: If not Achilles, sir,
What is your name?
Ac: If not Achilles, nothing.
Ae: Therefore Achilles; but, whate'er, know this...

Here three speakers are involved in a public exchange in which the rules have to be sought, to the point where Achilles interrupts the exchange between Aeneas and Agamemnon and has then to be indirectly identified. The difference from Act One, Scene Three is obvious, but equally this is in no way private speech. The men are speaking with each other, and as so often in this mode on public matters, informally exchanged. Another use of this mode is in semi-public banter, as earlier in the same scene with the arrival of Cressida in the Greek camp and the offers of the generals to kiss her.

A different example of a commonly employed intermediate kind is in Act Four, Scene One, where Aeneas, Paris, Diomedes, Deiphobus and others meet and pass, typically in a thoroughfare where the relationships are evidently different from either the rule-governed assembly or the private enclosure:

P: See, ho! who is that there?
De: It is the Lord Aeneas.
A: Is the prince there in person?
Had I so good occasion to lie long
As you, Prince Paris...

This is an inherently mobile kind of dialogue, involving within four lines the movement from spotting and recognition to direct address. Even where it settles, its level is that of everyday encounters in which a variety of matters, including some serious, are discussed, but not in the engaged, set ways of either D (i) or D (ii):

A: We know each other well.
Di: We do; and long to know each other worse.
P: This is the most despiteful gentle greeting,
The noblest hateful love, that e'er I heard of.

> What business, lord, so early?
> A: I was sent for to the king, but why, I know not.
> P: His purpose meets you: 'twas to bring this Greek
> To Calchas' house...

When these distinguishable basic forms of dialogue have been identified, it is necessary to return to the complex forms within which,
together with several distinguishable kinds of monologue, they are
integrated. This has eventually to be done at the level of whole plays,
but there is also some interesting integration in certain important
scenes and sequences, and there is an especially good example of this
in *Troilus and Cressida*. In Act Five, Scene Two, there is a complex
interweaving of two separate dialogues and a further separated
monologue. Diomedes meets Cressida, at night, and they speak
privately in the enclosed person-to-person mode:

> C: You shall not have it, Diomed; faith, you shall not;
> I'll give you something else.
> D: I will have this. Whose was it?
> C: 'Tis no matter.
> D: Come, tell me whose it was.
> C: 'Twas one's that loved me better than you will,
> But, now you have it, take it.
> D: Whose was it?

Yet they are actually being overheard by the conventionally concealed Troilus and Ulysses, who also speak privately:

> T: Behold, I pray you!
> U: Nay, good my lord, go off:
> You flow to great distraction; come, my lord.
> T: I pray thee, stay.
> U: You have not patience; come.
> T: I pray you, stay. By hell and all hell's torments,
> I will not speak a word.

The two private dialogues are then frequently interwoven:

> C: I prithee, do not hold me to mine oath;
> Bid me do anything but that, sweet Greek.
> D: Good night.
> T: Hold, patience!
> U: How now, Trojan!
> C: Diomed
> D: No, no; good night; I'll be your fool no more.
> T: Thy better must.

C: Hark! one word in your ear.
T: O plague and madness!

Thus two private dialogues are being simultaneously played, in a whole presentation, and with a further kind of speech, that of the common observer, Thersites, speaking in monologue (see below) Thus:

D: Give me some token for the surety of it.
C: I'll fetch you one.
U: You have sworn patience.
T: Fear me not, sweet lord.
　 I will not be myself, nor have cognition
　 Of what I feel: I am all patience.
T: Now the pledge! now, now, now!
C: Here, Diomed, keep this sleeve.·
T: O beauty! where is thy faith?

Here in nine lines there are two separate pairs and one single speaker. The flexibility but also the complex possible integrations must underline the impossibility of reducing the idea of dialogue to simple conversational exchange.

There are observable variations in the proportions of different kinds of dialogue and of monologue in different plays, and it may well be that some of these variations indicate significant differences of form in relation to differences of theme. This would require much further analysis, but a preliminary analysis of five plays has given the following results:

Play	D(i)	D(ii)	D(iii)	Mon
Troilus and Cressida	20	53	22	5
Hamlet	9	41	42	8
Macbeth	16	38	31	15
Julius Caesar	22	30	42	6
Coriolanus	16	30	53	1

Monologue

The first problem in an analysis of monologue and soliloquy is that there is a divergence between dictionary definitions and current literary usage. Thus in *The Oxford Dictionary of English Etymology* (1966):

> Monologue: dramatic scene or composition in which a single actor speaks. XVII (Dryden).—F.*monologue* (XV), after *dialogue*; cf. late Gr. *monologos* speaking alone.
>
> Soliloquy: talking aloud to oneself. XVII.—late L. *soliloquium* (Augustine).

Or in Fowler's *Modern English Usage* (1926), under 'Technical Terms':

> Monologue (Lit); 'sole speech'. This and *soliloquy* are precisely parallel terms of Greek, and Latin, origin; but usage tends to restrict *soliloquy* to talking to oneself or thinking aloud without consciousness of an audience, whether one is in fact overheard or not; while *monologue,* though not conversely restricted to a single person's discourse that *is* meant to be heard, has that sense much more often than not, and is especially used of a talker who monopolizes conversation, or of a dramatic performance or recitation in which there is one actor only.

What then is usage? I can say only that in forty years, in a relevant environment, I have never heard *soliloquy* and *soliloquize* used of 'talking to oneself', in any ordinary sense. Conversely, while I have heard *monologue* in Fowler's two senses, of monopolizing conversation and of dramatic performance or recitation by a single actor, and in a third sense of a kind of poem written as if spoken by a single character, I have regularly heard *soliloquy* in the sense of a 'dramatic scene or composition in which a single actor speaks' and especially in the sense of a speech in a play in which a *character* is taken to be at least temporarily alone and in that sense (but there, as we shall see, all the difficulties begin) as 'talking to himself'.

The problem is much wider than one of technical terms. Yet their history has some significance. It is the shift in *soliloquy* that has most importance. The late Latin *soliloquium* is commonly cited from the *Liber Soliloquiorum* of Augustine, which has the subtitles *Soliloquia animae ad Deum* and *Meditationes, soliloquia et manuali*. It was freely translated into Old English under Alfred, in the late ninth century. Most medieval English references are to the Augustinian soliloquy. But then *soliloquy,* in this line, is not a matter of represented singular speech. Indeed in Augustine it is often in dialogue form, as between the soul and God, or between different faculties of the mind. This sense of private meditation or prayer persisted as the primary meaning until at least the eighteenth century, though there is a recorded early-seventeenth-century use as 'private talk'. There is a characteristic title from 1738 : *Devout Exercises of the Heart in Meditation and Soliloquy.*

It is difficult to be certain when the sense of religious meditation went out or when the sense of a mode of composition in drama came in. Johnson, in his *Dictionary*, defined *soliloquy* as 'a discourse made by one in solitude to himself': the formal version of the twentieth century's 'talking to oneself'. He defined *monologue* as 'a scene in which a person of the drama speaks by himself, a soliloquy', where 'speaks *by*' (rather than *to*) may be important. The addition of *soliloquy,* in a dramatic context, is somewhere near the shift we are tracing, but not yet at it, since there is a citation of 'monologue, to which unnatural way of narration Terence is subject in all his plays', where the confusion between narrative and dramatic is historically significant, and where 'unnatural' is a key indicator of the problems of changing dramatic conventions.

On the other hand, there is a fully modern sense in a use by Vanbrugh, in *A Short Vindication of 'The Relapse' and 'The Provok'd Wife'* (1698) :

> ...upon the Stage the Person who speaks in a Soliloquy is always suppos'd to deliver his real Thoughts to the Audience.

It is probable that this use had been becoming more common in the Restoration theatre. Yet the most interesting moment in the history of the term occurs in Shaftesbury's essay *Soliloquy, or Advice to an Author* (1710), reprinted in *Characteristicks,* Volume One (1727). Shaftesbury is discussing the relations between experience and practice. Having insisted that we have ourselves to practise on, he supposes the objection:

'Who can thus multiply himself into *two Persons,* and be *his own Subject*?' To this he replies:

> Go to the *Poets*, and they will present you with many Instances. Nothing is more common with them, than this sort of SOLILOQUY. A Person of profound parts, or perhaps of ordinary Capacity, happens, on some occasion, to commit a Fault. He is concern'd for it. He comes alone upon the Stage; looks about him, to see if any body be near; then takes himself to task, without sparing himself in the least. You wou'd wonder to hear how close he pushes matters, and how thorowly he carrys on the business of *Self-dissection*. By virtue of this SOLILOQUY he becomes two distinct *Persons*. He is Pupil and Preceptor. He teaches, and he learns. And in good earnest, had I nothing else to plead in behalf of the Morals of our modern Dramatic Poets, I shou'd defend 'em still against their Accusers for the sake of this very Practice, which they have taken care to keep up in its full force. For whether the Practice be *natural* or no, in respect of common Custom and Usage; I take upon me to assert, that it is an honest and laudable Practice; and that if already it be not natural to us, we ought however to make it so, by Study and Application.

This passage may be decisive for subsequent usage (though it seems not to have penetrated the dictionaries). Yet Shaftesbury is concerned with the dramatic method only as example. His central argument is that such private practice is necessary:

> ...'tis a certain Observation in our Science, that they who are great Talkers *in Company*, have never been any Talkers *by themselves*... For which reason their Froth abounds;

yet that at the same time it is

> very indecent for any one to publish his *Meditations, Occasional Reflections, Solitary Thoughts*, or other such Exercises as come under the notion of this *self-discoursing Practice*.

A characteristic sense of decorum, with clearly distinguished rules for public and private behaviour, admitted one, but only one, written form of 'self-discoursing Practice', and even then, within the special case of dramatic speech 'by a character', only as private example. The full shift depended on a wide alteration of attitudes. It was above all in the Romantic movement, with its intense interest in new forms of subjectivity in verse, in its practice and popularization of the relatively new form of the autobiography, and in its attachment to new forms of self-reflective fiction and to forms of internal analysis of private thought and feeling within more general fiction, that a new strong emphasis and interpretation of this already available and apparently subjective form in drama developed and eventually became dominant. The centre of interest was in Shakespeare and above all in what came to be generalized as 'the soliloquies': in practice the major set speeches in which so many leading actors specialized. The shift was congruent with an increasingly internal 'psychological' analysis of characters. Critical and academic practice followed this line. *Soliloquy* was preferred to *monologue* since all the previous associations of *soliloquy* with private meditation and reverie—in a more modern term, 'inner speech'—supported the selected emphasis. The more technical *monologue*, without such associations, was in effect crowded out.

Yet the actual difficulties persist. It is possible to take *soliloquy*, with these associations, as an appropriate term for one kind of dramatic speech, to which such characteristics are commonly assigned: the 'great soliloquies', as it is put, of Hamlet or Macbeth. Yet it is not only that there are other kinds of monologue, to which such characteristics need not or can not be assigned. Nor only that such characteristics can also be discovered in *dialogue*; some 'well remembered' soliloquies turn out, in the text, to be dialogic. It is also that certain major problems of convention and definition, centred on the problem of subject and object in writing, and very actively present in the texts of dramatic writing for speech of various kinds before actual and presumed audiences, inhere not only in these wider forms but within the 'soliloquies' themselves.

I will try to set out, summarily, the actual range of monologue, for convenience in analysis but also as a deliberate break with the mystifying concept of *soliloquy* in current academic and critical usage.

It is necessary to begin rather far back, yet at a point so obvious that only conceptual confusion could obscure it. The preposition in Johnson's definition can help us here. A person in a drama may indeed speak *by* himself. He literally cannot speak *to* himself, in the sense in which that description is used for 'talking to oneself in private'. Always, and obviously, there is an audience, to whom, in some manner, his words are by deliberation made available.

It is within that general description, 'by deliberation made available', that the true varieties of dramatic speech must be distinguished. The relations of any speech to an audience can be inscribed within particular forms of composition, and are in any case governed by wider dramatic conventions. Thus some relations are evident, or can become evident by analysis, within texts. Other relations become evident only in analysis of the text within the dramatic conventions for which it was written. For a dramatic text, unlike texts written for silent reading (on which most studies of direction of address have been based), presumes both an inherent multivocal form—the composition is distributed between different speaking voices—and certain governing physical relations, in the relational presence of actors in a playing space and in the further (and often complex) relational presence of these actors with an audience.

These relations cannot be reduced to those of any particular dramatic convention. In the case of *soliloquy* there has been some unnecessary confusion because of an unnoticed assimilation, in the modern period, of the conventions of 'naturalist' drama. Here the relations between actors and audience are negatively defined. The audience is of course present, and the actors are conscious of it, but the controlling convention is that the actors do not *dramatically* notice the audience; instead they play out their action before it, in a space defined by the raising or lowering of curtains or lights. It usually follows from this that the actors are understood as invariably *talking to each other*. When only one actor is on the stage, he has then, within the convention, *nobody to speak to but himself*. Then since 'talking to oneself' carries certain habitual social and pyschological implications, what had once been the *soliloquy* is felt to be 'unnatural'. This is generally known, but what is less often noticed is the common (retroactive) conclusion that when an actor is alone on the stage and speaks he is 'talking to himself', as in the dominant sense of *soliloquy*. For who else, within the 'naturalist' convention, could he be talking to? That he might be talking *to*, rather than in the unnoticed presence of, an audience has been conventionally ruled out.

In fact monologue within a multivocal dramatic form can include, as we shall see, direct address to an audience. But there are then more complex relations: some of them very indirect, though not necessarily identical with the wholly enclosed and internal speech relations of the 'naturalist' convention. Between the explicitly direct and such indirect cases, there are intermediate cases, which we can properly call 'semi-direct', in which speech is given in full consciousness of the audience but without the marks of direct address. These three most general types, and the best-known variations within them, can be set out as follows, with brief examples from English Renaissance drama.

A. DIRECT
(i) Presentational
The most easily recognized form of direct address, commonly in Prologue and Epilogue of a certain type, preceding or succeeding the full dramatic action and relying on direct relation between *performer* and audience. E.g.,

> The general welcomes Tamburlaine receiv'd,
> When he arrived last upon our stage,
> Have made our poet pen his Second Part...
> > (*Tamburlaine the Great*, II, Prol).

Other examples: *Henry IV, 2*, Epilogue ('If you be not too much cloyed with fat meat, our humble author will continue the story...and make you merry...'); *Midsummer Night's Dream*, Puck epilogue ('If we shadows have offended...'): *All's Well that Ends Well*, Epilogue ('The king's a beggar now the play is done...')

(ii) Expository
A different use of Prologue especially, though it can appear elsewhere; at times combined with (i), as in the later lines of the Tamburlaine II epilogue. E.g.,

> Two households, both alike in dignity,
> In fair Verona, where we lay our scene,
> From ancient grudge break to new mutiny...
> > (*Romeo and Juliet*, Prol.)

Other examples: *Henry V*, Prologue (includes elements of (i)); *Troilus and Cressida*, Prologue ('In Troy there lies the scene. From isles of Greece...'); *Winter's Tale*, IV, i, spoken by Time; *Henry IV, 2*, Induction, spoken by Rumour. Though there is often combination of the expository with the presentational, the former function is typically more integrated with the dramatic action and the speaker then passes from performer to a certain kind of generalized character, often specified as Time, Rumour, Armed Chorus, etc. This mode is then close to certain kinds of expository self-introduction by a named character; cf Machevill prologue, *Jew of Malta*; Gloucester, *Richard III*, I, i (cf. B (ii) below); Autolycus in *Winter's Tale*, IV, iii; and cf. B (iii) below.

(iii) *Indicative* or *Homiletic*

Common as direct homily in medieval drama, presenting the religious and moral significance of the action. More generally indicative in Renaissance drama, though the range can be illustrated even there. E.g.,

> Cut is the branch that might have grown full straight,
> And burned is Apollo's laurel bough,
> That sometime grew within this learned man.
> Faustus is gone. Regard his hellish fall...
>
> *(Doctor Faustus*, Epil.)

(Homiletic)

> And my ending is despair,
> Unless I be relieved by prayer,
> Which pierces so that it assaults
> Mercy itself, and frees all faults.
> As you from crimes would pardon'd be,
> Let your indulgence set me free.
>
> *(The Tempest*, Epil.)

(In this epilogue by Prospero the indicative is combined with and qualified by the presentational.)

> Till then I'll sweat, and seek about for eases;
> And at that time bequeath you my diseases.
>
> *(Troilus and Cressida*, V, x)

(Not formal epilogue, and the *you* specified to 'as many as be here of pandar's hall'; this is the dramatically indicative at full development from the homiletic.)

B SEMI-DIRECT

(i) *Aside*

The most easily recognized form of semi-direct address, evidently spoken 'to' the audience but qualified by its placing as a short break within dialogue. E.g.,

> I know them all, though they suppose me mad,
> And will o'erreach them in their own devices;
> A pair of cursed hell-hounds and their dam.
>
> *(Titus Andronicus*, V, ii)

(ii) *Secretive/Explanatory*

In some ways a relatively complex development of the aside, but often tending towards the undifferentiated form of 'soliloquy', from which, however, in that usual sense, it can be functionally distinguished. E.g.,

> A credulous father! and a brother noble
> Whose nature is so far form doing harms
> That he suspects none;on whose foolish honesty
> My practices ride easy! I see the business.
> Let me, if not by birth,have lands by wit
> All's with me meet that I can fashion fit.
>
> *(Lear, I, ii,182-7)*

This can be functionally distinguished, in this case formally by the characteristic concluding rhymed 'sentence', from Edmund's monologue in I, ii, 1-22, which is relationally more indirect; cf. C (ii) and (iii) below. The point may be clearer in a comparison between Iago in Othello, I, iii ('Thus do I ever make my fool my purse') and in II, iii ('And what's he then that says I play the villain?'), where the matter is in both cases required to be secret, and is dramatically made so by the convention of monologue, but where the former more evidently includes necessary explanation of 'the business' in hand, so that the audience may understand its manoeuvres. This is the distinguishing element of conscious if semi-direct relation to an audience.

(iii) Characteristic

A very different kind of semi-direct monologue, with some functional relation to the indicative (A(iii) above). A certain type of self-introducing character functions, explicitly or implicitly, as a form of commentary upon the action, which within this formal mode is temporarily distanced. E.g. (Thersites):

> Now they are clapper-clawing one another; I'll go look on. That dissembling abominable varlet, Diomed, has got that same scurvy doting foolish young knave's sleeve of Troy there in his helm: I would fain see them meet...
>
> *(Troilus and Cressida, V, iv)*

Other monologue examples: *Cymbeline*, v, iv,end (First Gaoler: 'Unless a man would marry a gallows...'); Macbeth, II,iii,1-20. The linguistic markers on this type are especially evident: the composition is not only in 'prose' but is deliberately (and often in sharp contrast) popular in syntax and diction.

C. INDIRECT
(i) Rhetorical
This type answers, in general, to the description of mono-
logue/soliloquy as 'self-discoursing practice', but sets up a specific
linguistic relation between presumed subject and object. The type example is:

> Settle thy studies, Faustus, and begin
> To sound the depth of that thou wilt profess...
>
> (*Doctor Faustus*, I,i)

The long opening monologue of *Faustus* is a form of 'self-discourse'
predominantly written in a grammar of the self addressing the self as
if a second person. There are subordinate uses of the first-person
pronoun in lines 6, 36, 56, 62, but the second-person address controls
the overall style.The effect can be seen by contrast with the first-
person monologue that soon follows, lines 77-96, which is primarily
B (ii). The contrast can be seen again in the remarkable final monologue of Faustus,v, ii, 143-200, which begins (143-154) in second-
person address and then shifts dramatically to first-person.

> Oh, I'll leap up to my God: who pulls me down?

This continues to 168, and thereafter the monologue is a combination of first and second-person pronouns and forms.

Other known rhetorical figures for this type were also used,
especially the apostrophe (see below III & V)

(ii) Reflexive
This is the type which has been most widely generalized as *soliloquy*,
in which a self-discoursing practice is spoken, alone on the stage, in
the first person. It is clearly an extremely important kind. E.g.,

> O, what a rogue and peasant slave am I...
>
> (*Hamlet*, II, ii, 553-609)

In this type example, there is deliberate notation

> Ay, so, God bye to you! now I am alone.

Among numerous other examples, *Hamlet*, I, ii, 129-159 or IV, iv,
32-66.

It should be noted that the condition of being alone on the stage, though normal for this type, is not always fulfilled; there can be other forms of temporary isolation (see below).

(iii) Generic

This type is often, under the influence of general psychologizing or characterizing explanations of all monologue/soliloquy in terms of the private or the wholly subjective, reduced from its full function. It is usually apparently similar to the reflexive, but can often be linguistically distinguished by its use of the 'we' rather than the 'I' pronoun. E.g.,

> To be, or not to be...
> ...and by a sleep to say we end...
> ...When we have shuffled off this mortal coil
> Must give us pause...
> ...And makes us rather bear those ills we have
> Than fly to others that we know not of?
> Thus conscience does make cowards of us all.
>
> (*Hamlet*, iii, i, 56-88)

The need to distinguish the generic from the reflexive is more than formal. It is an indication of the true range and flexibility of this highly developed dramatic speech that there can be such transitions from the reflexive/subjective to the generic/objective. Whatever may be said of the reflexive, the generic is evidently not 'inner speech'. It is, rather, most notably through its selection of 'we', the realization of a communal mode which is not (as in some other communal forms) opposed to subjectivity but is a deepening and then a transformation of it: a common 'individual' condition in the old sense of 'individual' as that which is specific yet cannot be 'divided', that is, separated. It is essential that this type of indirect monologue should be distinguished from the post-Romantic version of 'soliloquy' as the 'private' or 'inner' (then 'deeper') self as distinct from 'public' and 'outer' identity.

The linguistic complexity of these types of monologue, as of types of dialogue, is the complexity of the written composition, and as such usually distinguishable in the text, but it is supported by a complexity of playing conditions, within a knowledge of which the writing was done. One important factor is the variety of available stage positions, from which variable relations between speakers(s) and audience could be defined. For a fuller discussion of this, see Weimann, *Shakespeare and the Popular Tradition in the Theatre* (1978), 73-85 and 215-45, and W.D. Smith, *Shakespeare's*

Playhouse Practice (1975). In monologue there is a centre downstage position for all types of A, and typically a move downstage to this position in B (ii) and C (i) and in some C (ii) and C (iii). Other moves include the turn towards the audience in most forms of B (i), and the move down and back again in some C (ii) and C (iii). B (iii) is more complex, since it is sometimes from the simple direct-address position but can be also from a downstage position while upstage is otherwise occupied in a different mode. This double or even triple layering is evident in *Troilus and Cressida*, v, ii, where Thersites is nearest the audience and is both observing the upstage action and turning to the audience to comment on it. There is a comparable but simpler layering of dialogue in D (i), when the formality of the occasion is marked by the upstage *state*, to which both the other actors and the audience are formally directed. The lingusitic and positional markers, while typically corresponding, cannot be read from the 'bare' text. Indeed, as more generally, the text has always to be read through the markers, and in the broadest sense through both linguistic and playing conventions.

Monologue in *Macbeth*

Macbeth contains several well-remembered 'soliloquies', but we may now make some more precise descriptions and distinctions. Monologue in general, and the reflexive monologue in particular, are extensively used in the play and comprise an unusually high proportion of it, at fifteen per cent. There is no monologue of the direct type, A, and the monologue aside, B (i), is very sparingly used; for one example see, iii, 116–7. It should be noted here that there are cases of the 'dialogue aside'—a detached and inset break from general dialogue exchange, as in II, iii, 119–24, in which Malcolm and Donalbain would move downstage; in the subsequent 135–46 they are left alone.

B (iii) is well represented by the Porter's monologue, II, iii, 1–20. Often dismissed as 'comic relief', this is in fact a typical example of what has been called in recent linguistics 'anti-language' but can be better called 'counter-language', in which the evident linguistic shift, to a traditional colloquial mode, is not empty 'relief' but a deliberate shift of dramatic perspective: a connecting communal mode, played very close to the audience, in which the action is seen from a different base.

B (ii) is often difficult to distinguish from the more indirect types in C. In two examples in *Macbeth* there are useful linguistic markers: the secretive/explanatory function is marked by rhymed sentences. In I, iv, 48–53 Macbeth is not left alone but moves downstage to speak three rhymed couplets:

> ...Stars hide your fires
> Let not light see my black and deep desires:
> The eye wink at the hand; yet let that be
> Which the eye fears, when it is done, to see.

Duncan, still formally upstage, speaks to Banquo *after* this typical summary exit. The more usual case in III, i, 140–1, in which Macbeth is left alone after speaking to the murderers:

> It is concluded: Banquo, thy soul's flight,
> If it find heaven, must find it out tonight.

On the other hand, there are cases which are clearly explanatory rather than self-discursive in function, without such evident markers; the best example is in II, ii, 1–13, notably in 'I have drugged their possets', though lines 12–13 ('Had he not resembled my father...') move towards the reflexive mode. Banquo's monologue in III, i, 1–10 seems to me also primarily explanatory, and therefore B (ii).

There are interesting examples of the rhetorical type of monologue, C (i). The most evident is in I, v, 1–29, where a mode of exchange, as in dialogue, is set up in Lady Macbeth's monologue by the device of her reading Macbeth's letter and then, in monologue, addressing him in a form of *apostrophe*, as if he were present:

> what thou wouldst highly,
> That wouldst thou holily.

A more arguable case is in III, iv, where Macbeth speaks in what is in effect inset monologue (50–1, 70–3, 93–6, 99–107) to the ghost of Banquo. It is not the ghost as such that makes this to some degree monologic; other ghosts, as in *Hamlet*, are both seen by others and themselves speak. Here it is only Macbeth *and the audience* who see the ghost, and it does not speak. The effect is very complex, but may be defined as speech without an object internal to the web of dramatic speech; hence (without the need for psychological explanation, though this may be added) as monologic projection of an object: commonly through use of the *apostrophe*—address to unseen forces or persons—but also in other ways. But this has in turn, since the audience sees the ghost, to be distinguished from a related form, itself fully reflexive, in which Macbeth, but now only Macbeth, 'sees' (imagines) the dagger: II, i, 33 *et seq*. The linguistic forms overlap, in projection of an object—'I see thee yet, in form as palpable'; but there is an easy transfer to the fully reflexive—'It is the bloody business which informs.' Interestingly, however, this whole monologue is markedly projective by apostrophe, 'Thou sure and firm-set earth'—and indeed invocative—'Hear not my steps.' It concludes with a summary rhymed sentence, in 63–4.

The fully reflexive is, as has been said, unusually frequent in *Macbeth*. Examples include, I, iii, 127–41, 143–5, 146–7; I, v, 37–53; I, vii, 1-28; II, i, 33–61; II, ii, 57–63; III, i, 47–71; IV, i, 144–55; IV, iii, 72–8; V, i, 31, 33–9, 41–4, 49–51, 61–3, 65–7; V, iii, 22–8; V, viii, 1–3. The mode, nevertheless, is sufficiently complex to include other functions; B (ii) is evident for example, in IV, i, 150–4, again concluding with a summary rhymed sentence. The purest kind of reflexive, with the characteristics so often assigned to the 'soliloquy', is to be found in the longer monologues, e.g., I, vii, 1–28. What Shaftesbury had in mind as 'self-discoursing practice' is evidently exemplified in lines 12–28:

> He's here in double trust:
> First...
>
> > ...then...
> > ...Besides...

This is argument in a single mind, spoken aloud. Another famous example is in I, iii, 130–42:

> If ill...
> If good...
> My thought...
> Shakes so my single state of man that function
> Is smothered in surmise...

These last lines indeed express, precisely, this situation of agitated and as yet indecisive 'self-discourse'. Yet this sense of internal argument, which is clearly a major function of the reflexive, should not be taken as exclusive. The mode of argument, so clear in I, vii,

12–18, is surpassed in lines 19–25, by a kind of speech which it would be seriously reductive to call argument. It is in this further mode that some of the most difficult questions arise.

Within the assumptions of 'soliloquy', and indeed within the categories of an older kind of literary linguistics, a relatively simple definition would be possible.

> And pity, like a naked new-born babe,
> Striding the blast...

Is this not 'emotive' rather than 'referential' language? Is it not Macbeth 'overcome' by powerful feeling, which transforms and intensifies his 'argument'? But this is not 'private' or 'internal' meditation. It is dramatic monologue, spoken, to be sure indirectly, before an audience. While the mode is construed solely in terms of a character as subject, whose 'thoughts' and 'feelings' have only this isolated and enclosed reference, some of this writing cannot be understood at all; cannot, that is to say, be fully 'read' by its actual conventions and notations. For even in this monologue, of a classically reflexive type, more complex linguistic and (even within monologue) dramatic relations are in fact composed. Thus the full transition to the first-person pronoun as subject—'First, as I am his kinsman'—does not occur until line 13. In the preceding lines, though the speech is of course directly relevant to Macbeth's specific situation, there is the characteristic use of the plural pronoun, which in more integral cases can be seen as marking the important C (iii), the 'generic':

> But in these cases
> We still have judgement here—that we but teach
> Bloody instructions, which being taught return
> To plague th' inventor: this even-handed justice
> Commends th' ingredience of our poisoned chalice
> To our own lips.

It would be absurd to reduce this deliberately engaging argument, of a common condition and consequence, to a mere generalization made by this isolated and agitated man. The relations implicit in such speech before an audience belong to an indirect communal mode rather than to the mode of expressive instances spoken by an isolated subject.

At this borderline between the reflexive and the generic we can look at one very interesting example which, if I am reading it rightly, reminds us to retain the reflexive in its most evidently subjective cases. The case is also interesting as dramatic construction. It is significant at this stage of the development of monologue, even in a play which uses conventional monologue so freely, that elements of explanation are entered at some points. See for example 'Look how our partner's rapt' (142), pointing Macbeth's reflexive monologue in I, iii, and Macbeth's own explanatory and apologetic 'my dull brain was wrought/With things forgotten' (149–50). But there is a more remarkable case in v, i, where Lady Macbeth's reflexive monologue (as it must surely be defined) is dramatically defined by the condition of sleepwalking: the true monologue but overheard within the play, as in other cases. Interestingly, her speech is predominantly projective and in its later parts a form of projected (but unanswered) dialogue with Macbeth:

> I tell you yet again...

But this is, we could say, the most fully internal mode. It is private guilt and only through overhearing confession. This use of monologue, for the representation of mental *process* (either disordered, as here, or simply unarranged) as distinct from the articulation of mental *product* (fixed attitudes and beliefs, ordered stages of an argument or event, settled feelings), is of great importance in English Renaissance drama. It is this element which has sustained the narrow sense of 'soliloquy'. Linguistically it is marked by strong uses of the dramatic present (as distinct from the historic present) tense, with relatively uncomposed—in fact often directly oral rather than 'written'—sentences:

> Whence is that knocking?
> How is't with me, when every noise appals me?
> What hands are here? ha! they pluck out mine eyes!
>
> (II, ii, 57–9)

Yet these same qualities of active presence and process are to be found also in dialogue:

> M: What soldiers, whey-face?
> S: The English force, so please you.
> M: Take thy face hence. Seton! I am sick at heart,
>   When I behold—Seton, I say! This push...
>
> (IV, iii, 17–20)

At the same time monologue, including reflexive monologue, can be quite differently composed, in weaker present or in perfect or past tenses:

> I have almost forgot the taste of fears:
> The time has been, my senses would have cooled
> To hear a night-shriek...
>
> (v, v, 9–11)

Thus there is no formal equivalence between presumed psychological content, of a subjective kind, and a mode of writing centred on a single and isolated speaker. The 'soliloquy', to put it another way, is not 'inner speech' in any defining or exclusive sense. The degrees of address, over a range from 'self-discoursing practice' to indirect and direct monologue of more outward kinds, control much more variable and complex relations, which the modern private/public dichotomy cannot construe; indeed often literally cannot read.

It is on this basis that we can return to the relations between the reflexive and the generic. For.the true generic is the completion of that common element of the reflexive which is not in any limiting sense 'inner speech' but is the engagement, often from within personal crisis, with a common condition. The most notable example in *Macbeth*, again linguistically marked by the plural pronoun, is the famous

> Tomorrow, and tomorrow, and tomorrow,
> Creeps in this petty pace from day to day,
> To the last syllable of recorded time;
> And all our yesterdays have lighted fools
> The way to dusty death...
>
> (IV, v, 19–23)

This is not to be reduced to the speech of a subjective psychological condition, as can be seen from its evident formal difference from a closely related speech in the same Act:

> I have lived long enough: my way of life
> Is fall'n into the sear, the yellow leaf...
>
> (V, iii, 22–3)

The latter is reflexive, within an individual condition; the former is generic, engaging a possible common response within a common condition. It is relevant to notice that the linguistic forms of the generic are often close to those of shared prayer, or prayer offered for sharing, within liturgy, though in the two most famous cases—this from *Macbeth* and 'To be or not to be' in *Hamlet*—the content has been transformed. The developed reflexive, in its more or less subjective forms, but also this dramatic rather than orthodox-liturgical generic, are then remarkable extensions of the range of public discourse, within the changing social and historical conditions of this secular drama.

The point of distinguishing and illustrating these types of monologue is not primarily classification, but an extension of vocabulary in the service of analytic rather than characterizing reading. There is room for argument about each of the types and their definitions, and of course for variation of judgment in the reading and assigning of any particular example. In my own analysis of *Macbeth* the distribution can be summarized as follows:

	Ai	Aii	Aiii	Bi	Bii	Biii	Ci	Cii	Ciii	Di	Dii	Diii
% of text:	–	–	–	O.2	1.5	1	2.2	9	1.1	16.6	31	37.4

Analysis of the variations of monologue leads necessarily into variations of dialogue and of the relations between monologue and dialogue. These, as has been argued, are especially complex in this unusually flexible dramatic form. Thus the generic quoted above occurs within very complex staging. v, v begins with Macbeth ordering his defences: therefore speaking to soldiers. There is a break at the 'cry within of women' and Macbeth's question to Seton, who has then perhaps been present from the beginning. Macbeth's reflexive 'I have almost forgot the taste of fears' is then not necessarily 'soliloquy' in the sense of being alone on the stage; it is, more strictly, inset indirect address. The next break is the question 'Wherefore was that cry?', which Seton answers. Has he left and returned? What matters more is the rapid and flexible shift between exchange, as in the question and answer, and both direct in-play ('Hang out our banners') and reflexive ('I have supped full with horrors') address. This kind of shift is especially notable in the movement from response (of its kind) to the news that the queen is dead—the reduced exchange—to the fully generic monologue, downstage but not necessarily 'alone', of 'Tomorrow, and tomorrow, and tomorrow', itself pointed by the next shift, with the certain entry of a messenger: 'Thou com'st to use thy tongue'.

Such relations between monologue and dialogue, and more crucially between levels and types of address, are also evident, as was argued, within different kinds of dialogue, where the 'object of address' can be variable and shifting. We can now turn to some important examples of such shifts and variations.

Monologue and Dialogue in *Hamlet*

Hamlet is often thought of as the very type of the soliloquizing play: the dramatic presentation of an isolated, introspective character within an action from which he is alienated. Yet the play is in no way exceptional for its proportion of monologue, at some eight per cent. There is almost twice as much in *Macbeth*. The monologues of *Hamlet* himself are well remembered, but they compose only some six per cent of the play. Of these, more than half are reflexive—C(ii):

> O, that this too too solid flesh would melt...(I,ii)
> O, what a rogue and peasant slave am I!...(II,ii)
> How all occasions do inform against me...(IV, iv)

There are elements of the secretive-explanatory in the first of these, just as there are elements of the reflexive in the primarily secretive-explanatory B (ii) examples: I, ii, 255–8; I, v, 92–112; III, ii; 391–402; III, iii, 72–96. The most famous monologue—'To be or not to be...', III, i,—is fully generic, C (iii), and there is a clear generic element in the mainly reflexive 'How all occasions...'. Taken together, and allowing for the fact that the power of the speeches may be much greater than their numerical proportion, there is no real basis for describing *Hamlet* as a mainly soliloquizing play. On the contrary, some of its unique effects depend not on monologue but on other forms.

What is indeed unusual in *Hamlet* is the proportion of the play in which Hamlet is present and talking, and the further proportion in which he is being talked about. The figures are:

Hamlet alone:	6%
Hamlet with one other:	20%
Hamlet with others:	31%

One on Hamlet:	1%
Two on Hamlet:	11%
More than two on Hamlet:	5%

We can then see that Hamlet is present and speaks in no less than fifty-seven per cent of the lines of the whole play, and is being spoken about in another seventeen per cent. Thus in virtually three quarters of the play the figure of Hamlet is central.

It is interesting to look at the kinds of speech that occur when Hamlet is present. Much more common than his isolated monologues are his essentially private speeches with others. But there is then a distinction. He talks privately with Horatio in scenes as long as his monologues, and this kind of speech is essentially that which became known in French drama as speech with a *confident*. Horatio is the respectful and loyal companion with whom Hamlet can speak his mind. Indeed what is often misremembered as a 'soliloquy' — 'Give me that man that is not passion's slave'—is an expression of this precise relationship:

> Ha: Horatio, thou art e'en as just a man
> As e'er my conversation coped withal
> Ho: O, my dear lord
> Ha: Nay, do not think I flatter,
> For what advancement may I hope from thee...
>   ...give me that man
> That is not passion's slave, and I will wear him
> In my heart's core, ay in my heart of heart,
> As I do thee.
>
> (III, ii)

What may then be seen as happening is that it is in this selected and confiding talk that there is, as it were, a norm for Hamlet: significantly different not only from his talk with others but also from his own dramatically differentiated monologues. The normative dialogue with Horatio is by definition of an enclosed kind—D (ii)—but it has different functions from the two other main kinds of apparently enclosed dialogue, with his mother and with Ophelia. The private talk with his mother (III, iv), though actually overheard by Polonius, is a quite different kind of enclosure: intensely personal but as dialogue mainly demonstrative and declamatory, in a development of what are elsewhere public forms. In a scene of 217 lines, the

Queen speaks only 38, and Hamlet's speeches—which have to be called that, though varying in mode from the rhetorically formal 'Look here, upon this picture, and on this...' to the personally direct 'Let the bloat king tempt you again to bed'—are a kind of public prosecution, to which no real defence is offered.

The talk with Ophelia is different again, for though in tone and manner private it is either actually or probably being overheard and observed (III, i and III, ii).

Already from the variation in what is technically enclosed dialogue with one other there are dramatic effects of a special kind. There is a central uncertainty in how Hamlet will speak, over a range from the steady norm with Horatio to the mischievous display with Ophelia. This uncertainty, which is often referred to the private character of Hamlet and then technically exemplified in soliloquy, is a function, primarily, of the unusual variation of modes and relationships within dialogue. Moreover it is significant that so much emphasis is given to other persons talking about Hamlet. The 'change' in his 'character', after he has been told by the Ghost of his father's murder, is actually presented through the view of him by others, which in its speculation and uncertainty is, as it were, negatively confirmed by his variable self-presentation in his subsequent speech to others. The normative *confident* relationship with Horatio holds, but is not in itself enough to control the dazzling and bewildering series of self-presentations, in dialogue as much as in monologue, which presents, openly and dramatically rather than introspectively, a radically uncertain and shifting identity. What is part stratagem, within a known dramatic convention of concealment or self-protection by feigned madness, is in its larger part an innovative dramatic presentation of problematic *relationships*, expressed in different kinds of dialogue, which go so far as to put the stable identity of the central speaking character (who cannot be abstracted from these modes) in open question.

It is interesting that this radical uncertainty about Hamlet is introduced not by monologue or soliloquy, and not first by his shifting and problematic dialogue with others, but by others discussing him: Ophelia and Polonius in II, i; the King and Queen with Rosencrantz and Guildenstern in II, ii, and then the King and Queen with Polonius later in the same scene. It is only then, under observation from the audience, that the unfamiliar Hamlet appears:

> But look where sadly the poor wretch comes reading.

This is crucially different, for example, from the mad guise of Edgar in *King Lear*, where the conventional presentation in III, iv is dramatically preceded by his own explanation of the assumption of the guise, in II, iii. To the audience, also, from this point in the play, the speaking Hamlet is problematic.

What is unusual and perhaps unique, then, in *Hamlet* is not the emphasis of 'soliloquy' or reflexive or other kinds of monologue, but a set of variations in dialogue in relation with monologue in which both the central speaking subject and the central object of speech are dispersed from stable and persistent identity and relationships. The common effect of the play, wrongly identified with an abstracted character and his soliloquizing, is a more general and conscious effect of a wider range of shifting speech forms. .

Beyond Dialogue

The idea of dialogue, even in its variable forms, presumes a form of exchange. This is represented in modern information theory in A–B or A–B–C models and diagrams, with arrows of interaction. Monologue, in all its uses, can be made congruent with such models, taking the audience as B. Yet it is not only that the function of exchange is then altered, often to the point where it is only tacitly presumed. It is that any attempted assimilation of monologue, but then also of certain kinds of dramatic dialogue, to the theoretical function of exchange comes to exclude other possible relations which are of great importance in certain types and moments of drama. This can be seen most clearly in three scenes of *King Lear*: Act Three, Scenes Two and Four (usually known as the storm scenes) and Act Four, Scene Six. The central point in these scenes is the disorder of normal relations and functions, yet it cannot be said (as, glibly, of certain kinds of modern drama) that this is the drama of 'non-communication'. Rational, ordered and connecting exchange indeed breaks down, with the social relations that necessarily underlie its forms. But it is very far from 'non-communication', in the cant contemporary sense in which the 'fact' that 'human beings cannot fully communicate' is offered as a flat datum. What actually happens is a very powerful kind of dramatic writing which is linguistically beyond the limited theoretical assumptions of exchange, just as Lear and his family and kingdom are beyond the limited political assumptions of the feudal state and its formal relations. At certain points there is absolute exposure and breakdown, but these are still *formally* written and shown.

Thus Act Three, Scene Two, begins with a variation of monologue, essentially of the generic type, C (iii). It is predominantly first-person in its pronouns, as in the reflexive monologue, but it is wholly different in mood. Formally, in fact, it is an *apostrophe*, an exclamatory address: not in its original negative Greek sense, of turning away to no one in particular, but in the developed dramatic sense of an exclamatory address to persons not present on the stage or, as here, to powers wholly beyond the human action. Lear addresses the winds and thunder and lightning of the storm, in defiance and personal complaint. The Fool is with him, and addresses him directly, to take shelter, but the apostrophe is unbroken. When the Fool next speaks, he too is in a singular dimension: in fact the characteristic wit and song of the traditional fool, as in monologue B (iii). It is the coexistence of these different singular dimensions that produces a specific general form, beyond dialogue.

When Kent enters, there is a move back towards dialogue. Both Kent and the Fool attempt exchange, and Lear rejoins this from line 68—'Come on, my boy', after the further apostrophe of lines 49 to 58 has passed and then begun to move back, in 58–59, to the reflexive. The general tenor of the scene is confirmed, however, when Lear and Kent go in and the Fool is left to characteristic monologue, with his prophecy, in a popular idiom, of a world turned upside down.

Act Three, Scene Four, is more complex, and takes us further beyond speech as exchange. It begins, to line 26, with relatively normal dialogue, in the move to shelter, though with no real exchange, since Lear continues (8 to 19) his essentially monologic preoccupation. When he is left alone, there is pure monologue (28 to 36) which moves from apostrophe to reflexive:

> Poor naked wretches, whereso'er you are,
> That bide the pelting of this pitiless storm...
>   ...O, I have ta'en
> Too little care of this!

But then the mode changes again, with the emergence of Edgar disguised as a madman. This has been conventionally prepared in Edgar's explanatory (B ii) monologue in Act Two, Scene Three, but now throughout the scene the disguise is absolute: the individual character has shifted to the characteristic type. Through the whole middle part of the scene (45 to 124), and at one coexistent level beyond it, speech is moved into a different dimension. It is not in itself disordered. Syntactic forms are carefully retained:

> E: ...Wine loved I deeply, dice dearly; and in woman out-paramoured the Turk. False of heart, light of ear, bloody of hand; hog in sloth, fox in stealth, wolf in greediness, dog in madness, lion in prey...
>
> L: ...Consider him well, Thou ow'st the worm no silk, the beast no hide, the sheep no wool, the cat no perfume. Ha! Here's three on's are sophisticated: thou art the thing itself. Unaccommodated man is no more but such a poor, bare, forked animal as thou art.

Edgar as madman answers questions, but within his own forms. Lear addresses him, but in exclamation, not exchange. The Fool's comments are within his own fixed character. Kent's would-be normative intervention is ignored.

In the broadest technical sense this is dramatic dialogue, and it is important to emphasize that conscious dramatic writing can compose even this extremity of exposure and breakdown. Yet the scene is also beyond dialogue in all its ordinary connotations of exchange. What is both written and powerfully communicated is a complex speech form within which singular non-exchange modes coexist but in their own kind of relationship: beyond reason for a reason; beyond the formalities of accommodation to the intensities and extremities of exposure. The whole writing is not to be divided into A–B–C but is a form for orchestrated voices, carrying its specific whole meaning. Then it changes again, with the arrival of Gloucester, and within a re-established dialogue of known identities Lear attempts a fantastic relationship with the madman as philosopher. The limits of exchange are reached yet again, significantly marked by Gloucester's 'No words, no words; hush!' and Edgar's closing traditional rhyme.

There is a different but comparable form in that part of Act Four, Scene Six in which Lear is present (81–201). Here the form is that of a complex monologic type of speech, to which Edgar and Gloucester, and later the Gentleman, are in effect witnesses, though they may speak aside or, in an attempt at exchange dialogue, give cues. It is a form in which, as often in other ways, what we separate as monologue and dialogue are not distinctly arranged forms but are elements in a whole form in which one or other may become, as here, temporarily dominant. What Lear says is not soliloquy, in the sense of private reflection. It is in part characteristic discourse, in the convention of madness—

> There's my gauntlet; I'll prove it on a giant. Bring up the brown bills. O, well flown, bird...;

in part a form consciously based on formal address, as from the seat of power—'I pardon that man's life'—but with the power and its confirming relations gone, and then with authority itself subverted:

> ...See how yond justice rails upon yond simple thief. Hark in thine ear: change places and, handy-dandy, which is the justice, which is the thief? Thou hast seen a farmer's dog bark at a beggar?
> Ay, sir.
> And the creature run from the cur? there thou mightst behold the great image of authority—a dog's obeyed in office.

The underlying mode is one of royal argument, to be respectfully attended. Yet it has either to be whispered ('in thine ear') or break towards exclamation, denunciation and rage. What wells up through the lost but remembered formalities of state is a disordered because decentred homily:

> I will preach to thee: mark!
> ...When we are born, we cry that we are come
> To this great stage of fools.

The world-view of this is a loss of state and a religious critique of power and vanity, written in the powerful and protected form of a personal disorder that is both apparent and real. The communicative level of this kind of drama is a creative composition beyond the dialogue of fixed and reliable relationships. When neither the preacher's assigned homily nor the addressable presence of God is available, the modes of necessary speech beyond the forms of social exchange belong neither to the self, as in private soliloquy, nor to the exchange of selves, as in ordinary dialogue, but to a generic form drawing on and moving beyond both:

> Let me have surgeons;
> I am cut to th'brains...

It is an appeal or a prayer, but though Gloucester can answer, conventionally, 'You shall have anything', neither appeal nor prayer will be answered, though both, in a common voice, will be heard.

2

Notes on English Prose:
1780–1950

Some of the prose being written at the end of the eighteenth century
is not very different from some of the prose being written today. We
can usually notice words, phrases, sentences, constructions, which
would not now normally be used, but in many other words and
phrases and sentences we are aware mainly of continuity, within a
relatively stable modern English. Most of the prose forms with which
we are now familiar—the novel, the essay, the treatise, the journal—
were then in regular use, and there are also some important continuities in ideas and feelings.

We shall see, on closer examination, how much has changed in
English prose, but the stress on continuity is worth making at the
beginning. The two centuries since 1780 are the making of modern
Britain. Both the connections and the gaps between some of the early
and some of the later stages are significant. There are moments when
we know Coleridge or Cobbett or Paine or Jane Austen as ancestors:
as connected with us in a land and through a language, but across an
evident gap of historical time. There are also moments when in a
thing seen, a thing said, a thing written in a particular way, we feel
not distance but closeness: a man or woman; a writer; a known experience or idea; a known country.

We can see how much has changed in these centuries, in the social
and physical landscape of Britain. Here I want to consider how the
writer's landscape has changed: in connection, undoubtedly, with
the more general changes; but specifically, also, in his or her position
as writer, and in the consequent relations with readers. I find I have
always to remind myself, as I read the prose of these centuries, how
substantial these changes have been. In some simple ways, the signs
are everywhere, but certain important kinds of prose, now as then,

are written and read by a minority, in which there is less apparent change. To what extent can I feel, passing, say, from Coleridge to Eliot, that in the years between them literacy has become a quite different kind of social fact?

> There remains but one other point of distinction possible, and this must be, and in fact is, the true cause of the impression made on us. It is the unpremeditated and evidently habitual *arrangement* of his words, grounded on the habit of foreseeing in each integral part, or (more plainly) in every sentence, the whole that he then intends to communicate. (*The Friend*, 1818)

> The existing monuments form an ideal order among themselves, which is modified by the introduction of the new (the really new) work of art among them. The existing order is complete before the new work arrives; for order to persist after the supervention of novelty, the *whole* existing order must be, if ever so slightly, altered; and so the relations, proportions, values of each work of art toward the whole are readjusted: and this is conformity between the old and the new. (*Tradition and the Individual Talent*, 1917)

Each man is writing, in these instances, for readers with his own particular interests (interests, as it happens, in *order*); the reader, in a critical way, seems in each case to include the writer. It can be different with their contemporaries: Cobbett writing in the *Political Register*; Lawrence in a popular magazine.

> I never before saw *country* people, and reapers too, observe, so miserable in appearance as these. There were some very pretty girls, but ragged as colts and as pale as ashes. The day was cold too, and frost hardly off the ground; and their blue arms and lips would have made any heart ache but that of a seat-seller or a loan-jobber. A little after passing by these poor things, whom I left, cursing, as I went, those who had brought them to this state, I came to a group of shabby houses upon a hill. (*Rural Rides*, 1821)

> I am so tired of being told that I want mankind to go back to the condition of savages. As if modern city people weren't about the crudest, rawest, most crassly savage monkeys that ever existed, when it comes to the relation of man and woman. All I see in our vaunted civilization is men and women smashing each other emotionally and physically to bits, and all I ask is that they should pause and consider. (*We Need One Another*, 1930)

Here the flow is all outward, and the writer is not—does not seem to be—speaking in any way to himself; he is writing (though speaking is a good way of putting it, as we listen to the sentences) *for* himself, *in front of* a public. There are strengths and weaknesses in each mode; I give the examples, at this stage, simply to indicate the complexity of the actual history.

On the British mainland, at the end of the eighteenth century, there were less than eleven million people. By the middle of the nineteenth century there were twice as many; by the early twentieth century twice as many again. In our own period, there are more than fifty-one millions. At the end of the eighteenth century, most people were living in country areas. By 1851, the urban population exceeded the rural, for the first time in any society in the history of the world. By the end of the nineteenth century three people lived in towns, for every one in the country. In our own period the proportion is four to one. These extraordinary changes, in numbers and in kinds of community, were bound to affect, though in complicated ways, so important a means of communication as prose. When we feel this history not as figures but as people and places, we know that this must be so.

In the same history, more people were learning to read. We cannot tell exactly how many readers there were at the end of the eighteenth century. The nearest estimate I can make is some four or five million. But from just this time, standards of literacy were rising, and when we put these to the increasing number of people, the number of readers was increasing remarkably. By 1840 it was getting on for twelve million; by 1870, it was more than twenty million; by 1900, more than thirty million. In our own century, with nearly universal literacy, readers on the British mainland have grown to between forty and fifty million: about ten times as many as when Cobbelt and Coleridge were writing.

Much depends, then, not on the simple increase in numbers of readers, though this is in many ways a transforming social fact; but on the kinds of writing made available to them, and thus on the real relations between so many different readers and so many kinds of writers. If we look first at books, we see, as a matter of numbers, the kinds of change we would expect. At the end of the eighteenth century the number of titles published each year was rising sharply. It had been stuck at about 100 a year in the middle of the century, but in the 1790s it averages 372, and was continuing to rise. Between

1802 and 1827, the annual number of titles (new books and reissues) averaged 580; an important part of this increase was in novels, as it had been since 1780. By the middle of the nineteenth century, the average annual figure was more than 2,600; by 1901, more than 6,000; by 1913, more than 12,000; by 1937, more than 17,000; by the 1960s, well over 20,000. Most of these books, throughout, were in prose, and this reminds us of the vastness of the period we are trying to understand.

Yet although the increase in titles almost matched the increase in literacy, the book-reading public increased only slowly and unevenly. Tom Paine's *Rights of Man*, in the 1790s, sold 50,000 copies in a few weeks, and much more widely in a cheap edition. But the average size of an edition was about 1,250 for a novel, 750 for more general works. Walter Scott, the most popular novelist of the early nineteenth century, sold 10,000 copies of *Rob Roy* in a fortnight, but this was not a much higher figure than those of earlier popular successes, in the mid-eighteenth century. Twenty years later, the edition of the first number of Dickens's *Pickwick Papers* was 400; this had climbed, by the fifteenth number, to 40,000. This was in serial publication, of course. *Uncle Tom's Cabin*, in book form, sold 150,000 in its first six months, but George Eliot's popular success, *Adam Bede*, in the same decade (the 1850s) sold some 14,000–15,000. A main obstacle was cost. Books became markedly cheaper in the 1830s and 1840s, with new printing methods and cloth instead of leather binding. There had been many ventures, since the 1780s, in cheap reprint series. Yet in a wretched general standard of living, books were still, for most people, occasional luxuries; and for all the devices of libraries and other corporate buying, the book-reading public was largely defined by social and economic class, and continued to be so even as literacy was becoming universal. It is only in our own century, and still in incomplete ways, that books began to come with any convenience to the majority of people. If, today, we take all kinds of distribution into account (including the important and spectacular growth of public-library issues) we find some fifteen to twenty books read each year for every adult in the population; but this average figure conceals extremely unequal individual uses. I have estimated that it was only in the 1950s, when a majority of the population had been literate for well over a century, that a majority came to read books with any sort of regularity; and since this majority is a bare one, the development of the book-reading public has still a considerable way to go.

The increases in population and literacy were matched much earlier by other kinds of writing, in newspapers and magazines. Already in the 1820s people bought more than a million copies of the *Last Dying Speech and Confession* of the murderer of Maria Marten, but this was occasional reading; the regular reading of newspapers and magazines had to wait on lower costs and improved distribution. I have estimated that in 1820 about one person in a hundred read daily or Sunday newspapers; about ten in a hundred the occasional broadsheet. In 1860 about three in a hundred read a daily newspaper, twelve in a hundred a Sunday paper. These figures are of course very markedly lower than the actually literate population. Eventually, a majority read Sunday papers by about 1910, and daily papers by about 1920. Sunday papers reached nearly universal distribution between the wars, and daily papers during the Second World War. Here then, in newspapers, was the most widely distributed prose. The prose of books, in relation to it, was and is a minority matter.

This history has important implications in the tones and styles of prose, though they are not all on the surface, as we shall see. Yet it is still only part of the real history of the relations between writers and readers. When we consider those writers who are still read, we find that here, also, there is a social history. From the mid-eighteenth century the social and educational background of the most important writers was beginning to change, with many more from middle-class and professional families, and less, in proportion, who had passed through the universities of Oxford and Cambridge. More, too, were becoming professional writers, in the sense of having no independent income or other employment, though the really marked period for this change does not begin until the 1830s. In the late eighteenth and early nineteenth centuries, the relative importance of middle-class writers continued, but new social groups began to be better represented, with writers born in the families of tradesmen, farmers and craftsmen. This trend, together with the increasing importance of women writers, continued through the nineteenth century, but it was modified by the extensive reorganization of education in the period, especially in the universities and the new private schools. In some ways, English writers of the late nineteenth and early twentieth century are more homogeneous as a class than their early Victorian predecessors; and it has remained a decisive element in the relation of writers to readers that even where social origins have become more varied, the educational pattern has been more uniform; this is particularly important in such kinds of writing as history, philosophy, social criticism and science. In the twentieth century, as a result of some improved access from elementary to higher education, writers have had more varied social origins than their immediate predecessors, but many of their ideas about writing have been mediated through a minority area of higher education, both directly and indirectly. It is still quite clear in Britain today that there is not only a marked inequality of representation in writers, as between different social groups, with the majority of writing still coming from a highly organized middle class; but also, in relation to this, a definition of interest which has to do with their quite common educational background, which only a few share with the majority of their potential readers.

The results of this situation, in actual prose, are very difficult to analyse; we shall consider some important examples, from different periods and in very different men. But it is necessary to be aware of it, from the beginning. In its most general sense, the writing of prose is a transaction between discoverable numbers of writers and readers, organized in certain changing social relations which include education, class habits, distribution and publishing costs. At the same time, in its most important sense, the writing of prose is a sharing of experience which, in its human qualities, is both affected by and can transcend the received social relations. It is always so, in the relation between literature and society: that the society determines, much more than we realize and at deeper levels than we ordinarily admit, the writing of literature; but also that the society is not complete, not fully and immediately present, until the literature has been written, and that this literature, in prose as often as in any other form, can come through to stand as if on its own, with an intrinsic and permanent importance, so that we can see the rest of our living through it as well as it through the rest of our living.

The most important single development, in English prose since 1780, is the emergence of the novel as the major literary form. Perhaps between 1730 and 1750 it was temporarily dominant, but it is from the 1830s that it is regularly the form in which most of the major writers of the period work. Before the 1830s, such important novelists as Jane Austen and Scott seem relatively isolated figures beside the two generations of Romantic poets. After the 1830s, it is the generations of novelists which are most marked, and it is in the novel, primarily, that the great creative discoveries are made. It is not only, as it is sometimes put, that the novel began to include kinds of experience which would have been previously written in verse. It is mainly that new kinds of experience, in an essentially different civilization, flowed into the novel and were the bases of its new and extraordinary growth and achievement.

The effects on prose are then very marked. It becomes normal to look, in prose, for much of the finest writing of the age. But, further, this development of the novel transforms many received ideas of what literature is, and among these received ideas is the traditional assumption of the character of good prose. It is still remarkable, in a persistently narrow critical tradition, that the contrast between verse and prose can be made as if it were self-evidently a contrast between the 'imaginative' and the 'prosaic'. This is related to the still common habit of using 'poetry' as a normal and adequate synonym for 'literature', and to such symptoms, even in some of the best critical writing on the novel, as describing its organization as that of a 'dramatic poem'. What needs to be stressed is the originality of every kind, in form, language and subject, which can be found in the English novel from Dickens to Lawrence. This originality requires its own and specific critical recognitions, but it throws light, also, on kinds of writing outside itself. Before the novel was the major literary form, the best prose was normally looked for in essays and in similar kinds of general discourse. Such prose, of course, has continued to be important, but the notions of style derived from it have been damaging, not only to the novel, but to other kinds of writing. It is at this point, and especially as it refers to a polite and learned tradition, that the altered relations of writers and readers, which we have already discussed in a general way, become evident in new and particular ways.

One of the marks of a conservative society is that it regards style as an absolute. A style of writing or speaking is judged as a question of manners, and appreciation of this style as a question of breeding and taste. In important literary criticism, since Coleridge, this conventional assumption has been set aside. Style is known, not as an abstract quality, but as inseparable from the substance of the ideas and feelings expressed. In modern communication theory, a new dimension has been added: style is inseparable also from the precise relationship of which it is a form: commonly the relationship, whether explicit or implicit, between a writer or speaker and his or her expected reader or audience. This relationship is never mechanical. The ordinary formula in communication theory —'who says what, how, to whom, with what effect?'—characteristically neglects the real sources of communication. In practice, in studying communication, we have to add the question 'why?'. The precise relationship, which is only rarely static, is then inseparable from the substantial ideas and feelings, which might otherwise be abstracted as a 'content' without form. In almost all writing, the language which is at once form and content includes, though often unconsciously, the real relationships, and the tension between these and the conscious relationship, of the writer and others.

It is remarkable how often, in literary criticism but especially in ephemeral commentary, the mechanical version of style as an abstract quality, supported of course by the unnoticed conventions and traditions of particular groups, is still in practice assumed. But when the writing or speaking in question is not literary, the assumption is almost universal. Style is regarded as a decoration, a tasteful or mannered addition to substance, even in politics, where the kind of experience being drawn on and the version of other men indicated by a particular way of talking to them are not only substantial but are even crucial to the precise nature of a political act. It is especially significant in our own political world, of public relations and managed political images, that this connection between a way of living and a way of speaking to others should be so often suppressed. Such a connection, in a democracy, should be open and central, and its theoretical suppression is evidently related to the many practical devices for limiting or circumventing or managing democracy, which continually reveal themselves in particular ways of speaking and writing.

The most evident crisis in the language of politics occurred, not surprisingly, in the years between 1770 and 1830, when the struggle for and against democracy was taking place in an England being radically transformed by major social and economic changes. There have been equally important periods of crisis, of just this kind, in our subsequent history—not least, perhaps, the years through which we have just been living. There is also that very remarkable earlier crisis, with even more decisive effects on the uses of English, in the Civil War and Commonwealth. But the period of Junius and Burke and Tom Paine, of Cobbett and Hazlitt and Carlyle, is remarkable by any standards. Consider these two passages, written within months of each other:

> Your Grace can best inform us for which of Mr. Wilkes's good qualities you first honoured him with your friendship, or how long it was before you discovered those bad ones in him at which, it seems, your delicacy was offended. Remember, my Lord, that you continued your connection with Mr. Wilkes long after he had been convicted of those crimes which you have since taken pains to represent in the blackest colours of blasphemy and treason. How unlucky it is that the first instance you have given us of a scrupulous regard to decorum is united with the breach of a moral obligation! For my own part, my Lord, I am proud enough to affirm that, if I had been weak enough to form such a friendship, I would never have been base enough to betray it. But, let Mr. Wilkes's character be what it may, this at least is certain, that, circumstanced as he is with regard to the public, even his vices plead for him. The people of England have too much discernment to suffer your Grace to take advantage of the failings of a private character, to establish a precedent by which the public liberty is affected, and which you may hereafter, with equal ease and satisfaction, employ to the ruin of the best men of the Kingdom. (*Junius Letters,* 1770)

> I will not believe, what no other man living believes, that Mr. Wilkes was punished for the indecency of his publications, or the impiety of his ransacked closet. If he had fallen in a common slaughter of libellers and blasphemers, I could well believe that nothing more was meant than was pretended. But when I see, that, for years together, full as impious, and perhaps more dangerous writings to religion, and virtue, and order, have not been punished, nor their authors discountenanced ... I must consider this as a shocking and shameless pretence ... Does not the public behold with indignation, persons not only generally scandalous in their lives, but the identical persons who, by their society, their instruction, their example, their encouragement, have drawn this man into the very faults which have furnished the Cabal with a pretence for his persecution, loaded with every kind of favour, honour and distinction, which a Court can bestow? ... When therefore I reflect upon this method pursued by the Cabal in distributing rewards and punishments, I must conclude that Mr. Wilkes is the object of persecu-

> tion, not on account of what he has done in common with others who
> are the objects of reward, but for that in which he differs from many
> of them: that he is pursued for the spirited dispositions which are
> blended with his vices; for his unconquerable firmness, for his
> resolute, indefatigable, strenuous resistance against oppression.
> (*Thoughts on the Causes of the Present Discontents*, 1770)

The first of these passages is by Junius; the second is by Burke. What
they have in common is sufficiently remarkable: the exposure of a
political move made under the cover of morality. The strength of the
argument, in each case, draws on an important assumption of public
candour. Yet the differences are equally interesting. Junius relies on
a distinction between public and private morality which is ultimately
a matter of aristocratic convention: Grafton's disloyalty to a friend
is a decisive breach of the decorum on which he relies, and even the
'best men of the kingdom' might be similarly ruined. The attack is
then on a personal hypocrisy, a failing within an agreed convention.
It is an *ad hominem* denunciation, within the moral conventions of a
ruling class. Burke takes account of the same perception, but he does
not rely on it. There is a radical difference between Junius's 'even his
vices plead for him' and Burke's distinction between 'what he has
done in common' and 'that in which he differs'. There is thus a
basis, in Burke, for an appeal to general principles, beyond the exposure of a personal failing within the convention. He can at least
approach the moral judgement of a system of government, as
something more general and more important than the faults of a particular man in power.

This substantial difference of political interest is embodied in the
contrasted forms of writing. Junius, necessarily, extends political
controversy by the device of the open letter: the personal denunciation put into general print. Burke, on the other hand, while no less
immediate, is writing in a genuinely public way, not only referring
the question to general principles, but describing a system of government as part of a public inquiry. The important shift from the style
of eighteenth-century politics, within a ruling class, to the style of a
more public and open politics, can then be decisively observed.
Junius attacks by breaking the convention: he publishes and cir-
culates the personal denunciation. But this is a political challenge
within existing forms: an out-group using publication against an in-
group. Burke, although his immediate motives seem to have been of

much the same kind, is preparing a wholly different kind of argument. His degree of generalization and abstraction is the necessary basis of a more general and more abstract politics. What his style loses in liveliness it gains in seriousness. A genuinely public political argument could only begin when there was this kind of assertion of principles.

It is then ironic to go forward some twenty years, and find Burke in a paradoxical position. We have taken too little notice of the fact that the *Reflections on the Revolution in France* is in the form of an open letter. It is not, of course, the method of Junius, the scandalous challenge within as well as against a convention. Burke uses the letter to 'a very young gentleman at Paris' for more subtle effects. His essential argument is at least as much about English as about French politics, but by writing as an Englishman to a Frenchman he can assume (what he could not prove) a representative quality, describing the English constitution *as if* to a foreigner, and thus enlisting behind him the feelings of a united patriotism. Where Junius relied on the itch for scandal which could be directed into an indignation for liberty, Burke now relies on a pretended national unity of political feeling, to which in fact he is trying to persuade his *English* readers.

> You see, sir, that in this enlightened age I am bold enough to confess, that we are generally men of untaught feelings; that, instead of casting away all our old prejudices, we cherish them to a very considerable degree, and, to take more shame to ourselves, we cherish them because they are prejudices; and the longer they have lasted and the more generally they have prevailed, the more we cherish them...Your literary men, and your politicians, and so do the whole clan of the enlightened among us, essentially differ in these points. They have no respect for the wisdom of others; but they pay it off by a very full measure of confidence in their own.

In this form the literary method becomes, if we are not careful, the political proof. The youth of the 'very young gentleman at Paris' is a comparable device. It permits the decisive tone of the reflections, from settled wisdom (English politics) to inexperience (French politics), and the more subtle tactic of engaging sympathy in the very act of denunciation: the conventional presence of the correspondent, used only when it suits this particular appeal, supports the necessary distinction, for Burke's purposes, between what the French are and what they have done; the spirit of the people from the actual revolution. Thus an argument against revolution is developed by the set-ting-up, in form and language, of would-be and hoped-for relations, which in fact serve to disguise the actual relations. We can then understand why Tom Paine, in his reply, cut through to direct public address, against what he called Burke's theatrical performance.

> Lay then the axe to the root, and teach governments humanity. It is their sanguinary punishments which corrupt mankind. In England the punishment in certain cases is by *hanging, drawing,* and *quartering*: the heart of the sufferer is cut out and held up to the view of the populace. In France, under the former government, the punishments were not less barbarous. Who does not remember the execution of Da-mien, torn to pieces by horses? The effect of those cruel spectacles ex-hibited to the populace is to destroy tenderness or excite revenge; and by the base and false idea of governing men by terror, instead of reason, they become precedents. It is over the lowest class of mankind that government by terror is intended to operate, and it is on them that it operates to the worst effect. They have sense enough to feel they are the objects aimed at; and they inflict in their turn the examples of ter-ror they have been instructed to practise.
>
> There is in all European countries a large class of people of that description, which in England is called the '*mob*'. Of this class were those who committed the burnings and devastations in London in 1780, and of this class were those who carried the heads upon spikes in Paris.

Yet as we read *The Rights of Man* we find another uncertainty: the tone veers between open argument, in line with his appeal to govern-ment by reason, and what is really an anxious appeal to men of his own kind to understand the feelings of 'a large class of people of that description, which in England is called the "mob".'

Political prose then developed in two ways. It became open ra-tional argument, to men as such, and in doing so was *addressed* to nobody and was necessarily, in substance and manner, abstract. The strengths of this kind of prose have been underestimated, in a com-mon prejudice, but there is a real and inescapable weakness in that it assumes the political forms of open and rational discourse which in fact it is trying to create. Alternatively, it became direct address to an ever-widening public, having the strengths of contact, of the sounds of actual voices and experiences, as most notably in Cobbett, but in danger, always, of declining to opportunism—the devices of flattery, of any public, which could be easily learned—and to simplification, where the voice of plain man-to-man common sense could be used against connected reasoning and against real complexities.

My point is that when we read passages of these very different kinds of prose we cannot refer the question of their value to any simple criterion of style. What each method discloses is not only the general substance of the argument, but also that other substance which is the real relation of writer and reader, and at times a desired but not yet existing relation. It is difficult to feel, reading late eighteenth-century and early nineteenth-century political prose, that any of these relations was adequate, though the genius of some of the writers is very clear. But then to say that is only to say, in another way, that the new political feelings had as yet no adequate social forms. What we can learn from looking at the institutions we can learn also from looking at the prose; just as we can see in the prose, as in the history of the time, certain new relationships struggling to be formed.

In the development of the novel, the evidence is even more interesting. In descriptive power, prose was already mature, as we can see in the vividness of many journals and memoirs. But now two other uses were remarkably developed. First, there is the power of sustained analysis of a situation or state of mind. We can find in this period, from Jane Austen through George Eliot and Henry James to E.M. Forster, an assured mastery in just this faculty, though we notice also the problem of combining such analysis, isolating and static as it must often be, with the essentially different rhythms of narrative continuity. This problem appears sometimes more acute in the later examples, as increasingly, from George Eliot's later novels onward, the form of fiction of this kind comes to be determined, overall, by analysis rather than by narrative. Then, related to this, there is the second development, which appears to work, at times, in quite other directions. This is the incorporation, in prose, of spoken as opposed to written rhythms and constructions. The most evident local example of this development is in the reported direct speech (what is still, in the critical power of the dramatic tradition, called the dialogue) of the novels. Here undoubtedly, in the period we are examining, there are important developments and discoveries. But this is only one aspect of a general movement, running through the nineteenth century and reaching a climax in our own, towards the restoration of speech rhythms as the normal basis for many different kinds of prose. When we set this fact beside the increasing precision and refinement of analysis, we find some elements of contradiction and tension, which are enough in themselves to remind us, as the straight reading of the novels of course reminds us, that there is no single tradition of fiction in the period, and not even a single major tradition. We have to relate these tensions, I believe, to one of the most important results of the altering relations between writers and readers.

It seems clear that the base from which fictional analysis was developed is the important eighteenth-century tradition of philosophical and critical analysis, itself often well evidenced in the essay. The strengths of this tradition are, in a special way, the strengths of literacy. It is easy to react against the formalities of diction and construction which of course occur in such prose, but these are only the surface marks of an essential stance between writer and reader, willingly and habitually accepted on both sides, in which rationality, precision and sustained argument become possible, in new ways, once the language has been learned. It is true that this manner has been repeatedly imitated, as a kind of social manner: in sermons, correspondence columns, political speeches, we can hear the whirring sound of a merely polite mind putting pen to paper. But it is only in ignorance or prejudice that we would then disregard, for all the hated formality of the sound, the real reach of this prose: the composed page; the sense of time gained, time given; the mind working but also the mind prepared, in an exposition which assumes patience, reference, inspection, re-reading. Such prose, indeed, is a kind of climax of print, and especially of the printed book: a uniformity of tone and address; an impersonality, assuming no immediate relation between writer and reader but only possession, in a social way, of this language; a durability, as in the object itself, beyond any temporary impulse or occasion. Consider these examples:

> Offended by the frequency with which, in ethical and philosophical controversy, feeling is made the ultimate reason and justification of conduct, instead of being itself called on for a justification, while, in practice, actions the effect of which on human happiness is mischievous, are defended as being required by feeling, and the character of a person of feeling obtains a credit for desert, which he thought only due to actions, he had a real impatience of attributing praise to feeling, or of any but the most sparing reference to it, either

in the estimation of persons or in the discussion of things. In addition
to the influence which this characteristic in him, had on me and others,
we found all the opinions to which we attached most importance, constantly attacked on the ground of feeling. Utility was denounced as
cold calculation; political economy as hard-hearted; anti-population
doctrines as repulsive to the natural feelings of mankind. We retorted
by the word 'sentimentality', which along with 'declamation' and
'vague generalities', served us as common terms of opprobrium.
Although we were generally in the right, as against those who were opposed to us, the effect was that the cultivation of feeling (except the
feelings of public and private duty), was not in much esteem among us,
and had very little place in the thoughts of most of us, myself in particular. What we principally thought of, was to alter people's opinions;
to make them believe according to evidence, and know what was their
real interest, which when they once knew, they would, we thought, by
the instrument of opinion, enforce a regard to it upon one another.
(John Stuart Mill, *Autobiography* 1873)
The advantages and disabilities which these phenomena create are properly described as social, since they are the result of social institutions,
and can by the action of society be maintained or corrected. Experience shows that, when combined, as is normally the case, with extreme disparities of economic power between those who own and
direct, and those who execute and are directed, but rarely own, they
clog the mechanism of society and corrode its spirit. Except in so far as
they are modified, as they partially have been, by deliberate intervention, they produce results surprisingly similar to those foretold by the
genius of Marx. They divide what might have been a community into
contending classes, of which one is engaged in a struggle to share in advantages which it does not yet enjoy and to limit the exercise of
economic authority, while the other is occupied in a nervous effort to
defend its position against encroachments. (R.H. Tawney, *Equality*,
1931)

The evident gain, in this kind of prose, is a composed seriousness
capable of holding the fine distinctions and the sustained attention of
a certain necessary kind of argument. Yet this kind of composition is
effective also in a mode wider than that of argument, as we can see in
these three examples of analysis in fiction:

She had led her friend astray, and it would be a reproach to her for
ever; but her judgement was as strong as her feelings, and as strong as
it had ever been before, in reprobating any such alliance for him, as
most unequal and degrading. Her way was clear, though not quite
smooth. She spoke then, on being so entreated. What did she say? Just
what she ought, of course. A lady always does. She said enough to

show there need not be despair—and to invite him to say more himself. He *had* despaired at one period; he had received such an injunction to caution and silence, as for the time crushed every hope—she had begun by refusing to hear him. The change had perhaps been somewhat sudden—her proposal of taking another turn, her renewing the conversation which she had just put an end to, might be a little extraordinary. She felt its inconsistency; but Mr Knightley was so obliging as to put up with it, and seek no further explanation.

Seldom, very seldom, does complete truth belong to any human disclosure; seldom can it happen that something is not a little disguised, or a little mistaken; but where, as in this case, though the conduct is mistaken; the feelings are not, it may not be very material. Mr Knightley could not impute to Emma a more relenting heart than she possessed, or a heart more disposed to accept of his. (Jane Austen, *Emma*, 1816)

Lydgate was no Puritan, but he did not care for play, and winning money at it had always seemed a meanness to him; besides, he had an ideal of life which made this subservience of conduct to the gaining of small sums thoroughly hateful to him. Hitherto in his own life his wants had been supplied without any trouble to himself, and his first impulse was always to be liberal with half-crowns as matters of no importance to a gentleman; it had never occurred to him to devise a plan for getting half-crowns. He had always known in a general way that he was not rich, but he had never felt poor, and he had no power of imagining the part which the want of money plays in determining the actions of men. Money had never been a motive to him. Hence he was not ready to frame excuses for this deliberate pursuit of small gains. It was altogether repulsive to him, and he never entered into any calculation of the ratio between the Vicar's income and his more or less necessary expenditure. It was possible that he would not have made such a calculation in his own case. (George Eliot, *Middlemarch*, 1871-2)

It was the first allusion they had yet again made, needing any other hitherto so little; but when she replied, after having given him the news, that she was by no means satisfied with such a trifle as the climax to so special a suspense, she almost set him wondering if she hadn't even a larger conception of singularity for him than he had for himself. He was at all events destined to become aware little by little, as time went by, that she was all the while looking at his life, judging it, measuring it, in the light of the thing she knew, which grew to be at last, with the consecration of the years, never mentioned between them save as 'the real truth' about him. That had always been his own form of reference to it, but she adopted the form so quietly that, looking back at the end of a period, he knew there was no moment at which it was traceable that she had, as he might say, got inside his idea, or exchanged the attitude of beautifully indulging for that of still more beautifully believing him.

It was always open to him to accuse her of seeing him but as the most harmless of maniacs, and this, in the long run—since it covered so much ground—was his easiest description of their friendship. He had a screw loose for her but she liked him in spite of it and was practically, against the rest of the world, his kind wise keeper, unremunerated but fairly amused and, in the absence of other near ties, not disreputably occupied. The rest of the world of course thought him queer, but she, she only knew how, and above all why, queer; which was precisely what enabled her to dispose the concealing veil in the right fold. (Henry James, *The Beast in the Jungle*, 1903)

We can feel the strain certainly, the increasing strain, but we are not likely, in any settled judgement, to want or expect its relaxation. If we put such prose down, as we may well at times do, it is still with the certainty that in its special achievement it continues to be there; that it is not dependent, in obvious ways, on mood or address, which seem to belong elsewhere while this intent and particular analysis is composed.

Yet such a feeling is, in part, an illusion. What seems, in abstraction, simply a quality of prose is also, in fact, a community of language and sensibility: a precise community, which can by no means be taken for granted. In the long development of this particular manner, the evolution of what can be called in the best sense an educated style, there were decisive social relationships, no less so when these became habitual. It is not only the increasing separation of written language from ordinary speech. This has been masked, at times, by the adoption of habits of speech, even on private occasions, which derive from the printed forms: an increasingly self-conscious formality, dependent for its success on arranged and self-conscious circles of social conversation, which indeed one still hears but with a deep and eloquent release of breath and of tension as they break and disperse. Within a wholly written form, the distance between what can be written and what can normally be said is itself an accepted convention. It is what Jane Austen acknowledges when she writes: 'seldom, very seldom, does complete truth belong to any human disclosure': a recognition, certainly, of a general human fact, but one which impels the novelist to particular means of disclosure, beyond what can be represented in speech or even in behaviour. Consider a further example:

They had reached the house.

'You are going in, I suppose?' said he.

'No,' replied Emma, quite confirmed by the depressed manner in which he still spoke, 'I should like to take another turn. Mr Perry is not gone.' And, after proceeding a few steps, she added—'I stopped you ungraciously, just now, Mr Knightley, and, I am afraid, gave you pain. But if you have any wish to speak openly to me as a friend, or to ask my opinion of anything that you may have in contemplation—as a__ friend, indeed, you may command me. I will hear whatever you like. I will tell you exactly what I think.'

'As a friend!' repeated Mr Knightly. 'Emma, that, I fear is a word—no, I have no wish. Stay, yes, why should I hesitate? I have gone too far already for concealment. Emma, I accept your offer, extraordinary as it may seem, I accept it, and refer myself to you as a friend. Tell me, then, have I no chance of ever succeeding?'

He stopped in his earnestness to look the question, and the expression of his eyes overpowered her.

'My dearest Emma,' said he, 'for dearest you will always be, whatever the event of this hour's conversation, my dearest, most beloved Emma—tell me at once. Say "No," if it is to be said.' She could really say nothing. 'You are silent,' he cried, with great animation; 'absolutely silent! at present I ask no more.' (*Ibid.*)

Here there is a deliberate variation in levels of reported speech, from the simple representative ease of 'You are going in, I suppose?' to the anxious, qualifying formality, characteristically self-aware of the conventional danger of speechmaking, which is there in 'whatever the event of this hour's conversation' and its related, composed rhythms. This is in part a social problem, of polite speech. But it is more than that, in its best examples: we can see a comparable shift, from the representative to the composed, in the radically different sensibility of Emily Brontë.

'Why?' she asked, gazing nervously round.

'Joseph is here,' I answered, catching opportunely the roll of his cart-wheels up the road; 'and Heathcliff will come in with him. I'm not sure whether he were not at the door this moment.'

'Oh, he couldn't overhear me at the door!' said she. 'Give me Hareton, while you get the supper, and when it is ready ask me to sup with you. I want to cheat my uncomfortable conscience, and be convinced that Heathcliff has no notion of these things. He has not, has he? He does not know what being in love is?'

'I see no reason that he should not know, as well as you,' I returned; 'and *if you* are his choice, he will be the most unfortunate creature that ever was born! As soon as you become Mrs Linton, he loses friend,

and love, and all! Have you considered how you'll bear the separation,
and how he'll bear to be quite deserted in the world? Because, Miss
Catherine—'

'He quite deserted! We separated!' she exclaimed, with an accent of
indignation. 'Who is to separate us, pray? They'll meet the fate of
Milo! Not so long as I live, Ellen: for no mortal creature. Every Linton
on the face of the earth might melt into nothing, before I could consent to forsake Heathcliff. Oh, that's not what I intend— that's not
what I mean! I shouldn't be Mrs Linton were such a price demanded!
He'll be as much to me as he has been all his lifetime. Edgar must
shake off his antipathy, and tolerate him, at least. He will, when he
learns my true feelings towards him. Nelly, I see now, you think me a
selfish wretch; but did it never strike you that if Heathcliff and I married, we should be beggars? Whereas, if I marry Linton, I can aid
Heathcliff to rise, and place him out of my brother's power.'

'With your husband's money, Miss Catherine?' I asked.
'You'll find him not so pliable as you calculate upon: and though I'm
hardly a judge, I think that's the worst motive you've given yet for being the wife of young Linton.'

'It is not,' retorted she; 'it is the best! The others were the satisfaction of my whims: and for Edgar's sake, too, to satisfy him. This is
for the sake of one who comprehends in his person my feelings to
Edgar and myself. I cannot express it; but surely you and everybody
have a notion that there is or should be an existence of yours beyond
you. What were the use of my creation, if I were entirely contained
here? My great miseries in this world have been Heathcliff's miseries,
and I watched and felt each from the beginning: my great thought in
living is himself. If all else perished, and *he* remained, I should still
continue to be; and if all else remained, and he were annihilated, the
universe would turn to a mighty stranger: I should not seem a part of
it. (*Wuthering Heights,* 1847)

There is a shift from the simplicity of '"Why?", she asked, gazing
nervously round', to the full convention (acknowledged to the reader
in 'this speech' or again in 'I was only going to say that...' or 'I cannot express it; but surely...') of the central, composed manner, in the
sentences beginning 'What were the use of my creation, if I were entirely contained here?' The convention and the substance of the in-
sight are then one, but since, in the general development, the literary
and the social convention proved not to be identical, the real
strains—not of attention but of anxiety—increased. George Eliot, in
her brilliant chapter on Lydgate's vote, even exploits these strains:

'Mr Tykes's opponents have not asked any one to vote against his conscience, I believe,' said Mr Hackbutt, a rich tanner of fluent speech,

whose glittering spectacles and erect hair were turned with some severi-
ty towards innocent Mr Powderell. 'But in my judgement it behoves
us, as Directors, to consider whether we will regard it as our whole
business to carry out propositions emanating from a single quarter.
Will any member of the committe aver that he would have entertained
the idea of displacing the gentleman who has always discharged the
function of chaplain here, if it had not been suggested to him by par-
ties whose disposition it is to regard every institution of this town as a
machinery for carrying out their own views? I tax no man's motives:
let them lie between himself and a higher Power; but I do say, that
there are influences at work here which are incompatible with genuine
independence, and that a crawling servility is usually dictated by circumstances which gentlemen so conducting themselves could not af-
ford either morally or financially to avow. I myself am a layman, but I
have given no inconsiderable attention to the divisions in the Church
and...'

'Oh, damn the divisions!' burst in Mr Frank Hawley, lawyer and
town-clerk, who rarely presented himself at the board, but now looked
in hurriedly, whip in hand. (*Middlemarch*)

The language of analysis precedes the inadequacy of full disclosure
in the talk at the meeting, but also its rhythms, its formalities need be
only slightly displaced to represent the 'rich tanner of fluent speech',
with the 'glittering spectacles and erect hair', whose public manner
can be effectively broken in on, 'whip in hand', with a representative
'Oh, damn the divisions. Henry James shifts his analysis towards the
appearance of anxious, qualifying talk:

Oh he understood what she meant! 'For the thing to happen that never
does happen? For the Beast to jump out? No, I'm just where I was
about it. It isn't a matter as to which I can *choose*, I can decide for a
change. It isn't one as to which there *can* be a change. It's in the lap of
the gods. One's in the hands of one's law—there one is. As to the form
the law will take, the way it will operate, that's its own affair.'

'Yes,' Miss Bartram replied; 'of course one's fate's coming, of
course it *has* come in its own form and its own way, all the while.
Only, you know, the form and the way in your case were to have
been—well, something so exceptional and, as one may say, so particularly *your* own.'

Something in this made him look at her with suspicion. 'You say
"were to *have* been," as if in your heart you had begun to doubt.'

'Oh!' she vaguely protested.

'As if you believed,' he went on, 'that nothing will now take place'.

She shook her head slowly but rather inscrutably. 'You're far from
my thought'. (Henry James, *The Beast in the Jungle*)

To sustain a sense of talk James includes rather obvious colloquialisms—'he had a screw loose for her but she liked him in spite of it'; but at the same time, moving in from the other direction, incorporates almost every word spoken—even the vaguest 'Oh'—in a related and anxiously qualifying analysis. Within this tradition—there are of course many other examples—the relations between the received written language and the unevenness of the spoken language and of conversation forced a technical complication which came radically to affect the total form.

This is not, however, the whole tradition of major nineteenthcentury fiction. As we turn to Dickens, we find not only a different individual genuis, but a different underlying relationship between writer and reader. This is connected, of course, in obvious ways, with the expansion of the reading public, which was at an important new stage just as Dickens was beginning to write. But an altered relation, of this profound kind, is not only a consequence of altering general relationships. It is also something brought to an emerging situation: a voice, a structure of feeling, an habitual social tone. It would be fair to say that Dickens both formed and was formed by a new public for literature; but as we look at his very individual yet characteristic genius, we have to stress something more than formation and reaction; we have to insist, indeed, on an element which we can best describe as release: the bringing of a particular energy, already present in speech, to the new problems and opportunities of an expanding prose.

> WHY, yes. It cannot be disguised. There *are*, at Chesney Wold this January week, some ladies and gentlemen of the newest fashion, who have set up a Dandyism — in Religion, for instance. Who, in mere lackadaisical want of an emotion, have agreed upon a little dandy talk about the Vulgar wanting faith in things in general; meaning, in the things that have been tried and found wanting, as though a low fellow should unaccountably lose faith in a bad shilling, after finding it out! Who would make the Vulgar very picturesque and faithful, by putting back the hands upon the Clock of Time, and cancelling a few hundred years of history.
>
> There are also ladies and gentlemen of another fashion, not so new, but very elegant, who have agreed to put a smooth glaze on the world and to keep down all its realities. For whom everything must be languid and pretty. Who have found out the perpetual stoppage. Who are to rejoice at nothing, and be sorry for nothing. Who are not to be disturbed by ideas. (*Bleak House*, 1852-3)

Yet it is not only Dickens:

> WHO is that young gentleman on horseback? He is one of the young Walters of Bearwood. What! He who lately stood for Nottingham? No; a younger brother. And who are those in the carriage, those ladies? Those are his sisters, Mr Walter's daughters. A fine family! Oh, bless you, yes; a large family; very good people all of them, very.
>
> It is one o'clock. The various steeples proclaim the farmers' dinner hour. Every inn has a public ordinary; which shall we go to? The George is round here; the Angel is near at hand; here is the Broad Face; onward there is the Wheat Sheaf, the Wheel, the Elephant; and there is the White Hart, the Ship, the Black Horse, the Mitre, the Peacock, the Turk's Head, and several more to which we may go. This one round the corner will do; let us see, what is it called! Ah, never mind what its name is. Here we are in the public room, just in time. The clatter of knives and forks has just begun. Some of the guests are too busy filling themselves to speak; but the most are too full of the topics of the day to remain quiet. Let us open our ears.
>
> 'Roast beef, sir?—Robert Peel dare not—help you, Mr Jackson?— labourers' wages—potatoes?—Sir Robert Reel—salt?—waiter!—yes, sir—Robert Peel——potatoes—carve this pig—knife—cut of- fhishead—Peel—roast pig?—roast—Peel—waiter!—Canada flour— fowl?—majority of votes—this way, gentlemen, seats disengaged here—turn them out—Conservative ministry—boiled mut- ton—church extension—over done—take in—glass of ale—no relief this year—coming, sir—waiter, remove—county members—help you to—parliamentary—greens—Peel—no more tongue, thank you—two thousand miles off—American wheat—cheated—peti- tion—clear the table—thrown under and never read—petition— quite enough, thank you—Wallingford dinner, Mr Black- stone—powerless—nearly—false pretences—farmers—always suffering distress—Peel—so help me God...(Alexander Somerville, *The Whistler at the Plough*, 1843)

Or again:

> 'Well, I can't say as I thinks sweeping the streets is hard work. I'd rather sweep two hours than shovel one. It tires one's arms and back so, to go on shovelling. You can't change, you see, sir, and the same parts keeps getting gripped more and more. Then you must mind your eye, if you're shovelling slop into a cart, perticler so; or some feller may run off with a complaint that he's been splashed o' purpose. *Is* a man ever splashed o' purpose? No. sir, not as I knows on, in course not. [Laughing.] Why should he?
>
> 'The streets *must* be done as they're done now. It always was so, and will always be so. Did I ever hear what London streets were like a thou- sand years ago? It's nothing to me, but they must have been like what

they is now. Yes, there was always streets, or how was people that has tin to get their coals taken to them, and how was the public-houses to get their beer? It's talking nonsense, talking that way, a-asking sich questions.' [As the scavenger seemed likely to lose his temper, I changed the subject of conversation]. (*London Labour and the London Poor*, 1851)

The genius of Dickens was crucial, but as we read Somerville's description of the bustle and conversation at the inn, or Henry Mayhew's recording of the scavenger's description of his life, we can recognize behind the distinctive energy of Dickens's new rhythms a common pressure: restless, crowded, vivid: a social world of a radically different kind from that which was still there, and still important, as a basis for the composed, quiet and connected prose of the formally educated tradition. Whenever such a change happens, it is easy for those who are used to the existing conventions to see only the rough edges, hear only the loudness and crudeness, of this different manner. There is a kind of answer in Cobbett on the accusation of coarseness.

'*COARSE!*' the sons and daughters of Corruption will exclaim. '*Coarse!*' will echo back the scoundrel *seat-sellers*, each of whom ought to swing on one of the trees that he has acquired by the wages of Corruption. 'Coarse, coarse!' will cry the reptiles who are the seat-seller's understrappers, and who ought to swing from their heels. 'Vary coarse, ma'awm!' will some grinning Scotch sycophant observe to some she sinecurist or pensioner. '*Coarse as neck beef!*' will growl out some Englishman, who has filled his bags by oppressions of the poor; or, some other one, who, feeling in his very bones and marrow an instinctive horror *of work*, is desperately bent on getting *a share of the taxes*.

Yes, it is *coarse* indeed, and coarse it ought to be in a case like this. SWIFT has told us not to chop *blocks* with *razors*. Any *edge*-tool is too fine for work like this: a pick-axe, that perforates with one end and drags about with the other, is the tool for this sort of business. (*Political Register*, May 1828)

But there is also a quieter answer, of particular interest because it comes from a writer whose own settled manner is in the formal tradition:

In writing the history of unfashionable families, one is apt to fall into a tone of emphasis which is very far from being the tone of good society, where principles and beliefs are not only of an extremely moderate kind, but are always presupposed, no subjects being eligible but such

as can be touched with a light and graceful irony. But then, good society has its claret and its velvet carpets, its dinner-engagements six weeks
deep, its opera and its fairy ballrooms; rides off its *ennui* on thorough-
bred horses, lounges at the club, has to keep clear of crinoline vortices,
gets its science done by Faraday, and its religion by the superior clergy
who are to be met in the best houses: how should it have time or need
for belief and emphasis? But good society, floated on gossamer wings
of light irony, is of very expensive production; requiring nothing less
than a wide and arduous national life condensed in unfragrant,
deafening factories, cramping itself in mines, sweating at furnaces,
grinding, hammering, weaving under more or less oppression of car-
bonic acid—or else, spread over sheep-walks, and scattered in lonely
houses and huts on the clayey or chalky corn-lands, where the rainy
days look dreary. This wide national life is based entirely on emphasis—the emphasis of want...(*The Mill on the Floss*, 1860)

What George Eliot says about emphasis is important not only as a
way of approaching the new prose of Dickens and his successors, but
as the mark of a critical and increasingly important cultural change.
It is not only the material life of 'good society', but, she argues, its
associated tones of moderation and irony, which are a 'very expensive production'. It is not only luxury, but the leisure, the confidence, the assurance of continuity, which are in fact enjoyed at the
expense of a 'wide national life ... based entirely on emphasis—the
emphasis of want'. The complexity of this situation needs the most
careful analysis. The strengths of the social prose based on a small
educated class have already been acknowledged, and indeed they
continue to be relevant, for certain definite purposes, in a society in
which more and more people have been gaining education and an access to books. Yet for other purposes, and in particular for expressing the actual life of a hard-pressed, hard-driven, excluded majority,
a different prose was absolutely required; a different language as
expressing the altered relation of writer and reader. The new writers
and the new readers, in such a moment of change, often appear
together. Much is gained, of a permanent kind, as the achievement
of Dickens continues to remind us. But we have also to notice that
something is lost, or can be lost: not the older assurance and
seriousness, which with only the normal modifications of time has
continued to be available for certain precise purposes; but the common and intrinsic assumption of a natural equality; an effective continuity, between writer and reader, which of course at times is only a

matter of polite address but which is capable also of limiting the opportunities for mere exploitation: exploitation of the reader; exploitation of the experience; exploitation, in the bad sense, of the resources of the language. Much restless and superficially vivid prose has been exploiting in just these ways; the examples are everywhere in routine popular journalism, and it is easy to trace a bad as well as a good inheritance from Cobbett—the fearless, radical-sounding oracle, exploiting his personality and his assumed relationship with his readers, has unfortunately been a good deal more common than that actual radical, closely and seriously engaged with the central issues of his time, and putting himself at risk, with a necessary and urgent defiance, in every sentence and every opinion.

To reach the right way of describing the change, we have to recognize that the relation between writer and reader is not abstract; indeed cannot be, without corruption, a matter of address alone; of presentation, as a technique separable from substance. The deadness we noticed earlier, when a merely polite mind puts pen to paper, and the formalities of diction and construction merely suggest a seriousness which is never in substance confirmed, is perhaps easier to spot than that other deadness, when a merely restless mind makes a vivid scrawl at experience, with the words and rhythms of a close excited colloquialism, suggesting immediacy but never, past its weighed condiments of adjectives and its snatching, elbow-pulling rhythms, really engaging with anything. What is happening then is a writing not to the hard-pressed but to the jaded mind; it is this crucial distinction which the abstraction of presentation, the reification of style, simply blur and hide.

The most important thing to say about Dickens, then, is not that he is writing in a new way, but that he is experiencing in a new way, and that this is the substance of his language.

> The first shock of a great earthquake had, just at that period, rent the whole neighbourhood to its centre. Traces of its course were visible on every side. Houses were knocked down; streets broken through and stopped; deep pits and trenches dug in the ground; enormous heaps of earth and clay thrown up; buildings that were undermined and shaking, propped by great beams of wood. Here, a chaos of carts, overthrown and jumbled together, lay topsy-turvy at the bottom of a steep unnatural hill; there, confused treasures of iron soaked and rusted in something that had accidentally become a pond. Everywhere were bridges that led nowhere; thoroughfares that were wholly impassable;

Babel towers of chimneys, wanting half their height; temporary wooden houses and enclosures, in the most unlikely situations; carcases of ragged tenements, and fragments of unfinished walls and arches, and piles of scaffolding, and wildernesses of bricks, and giant forms of cranes, and tripods straddling above nothing. There were a hundred thousand shapes and substances of incompleteness, wildly mingled out of their places, upside down, burrowing in the earth, aspiring in the air, mouldering in the water, and unintelligible as any dream. Hot springs and fiery eruptions, the usual attendants upon earthquakes, lent their contributions of confusion to the scene. Boiling water hissed and heaved within dilapidated walls; whence also, the glare and roar of flames came issuing forth; and mounds of ashes blocked up rights of way, and wholly changed the law and custom of the neighbourhood.

In short, the yet unfinished and unopened railroad was in progress; and from the very core of all this dire disorder, trailed smoothly away, upon its mighty course of civilization and improvement.

This change in Staggs's Gardens, when the railway comes, is a change of a new kind, as we can see in a comparison with Jane Austen:

UPPERCROSS was a moderate-sized village, which a few years back had been completely in the old English style, containing only two houses superior in appearance to those of the yeomen and labourers; the mansion of the squire, with its high walls, great gates, and old trees, substantial and unmodernized, and the compact, tight parsonage, enclosed in its own neat garden, with a vine and a pear-tree, trained round its casements; but upon the marriage of the young squire, it had received the improvement of a farm-house, elevated into a cottage, for his residence, and Uppercross Cottage, with its veranda, French windows, and other prettinesses, was quite as likely to catch the traveller's eye as the more consistent and considerable aspect and premises of the Great House, about a quarter of a mile farther on.

The Musgroves, like their houses, were in a state of alteration, perhaps of improvement. The father and mother were in the old English style, and the young people in the new. Mr and Mrs Musgrove were a very good sort of people; friendly and hospitable, not much educated, and not at all elegant. Their children had more modern minds and manners. There was a numerous family; but the only two grown up, excepting Charles, were Henrietta and Louisa, young ladies of nineteen and twenty, who had brought from a school at Exeter all the usual stock of accomplishments, and were now, like thousands of other young ladies, living to be fashionable, happy, and merry. Their dress had every advantage, their faces were rather pretty, their spirits extremely good, their manners unembarrassed and pleasant; they were of consequence at home, and favourites abroad. Anne always contemplated them as some of the happiest creatures of her acquaintance: but still, saved, as we all are, by some comfortable feeling of superiority from wishing for the possibility of exchange, she would not have given up her own more elegant and cultivated mind for all their enjoyments; and envied them nothing but that seemingly perfect good understanding and agreement together, that good-humoured, mutual affection, of which she had known so little herself with either of her sisters. (*Persuasion*, 1818)

Here there is precise and visible change, but it is still, as it were, socially contained, as the language of formal description and analysis similarly contains it. In Dickens the scale and nature of the change break through the composed forms and set out in new ways. The linguistic innovations did not come by themselves, just because the scale of the change was so much greater. In some other writers the clear composition still held, as in this measured, reminiscent account by Nasmyth, the inventor of the steam-hammer but here a public figure, mediated by Samuel Smiles:

Amidst these flaming, smoky, clanging works, I beheld the remains of what had once been happy farmhouses, now ruined and deserted. The ground underneath them had sunk by the working out of the coal, and they were falling to pieces. They had in former times been surrounded by clumps of trees; but only the skeletons of them remained, dilapidated, black, and lifeless. The grass had been parched and killed by the vapours of sulphureous acid thrown out by the chimneys; and every herbaceous object was of a ghastly gray—the emblem of vegetable death in its saddest aspect. Vulcan had driven out Ceres. In some places I heard a sort of chirruping sound, as of some forlorn bird haunting the ruins of the old farmsteads. But no! the chirrup was a vile delusion. It proceeded from the shrill creaking of the coal-winding chains, which were placed in small tunnels beneath the hedgeless road. (*Autobiography*, c.1830, ed. 1833)

The phenomenon is Coalbrookdale, but the mind, for all its attention, still follows the polite allusions to Vulcan and Ceres. We can then see more clearly what Dickens is doing: altering, transforming a whole way of writing, rather than putting an old style at a new experience. It is not the method of the more formal novelists, including the sounds of measured or occasional speech in a solid frame of analysis and settled exposition. Rather, it is a speaking, persuading, directing voice, of a new kind, which has taken over the narrative, the exposition, the analysis, in a single operation. Here, there, everywhere: the restless production of a seemingly chaotic detail; the hurrying, pressing, miscellaneous clauses, with here a gap to push through, there a restless pushing at repeated obstacles, everywhere a crowding of objects, forcing attention; the prose, in fact, of a new order of experience; the prose of the city. It is not only disturbance; it is also a new kind of settlement.

> As to the neighbourhood which had hesitated to acknowledge the railroad in its struggling days, that had grown wise and penitent, as any Christian might in such a case, and now boasted of its powerful and prosperous relation. There were railway patterns in its drapers' shops, and railway journals in the windows of its newsmen. There were railway hotels, coffee-houses, lodging-houses, boarding-houses; railway plans, maps, views, wrappers, bottles, sandwich-boxes, and timetables; railway hackney-coach and cabstands; railway omnibuses, railway streets and buildings, railway hangers-on and parasites, and flatterers out of all calculation. There was even railway time observed in clocks, as if the sun itself had given in. Among the vanquished was the master chimney-sweeper, whilom incredulous at Staggs's Gardens, who now lived in a stuccoed house three stories high, and gave himself out, with golden flourishes upon a varnished board, as contractor for the cleansing of railway chimneys by machinery.
>
> To and from the heart of this great change, all day and night, throbbing currents rushed and returned, incessantly like its life's blood. Crowds of people and mountains of goods, departing and arriving scores upon scores of times in every four-and-twenty hours, produced a fermentation in the place that was always in action. The very houses seemed disposed to pack up and take trips. (*Dombey and Son*, 1848)

'Railway patterns...railway journals...railway hotels...railway plans...railway...railway...railway...railway...even railway time.' This is more than the excited emphasis of objects; it is the reorganization, through a single and repeated emphasis, of a whole way of life by a newly dominant element. The generalization, that is to say, is of a different order. It is not outward, by allusion or reference, to a familiar world; it is from inside, by the mounting emphasis of a new radical and organizing principle. Seriousness, connection, intelligent demonstration are not lost but transformed. A new prose has come to inhabit and to organize an essentially different world.

Or consider Dickens in a different manner:

> ...The limited choice of the Crown, in the formation of a new Ministry, would lie between Lord Coodle and Sir Thomas Doodle— supposing it to be impossible for the Duke of Foodle to act with

Goodle, which may be assumed to be the case in consequence of the breach arising out of that affair with Hoodle. Then, giving the Home Department and the Leadership of the House of Commons to Joodle, the Exchequer to Koodle, the Colonies to Loodle, and the Foreign Office to Moodle, what are you to do with Noodle? You can't offer him the Presidency of the Council; that is reserved for Poodle. You can't put him in the Woods and Forests; that is hardly good enough for Quoodle. What follows? That the country is shipwrecked, lost, and gone to pieces (as is made manifest to the patriotism of Sir Leicester Dedlock), because you can't provide for Noodle! (*Bleak House*, 1862–3)

This verbal parade is a kind of writing that can be dismissed (is still often dismissed) as a superficial, ranting prejudice. It is nothing of the kind; it is a new way of seeing a system. Not here a new system but an old system seen from a new point of view.

Junius denouncing Grafton was person-to-person, through the extending device of the open letter. But what Dickens sees and seizes on, from Boodle to Noodle, is a class: with individual differences no doubt, varying claims and prejudices, but as seen from outside the 'brilliant and distinguished circle', by those who are not the 'born first-actors, managers and leaders', differing by no more than a passing initial in a chiming community: what they have in common—the party from Boodle to Noodle and the party from Buffy to Puffy—being more important to those who have to watch and live under them than the distinctions they would make, in obviously different tones, among themselves. Then a way of seeing, a necessary way of seeing, has been learned and communicated, in an altered prose. 'Who have found out the perpetual stoppage. Who are to rejoice at nothing, and be sorry for nothing. Who are not to be disturbed by ideas.' The capital, general, dissected Who.

Just as clearly, however, in other parts of his writing, Dickens exploits the tension between the two kinds of language. This is a basic source of his comedy. Pecksniff's conversational style, to take only one example, is a demonstration of pompous emptiness in its mechanical reproduction of a familiar formal rhythm:

'When your mind requires to be refreshed, by change of occupation, Thomas Pinch will instruct you in the art of surveying the back garden, or in ascertaining the dead level of the road between this house and the finger-post, or in any other practical and pleasing pursuit'.

Whenever something is seen as ridiculous, in just this unconnected way, the decayed rhythm of a formal prose is likely to be used. On the origin of the name of Staggs's Gardens, for example:

> Others, who had a natural taste for the country, held that it dated from those rural times when the antlered herd, under the familiar denomination of Staggses, had resorted to its shady precincts.

Or, making the contrast more explicit:

> Bending over a steaming vessel of tea, and looking through the steam, and breathing forth the steam, like a malignant Chinese enchantress engaged in the performance of unholy rites, Mr F's Aunt put down her great teacup and exclaimed, 'Drat him, if he an't come back again!' It would seem from the foregoing exclamation that this uncompromising relative of the lamented Mr F, measuring time by the acuteness of her sensations and not by the clock, supposed Clennam to have lately gone away; whereas at least a quarter of a year had elapsed since he had had the temerity to present himself before her. (*Little Dorrit*, 1867)

This example reminds us that the comic effect is two-way. As in other periods of deep and uncomfortable cultural change, the habit of what is still felt as vulgar speech is as often the target as a decaying formality; indeed it is the cultural distance between them, when they are suddenly slapped together, that brings the uneasy but relieving laugh.

> 'In Italy is she really?' said Flora, 'with the grapes and figs growing everywhere and lava necklaces and bracelets too that land of poetry with burning mountains pictureque beyond belief though if the organ-boys come away from the neigbourhood not to be scorched nobody can wonder being so young and bringing their white mice with them most humane, and is she really in that favoured land with nothing but blue about her and dying gladiators and Belvederas though Mr F himself did not believe for his objection when in spirits was that the images could not be true there being no medium between expensive quantities of linen badly got up and all in creases and none whatever, which certainly does not seem probable though perhaps in consequence of the extremes of rich and poor which may account for it.'

This is a version of the full stream of Flora's miscellaneous consciousness, in a passage which may technically anticipate the famous last chapter of *Ulysses* but which is radically different in feeling because it is not taken seriously. It is not yet the spontaneity, the feeling association, of a reflecting and private mind; it is rather the unorganized jumble of the nervous, the pretentious and the ignorant. In his observation on method as the mark of an educated mind, Coleridge had instanced, as a contrast, the process of untrained speech, which can still often be heard:

> The necessity of taking breath, the efforts of recollection, and the abrupt rectification of its failures, produce all his pauses; and with exception of the '*and then*', and '*and there*,' and the still less significant '*and so*', they constitute likewise all his connections.

It is a fair comment, but that it should come from Coleridge is especially significant evidence of the power of the formal tradition: a rational and public habit of mind is unquestioningly preferred to the essentially different organization of ordinary speech and thought. Eventually, in our prose, and especially in the novel, the resources of this spoken and thinking dimension were to be brought to full use; but this is not Dickens's achievement; what happened there was the discovery of a new and more emphatic but still public mode.

It is in another kind of novel, feeling its way simultaneously towards the lives of ordinary people and towards a respecting naturalism of reported speech, that one element of the larger change can be seen to begin.

> 'Going—art thou going to work this time o'day?'
> 'No, stupid, to be sure not. Going to see the chap thou spoke-on.' So they put on their hats and set out. On the way Wilson said Davenport was a good fellow, though too much of the Methodee; that his children were too young to work, but not too young to be cold and hungry; that they had sunk lower and lower, and pawned thing after thing, and that they now lived in a cellar in Berry Street, off Store Street. Barton growled inarticulate words of no benevolent import to a large class of mankind, and so they went along till they arrived in Berry Street. It was unpaved: and down the middle a gutter forced its way, every now and then forming pools in the holes with which the street abounded. Never was the old Edinburgh cry of *Gardez l'eau!* more necessary than in this street. As they passed, women from their doors tossed household slops of *every* description into the gutter; they ran into the next pool, which overflowed and stagnated. Heaps of ashes were the stepping-stones, on which the passer-by, who cared in the least for cleanliness, took care not to put his foot. Our friends were not dainty, but even they picked their way, till they got to some steps leading down to a small area, where a person standing would have his head about one foot below the level of the street, and might at the same time, without the least motion of his body, touch the window of the cellar and

the damp muddy wall right opposite. You went down one step even from the foul area into the cellar in which a family of human beings lived. It was very dark inside. The window-panes, many of them, were broken and stuffed with rags, which was reason enough for the dusky light that pervaded the place even at midday. After the account I have given of the state of the street, no one can be surprised that on going into the cellar inhabited by Davenport, the smell was so foetid as almost to knock the two men down. Quickly recovering themselves, as those inured to such things do, they began to penetrate the thick darkness of the place, and to see three or four little children rolling on the damp, nay wet brick floor, through which the stagnant, filthy moisture of the street oozed up; the fire-place was empty and black; the wife sat on her husband's lair, and cried in the dark loneliness.

'See, missis, I'm back again.—Hold your noise, children, and don't mither your mammy for bread; here's a chap as has got some for you.'

In that dim light, which was darkness to strangers, they clustered round Barton, and tore from him the food he had brought with him. It was a large hunch of bread, but it vanished in an instant.

'We mun do summut for 'em,' said he to Wilson. 'Yo stop here, and I'll be back in half-an-hour.' (*Mary Barton*, 1848)

Mrs Gaskell, in her change of subject, in her altered relation to it, begins to acknowledge directly the positive resources of spoken English. It is a considerable achievement, but it is still qualified by reservations: in anxious footnotes explaining the meaning of unfamiliar dialect words—as if in anthropological presentation to a standard reader; and in the often unchanged prose of the main narrative, which includes such distancing devices as 'our friends were not dainty, but even they picked their way', even when at times it has the nerve to confront the experience directly and in its own terms. Mrs Gaskell's alternation between successful direct description and an anxious voice-over commentary is in fact her alternation between direct response to a humanity in poverty and a separated, sympathizing production of evidence and argument. It is an alternation towards which many novelists have been pressed, and which is a crucial phase in our social history. To the degree that there is still alienation between writers and most of the life around them, and uncertainty, then, in the relation of writer and reader, this problem in writing is still often unsolved. Yet we can look from Elizabeth Gaskell to D. H. Lawrence, in one of his early stories, and see that when these relations are (if only temporarily) right, a development in prose that is also a development in feeling is clearly achieved.

Elizabeth waited in suspense. The mother-in-law talked, with lapses into silence.

'But he wasn't your son, Lizzie, an' it makes a difference. Whatever he was, I remember him when he was little, an' I learned to understand him and to make allowances. You've got to make allowances for them—'

It was half-past ten, and the old woman was saying: 'But it's trouble from beginning to end; you're never too old for trouble, never too old for that—'when the gate banged back, and there were heavy feet on the steps.

'I'll go, Lizzie, let me go', cried the old woman, rising. But Elizabeth was at the door. It was a man in pit-clothes.

'They're bringin' 'im, Missis', he said. Elizabeth's heart halted a moment. Then it surged on again, almost suffocating her.

'Is he—is it bad?' she asked. (*Odour of Chrysanthemums*, 1914)

It is not only that the reported speech is an actual flow, in the course of living: at once serious and adequate, yet recognizing the limits of what can be ordinarily said, by anyone, in the deepest human crises. It is also that there is now a continuity between this speech and the hitherto separated modes of analysis and narrative. The sentence beginning 'It was half-past ten and the old woman was saying...' is constructed to achieve this integration—the words within the action as elsewhere the action within the words—but it is not only a matter of formal sentence construction; the integration is made possible by the shift of narrative vocabulary towards the colloquial. This shift was more available than the related shift in analysis, which is partly achieved by very short and simple sentences and by the inclusion of what read like spoken questions. On the other hand the analysis is developed in a different direction by the inclusion of some highly charged words from a literary rather than a colloquial range: as 'surged' or again at points in a subsequent passage:

'He went peaceful, Lizzie—peaceful as sleep. Isn't he beautiful, the lamb? Ay—he must ha' made his peace, Lizzie. 'Appen he made it all right, Lizzie, shut in there. He'd have time. He wouldn't look like this if he hadn't made his peace. The lamb, the dear lamb. Eh, but he had a hearty laugh. I loved to hear it. He had the heartiest laugh, Lizzie, as a lad—'

Elizabeth looked up. The man's mouth was fallen back, slightly open under the cover of the moustache. The eyes, half shut, did not show glazed in the obscurity. Life with its smoky burning gone from him, had left him apart and utterly alien to her. And she knew what a stranger he was to her. In her womb was ice of fear, because of this

separate stranger with whom she had been living as one flesh. Was this
what it all meant—utter, intact separateness, obscured by heat of living? In dread she turned her face away. The fact was too deadly. There
had been nothing between them, and yet they had come together, ex-
changing their nakedness repeatedly. Each time he had taken her, they
had been two isolated beings, far apart as now. He was no more
responsible than she. The child was like ice in her womb. For as she
looked at the dead man, her mind, cold and detached, said clearly:
'Who am I? What have I been doing? I have been fighting a husband
who did not exist. *He* existed all the time. What wrong have I done?
What was that I have been living with? There lies the reality, this man.'

This is the discovery, in prose, of a response to death, rather than a
reflection on it. The response is confused, painful; it is now deeply
moved, now flatly cutting off. By traditional formal standards it has
no method, no presentation at all; but it is not fragmentary or inarticulate. It is the response as it might be, in a composition based on
an oral mode but with sudden verbal intensifications ('ice of fear',
'utter, intact separateness') contained in rhythms connecting and extending only so much as to carry the brief exclamations, questions,
instructions, reassurances into a searching of heart and mind. It is
written speech; a written searching. But it is controlled by, as it is
based on, an ordinary voice.

   In other situations, Lawrence experienced and sometimes failed to
overcome the traditional difficulties. It is a problem of the most
acute and continuing kind, if we see it, as I think we must, as a still
unresolved social history. It would be very much simpler if we could
merely discard one of the contrasted methods, and the whole structure that supports it. Any individual writer may of course do this, or
think he has done it. If he never writes argument, or factual exposition, he can join in the reaction against the formal tradition; move
his prose, deliberately, towards the words and rhythms of ordinary
everyday speech. Or if he never writes of ordinary life processes, has
never to describe men speaking and thinking but only the results, the
products, of thought and behaviour, he can carry on with his own
variant of what is still an educated prose: insisting on formal arrangement; on certain complicated constructions which correspond
to his material; on words which although unfamiliar carry a precise,
identifying, discriminating meaning. One solution or the other may
be possible to the individual writer, but neither, evidently, is possible
to a culture or a language as a whole. For some writers now, since the

separated categories can and must overlap, in particular histories and circumstances, it is a matter of conscious choice, in this or that piece of writing. In which dimension, by what experience, is he now, in this writing, related? We can perhaps see this more clearly if we take it historically, for since George Eliot and Hardy this has been a general problem.

When a critic described George Eliot, Hardy and Lawrence as 'our three great autodidacts', he knew what he was doing, and it was just his bad luck that his audience included someone in the same separate and therefore critical position. For what his description depends on is an unstated and common assumption of what it is to have been properly taught. George Eliot, Hardy and Lawrence were all formally educated, to a standard still higher than that of three quarters of our children. All three, moreover, were in the most general sense intellectuals; they continued, after their formal education, to read, study, think and write for themselves. What they did not have—and it is all that they did not have, in this sense—was a standard upper-class English education, as this was coming to be in just their period: preparatory school; 'public' school; Oxford or Cambridge University. And yet there they are: add Dickens, another 'autodidact'; add Elizabeth Gaskell, Emily and Charlotte Brontë, all three in the same state; add Henry James and Joseph Conrad, educated quite elsewhere; add Wells and Gissing; and what you have is a list, with very few exceptions, of the major English novelists from 1840 to 1914. Only Forster, perhaps, among considerable figures, can be said *not* to have been an 'autodidact'.

I am considering this now as a question of prose. I think there is an important point about George Eliot, if we set what she had to say in *Mill on the Floss* about emphasis and irony beside parts of *Felix Holt* or against the detached, critically inspecting construction of *Middlemarch*. But the question is most immediately accessible in Hardy, who so often, we are told, 'wrote badly'. It is a question about language, but in an emphatic context of everyday life and labour. This is a recurrent theme of the novels: in the relationship of Tess and Angel, for example; in the whole of *Return of the Native*; in Jude and Arabella and Sue. Tess, we remember, had 'two languages':

> Mrs Durbeyfield habitually spoke the dialect; her daughter, who had passed the Sixth Standard in the National School under a London-trained mistress, spoke two languages; the dialect at home, more or less; ordinary English abroad and to persons of quality.

But this situation, which has since become so familiar, is seen from a particular viewpoint; the easy contrast between the 'dialect' and 'ordinary English', which, left like that, raises none of the real questions. We have to consider, for example, the confidence of that 'ordinary English', and ask how ordinary it was, and where, ultimately, the standard was set. It is here that Angel's reflections on his brothers can help us.

> As they walked along the hillside Angel's former feeling revived in him—that whatever their advantages by comparison with himself, neither saw or set forth life as it really was lived. Perhaps, as with many men, their opportunities of observation were not so good as their opportunities of expression. Neither had an adequate conception of the complicated forces at work outside the smooth and gentle current in which they and their associates floated. Neither saw the difference between local truth and universal truth; that what the inner world said in their clerical and academic hearing was quite a different thing from what the outer world was thinking. (*Tess of the D'urbervilles*, 1891)

But the connection Hardy is trying to trace, between observation and expression, is complicated. It is a matter, ultimately, of how he himself is to write. We know that he was worried about his prose, and that he was reduced by the educated assumptions of his period to studying Defoe, Fielding, Addison, Scott and *The Times*, as if they could have helped him. The real difficulty came from the complexity of his own position as an observer: a complexity that can be seen now as representative. His problem of style is not quite that of the two languages of Tess: the consciously educated and the unconsciously customary. This situation, however embarrassing, can often be lived with: in distinct social groups, one or other language is evident and available. But Hardy as a writer was mainly concerned with the interaction between the two conditions—the educated and the customary: not just as the characteristics of social groups, but as ways of seeing and feeling, within a single mind. And then neither established language would serve, to express this tension and disturbance. Neither, in fact, was sufficiently articulate. An educated style, as it had developed in a particular and exclusive group, could be dumb in intensity and limited in humanity. A customary style, while carrying the voice of feeling, could be still thwarted by ignorance and complacent in repetition and habit. Hardy veered between them, and the idiosyncrasy of his writing is related to this: the unusual combination of formal and colloquial words; of simple and elaborate rhythms. For example;

> Marty South alone, of all the women in Hintock and the world, had approximated to Winterborne's level of intelligent intercourse with Nature. In that respect she had formed his true complement in the other sex, had lived as his counterpart, had subjoined her thoughts to his as a corollary.
>
> The casual glimpses which the ordinary population bestowed upon that wondrous world of sap and leaves called the Hintock woods had been with these two, Giles and Marty, a clear gaze. They had been possessed of its finer mysteries as of commonplace knowledge; had been able to read its hieroglyphs as ordinary writing; to them the sights and sounds of night, winter, wind, storm, amid those dense boughs, which had to Grace a touch of the uncanny, and even of the supernatural, were simple occurences whose origin, continuance, and laws they foreknew. They had planted together, and together they had felled; together they had, with the run of the years, mentally collected those remoter signs and symbols, which seen in few were of runic obscurity, but all together made an alphabet. From the light lashing of the twigs upon their faces when brushing through them in the dark either could pronounce upon the species of the tree whence they stretched; from the quality of the wind's murmur through a bough either could in like manner name its sort afar off. They knew by a glance at a trunk if its heart were sound, or tainted with incipient decay; and by the state of its upper twigs the stratum that had been reached by its roots. The artifices of the seasons were seen by them from the conjuror's own point of view, and not from that of the spectator.
>
> 'He ought to have married *you*, Marty, and nobody else in the world!' said Grace with conviction, after thinking in the above strain.
>
> Marty shook her head. 'In all our outdoor days and years together, ma'am,' she replied, 'the one thing he never spoke of to me was love; nor I to him.'
>
> 'Yet you and he could speak in a tongue that nobody else knew—not even my father, though he came nearest knowing—the tongue of the trees and fruits and flowers themselves.'
>
> She could indulge in mournful fancies like this to Marty; but the hard core to her grief—which Marty's had not—remained. (*The Woodlanders*, 1887)

Here the central problem is expressed in terms of a problem of language. The central emphasis is on learning through work. The detailed knowledge of trees and of weather is seen as making 'an alphabet', and this knowledge is deeply respected. At the same time, when it really comes to be verbalized, a different and often remote kind of language appears necessary: 'intelligent intercourse', 'hieroglyphs', 'runic obscurity'. There is occasional integration in direct observation—'knew by a glance at a trunk if its heart were question. It is only from an external and romantic viewpoint that there is a *human* 'tongue of the trees'. Those who knew this 'tongue' as Hardy has Grace think of it could not fully speak of themselves.

This is in part Hardy's special viewpoint, but the underlying problem is general. It is a problem of how people can speak—and be written as speaking—more fully *and* as themselves. In narrative and description there is less of a problem. What Hardy is reaching for, always, is unambiguously an educated style, in which the extension of vocabulary and the complication of construction are necessary to the intensity and precision of the observation:

> The gray tones of daybreak are not the gray half-tones of the day's close, though the degree of their shade may be the same. In the twilight of the morning, light seems active, darkness passive; in the twilight of evening, it is the darkness which is active and crescent, and the light which is the drowsy reverse.

This successful observation and description is in a manner characteristic of some of the best nineteenth-century prose: compare Ruskin's observations of clouds, and Richard Jefferies's description of the early morning to which the reaper goes out.

> It is the first of July, and I sit down to write by the dismallest light that ever yet I wrote by; namely, the light of this midsummer morning, in mid-England (Matlock, Derbyshire), in the year 1871.
>
> For the sky is covered with grey cloud;—not rain-cloud, but a dry black veil, which no ray of sunshine can pierce; partly diffused in mist, feeble mist, enough to make distant objects unintelligible, yet without any substance, or wreathing, or colour of its own. And everywhere the leaves of the trees are shaking fitfully, as they do before a thunderstorm; only not violently, but enough to show the passing to and fro of a strange, bitter, blighting wind. Dismal enough, had it been the first morning of its kind that summer had sent. But during all this spring, in London, and at Oxford, through

meagre March, through changelessly sullen April, through despondent May, and darkened June, morning after morning has come grey-shrouded thus.

And it is a new thing to me, and a very dreadful one. I am fifty years old, and more; and since I was five, have gleaned the best hours of my life in the sun of spring and summer mornings; and I never saw such as these, till now. (*Fors Clavigera*, 1871)

THE reaper had risen early to his labour, but the birds had preceded him hours. Before the sun was up the swallows had left their beams in the cowshed and twittered out into the air. The rooks and woodpigeons and doves had gone to the corn, the blackbird to the stream, the finch to the hedgerow, the bees to the heath on the hills, the humble-bees to the clover in the plain. Butterflies rose from the flowers by the footpath, and fluttered before him to and fro and round and back again to the place whence they had been driven. Goldfinches tasting the first thistledown rose from the corner where the thistles grew thickly. A hundred sparrows came rushing up into the hedge, suddenly filling the boughs with brown fruit; they chirped and quarrelled in their talk, and rushed away again back to the corn as he stepped nearer. The boughs were stripped of their winged brown berries as quickly as they had grown. Starlings ran before the cows feeding in the aftermath, so close to their mouths as to seem in danger of being licked up by their broad tongues. All creatures, from the tiniest insect upward, were in reality busy under that curtain of white-heat haze. It looked so still, so quiet, from afar; entering it and passing among the fields, all that lived was found busy at its long day's work. Roger did not interest himself in these things, in the wasps that left the gate as he approached—they were making *papier-maché* from the wood of the top bar—in the bright poppies brushing against his drab unpolished boots, in the hue of the wheat or the white convolvulus; they were nothing to him.

Why should they be? (*One of the New Voters*, 1885)

But what we notice in Jefferies, as in Hardy, is the human problem: that this is a kind of observation which seems to depend on detachment. And then, if this is a detachment from human beings, or from a whole class of human beings, the manner itself can wither. Jefferies tells us that the reaper, with his day's work in front of him, does not see what the observer is seeing. What is also relevant, as Jefferies in his later work recognized, is that the educated observer, seeing nature, does not see the human being who is the reaper; or, if he sees him, sees him as only a figure in a landscape. Hardy, in more extended and complicated ways, works through this complexity of choice. Without the insights of consciously learned history, and of the educated understanding of nature and behaviour, he cannot really observe at all, either with adequate precision or with an adequately extending human respect. But then the ordinary social model, the learned language, which includes these capacities, is, very clearly, in a divided culture, a form which includes an alienation—'a few unimportant scores of millions of outsiders'—and a nullity—'to be tolerated rather than reckoned with and respected.' The tension which then follows, when the observer holds to educated procedures but is unable to feel with the existing educated class, is severe. It is not the countryman awkward in his town clothes, or the 'autodidact' awkward among people of settled learning. It is the more significant tension, of course with its awkwardnesses, its frequent uncertainties of tone, its spurts of bitterness and nostalgia, of the man caught by his personal history in the general crisis of the relation between education and class. What that crisis comes out as, in real terms, is the relation between intelligence and fellow-feeling, but this relation in the nineteenth and twentieth centuries had to be worked out at a time when education was consciously used to train members of a class and to divide them from their own passions as surely as from other men: the two processes, inevitably, are deeply connected. The writer moving through his history had to explore, as if on his own, the resources of what seemed to be but was not yet in fact a common language. In the novel, especially, this is the significant line of development.

Though the novel is the greatest achievement, in prose, of the period with which we are concerned, it is a more disturbed form than other kinds of writing. Some of the difficulties we have noticed in the novel were also present in social criticism: in Carlyle, for example, where the use of the persuading, presenting voice is very like that of Dickens, but is now often more difficult to read because of its formal quality, with certain formal expectations, as argument.

> Do not Books still accomplish *miracles* as *Runes* were fabled to do? They persuade men. Not the wretchedest circulating-library novel, which foolish girls thumb and con in remote villages but will help to regulate the actual practical weddings and households of those foolish girls. So 'Celia' felt, so 'Clifford' acted: the foolish Theorem of Life, stamped into those young brains, comes out as a solid Practice one

day. Consider whether any *Rune* in the wildest imagination of Mythologist ever did such wonders as, on the actual firm Earth, some Books have done! What built St Paul's Cathedral? Look at the heart of the matter, it was that divine Hebrew BOOK,— the word partly of the man Moses, an out-law tending his Midianitish herds, four thousand years ago, in the wildernesses of Sinai! It is the strangest of things, yet nothing is truer. With the art of Writing, of which Printing is a simple, an inevitable and comparatively insignificant corollary, the true reign of miracles of mankind commenced. It related, with a wondrous new contiguity and perpetual closeness, the Past and Distant with the Present in time and place; all times and all places with this our actual Here and Now. All things were altered for men; all modes of important work of men: teaching, preaching, governing, and all else. (*On Heroes...*, 1841)

Wherever really new ways of seeing and feeling are in question, Victorian prose is disturbed. Yet the bulk of Victorian prose is remarkably settled and solid: an achieved, confident and still powerful manner. Where a novelist shared this essential outlook, he could write so simply that he hardly seems to be writing: Trollope is an obvious example, and he has had many successors.

If the flour-mill had frightened him, what must the present project have done! Fisker explained that he had come with two objects,— first to ask the consent of the English partner to the proposed change in their business, and secondly to obtain the co-operation of English capitalists. The proposed change in the business meant simply the entire sale of the establishment at Fiskerville, and the absorption of the whole capital in the work of getting up the railway. 'If you could realise all the money it wouldn't make a mile of the railway,' said Paul. Mr Fisker laughed at him. The object of Fisker, Montague, and Montague was not to make a railway to Vera Cruz, but to float a company. Paul thought that Mr Fisker seemed to be indifferent whether the railway should ever be constructed or not. It was clearly his idea that fortunes were to be made out of the concern before a spadeful of earth had been moved. If brilliantly printed programmes might avail anything, with gorgeous maps, and beautiful little pictures of trains running into tunnels beneath snowy mountains and coming out of them on the margin of sunlit lakes, Mr Fisker had certainly done much. But Paul, when he saw all these pretty things, could not keep his mind from thinking whence had come the money to pay for them. Mr Fisker had declared that he had come over to obtain his partner's consent, but it seemed to that partner that a great deal had been done without any consent. And Paul's fears on this hand were not allayed by finding that on all these beautiful papers he himself was described as one of the agents and general managers of the company. Each document was signed Fisker, Montague, and Montague. (*The Way We Live Now*, 1875)

It is often said that this manner is heavy, but look at a passage from Macaulay and then at Bagehot.

It is not by the intermeddling of Mr Southey's idol, the omniscient and omnipotent State, but by the prudence and energy of the people, that England has hitherto been carried forward in civilisation; and it is to the same prudence and the same energy that we now look with comfort and good hope. Our rulers will best promote the improvement of the nation by strictly confining themselves to their own legitimate duties, by leaving capital to find its most lucrative course, commodities their fair price, industry and intelligence their natural reward, idleness and folly their natural punishment, by maintaining peace, by defending property, by diminishing the price of law, and by observing strict economy in every department of the state. Let the Government do this: the People will assuredly do the rest. (*Critical and Historical Essays*, 1830)

ENGLAND is the type of deferential countries, and the manner in which it is so, and has become so, is extremely curious. The middle classes—the ordinary majority of educated men—are in the present day the despotic power in England. 'Public opinion', nowadays, is the opinion of the bald-headed man at the back of the omnibus. It is *not* the opinion of the aristocratical classes as such; or of the most educated or refined classes as such; it is simply the opinion of the ordinary mass of educated, but still commonplace mankind. If you look at the mass of the constituencies, you will see that they are not very interesting people; and perhaps if you look behind the scenes and see the people who manipulate and work the constituencies, you will find that these are yet more uninteresting. The English constitution in its palpable form is this—the mass of the people yield obedience to a select few; and when you see this select few, you perceive that though not of the lowest class, nor of an unrespectable class, they are yet of a heavy sensible class—the last people in the world to whom, if they were drawn up in a row, an immense nation would ever give an exclusive preference.

In fact, the mass of the English people yield a deference rather to something else than to their rulers. They defer to what we may call the *theatrical show* of society. A certain state passes before them; a certain pomp of great men; a certain spectacle of beautiful women; a wonderful scene of wealth and enjoyment is displayed, and they are coerced by it. Their imagination is bowed down; they feel they are not equal to the life which is revealed to them. (*The English Constitution*, 1867)

It is just Macaulay's silvery confidence that now divides us. He shares so much with his readers, in ways of seeing and dealing with the world, that he becomes a kind of model: an admirable style. While the ways of seeing and dealing last, that is English, and schoolboys can be set to learn it: the attitudes and the style in a single operation: *Let the Government do this: the People will assuredly do the rest.* Or, as we might say, see Hansard, *passim*.

This division between the confident and the disturbed, in the long crisis of an industrial civilization, can hardly be overstressed. It is in effect a division between a prose with many strengths, of clarity and fluency, and a prose often tortured, uncertain, obscure—its lucidities dependent on new ways of seeing and feeling being learned; its strengths on unexpected connections; its flow on inarticulate and still struggling emotions. The confident prose is not just a matter of optimism, of a belief in progress. Bagehot is very remarkable as a pioneer of a style now very common but still difficult to describe: a complacency and a cynicism, which might appear opposite qualities, are brilliantly fused, into a sort of brittle durability, a penetrating reassurance. It is a style admirably suited to expose illusions as a way of maintaining them: the accent, the new poise, of a ruling class under pressure and using a style as a control. Bagehot is full of insights and illuminations, and among them, as we consider the subsequent history of this manner, we must insist on including, as an observation of the effect on others:

> Their imagination is bowed down: they feel they are not equal to the life which is revealed to them.

We can then add that this result—a bowing down of the imagination—is often evident, also, in those who are using such a style to impress others. The poise can replace and annihilate the man.

Much depends here on the immediate subject. Parts of Leslie Stephen's 'agnostic's apology' are straightforward and serious: an obstinate, solid questioning.

> I have said that our knowledge is in any case limited. I may add that, on any showing, there is a danger in failing to recognise the limits of possible knowledge. The word Gnostic has some awkward associations. It once described certain heretics who got into trouble from fancying that men could frame theories of the Divine mode of existence. The sects have been dead for many centuries. Their funda-

mental assumptions can hardly be quite extinct. Not long ago, at least, there appeared in the papers a string of propositions framed—so we were assured—by some of the most candid and most learned of living theologians. These propositions defined by the help of various languages the precise relations which exist between the persons of the Trinity. It is an odd, though far from an unprecedented, circumstance that the unbeliever cannot quote them for fear of profanity. If they were transplanted into the pages of the *Fortnightly Review*, it would be impossible to convince anyone that the intention was not to mock the simple-minded persons who, we must suppose, were not themselves intentionally irreverent. It is enough to say that they defined the nature of God Almighty with an accuracy from which modest naturalists would shrink in describing the genesis of a black-beetle. I know not whether these dogmas were put forward as articles of faith, as pious conjectures, or as tentative contributions to a sound theory. At any rate, it was supposed that they were interesting to beings of flesh and blood. If so, one can only ask in wonder whether an utter want of reverence is most strongly implied in this mode of dealing with sacred mysteries; or an utter ignorance of the existing state of the world in the assumption that the question which really divides mankind is the double procession of the Holy Ghost; or an utter incapacity for speculation in the confusion of these dead exuviæ of long-past modes of thought with living intellectual tissue; or an utter want of imagination, or of even a rudimentary sense of humour, in the hypothesis that the promulgation of such dogmas could produce anything but the laughter of sceptics and the contempt of the healthy human intellect? (*An Agnostic's Apology*, 1893)

But as Stephen approaches a climax of his argument, in the last sentence, he begins to use 'utter' as a repetitive adjective: 'utter want', 'utter ignorance', 'utter incapacity'; and we catch in this a kind of domineering scepticism, which has since been widely prevalent: in some serious argument, but more generally in a persistent type of conservative journalism. 'Anything but the laughter of sceptics and the contempt of the healthy human intellect' has behind it the admirable rationality of much earlier prose; but a long way behind it, for what has entered and weakened it is a confident social tone which depends, and knows it can depend on a certain kind of reader doing most of the work of the apparent proof. Matthew Arnold, similarly, is at a point of transition.

> So to this idea of glory and greatness the free-trade which our Liberal friends extol so solemnly and devoutly has served,—to the increase of trade, business, and population; and for this it is prized. Therefore,

the untaxing of the poor man's bread has, with this view of national happiness, been used not so much to make the existing poor man's bread cheaper or more abundant, but rather to create more poor men to eat it; so that we cannot precisely say that we have fewer poor men than we had before free-trade, but we can say with truth that we have many more centres of industry, as they are called, and much more business, population, and manufactures. And if we are sometimes a little troubled by our multitude of poor men, yet we know the increase of manufactures and population to be such a salutary thing in itself, and our free-trade policy begets such an admirable movement, creating fresh centres of industry and fresh poor men here, while we were thinking about our poor men there, that we are quite dazzled and borne away, and more and more industrial movement is called for and our social progress seems to become one triumphant and enjoyable course of what is sometimes called, vulgarly, outrunning the constable. (*Culture and Anarchy*, 1869)

We can see in this prose a genuinely questioning, flexible mind: an actual openness, which gets beyond 'stock notions' and 'mechanical pursuits'. But Arnold also relies, at certain crucial points, on a kind of complacent raillery; an overbearing by style: not the heavy or the pompous, certainly, but the engaging compact with the reader that he and the author share the only relevant kind of intelligence, so that certain positions do not have to be really weighed, but can be smiled or shrugged off into a pathetic inadequacy. There is a relation between this and the fully controlled irony of Samuel Butler in *Erewhon*, where the total convention of an ironically conceived world allows a singular purity: from which, all the same, a disturbing imagination, a disturbing engagement, are deliberately excluded.

The arguments in favour of the deliberate development of the unreasoning faculties were much more cogent. But here they depart from the principles on which they justify their study of hypothetics; for they base the importance which they assign to hypothetics upon the fact of their being a preparation for the extraordinary, while their study of Unreason rests upon its developing those faculties which are required for the daily conduct of affairs. Hence their professorships of Inconsistency and Evasion, in both of which studies the youths are examined before being allowed to proceed to their degree in hypothetics. The more earnest and conscientious students attain to a proficiency in these subjects which is quite surprising; there is hardly any inconsistency so glaring but they soon learn to defend it, or injunction so clear that they cannot find some pretext for disregarding it.

Life, they urge, would be intolerable if men were to be guided in all

they did by reason and reason only. Reason betrays men into the drawing of hard-and-fast lines, and to the defining by language—language
being like the sun, which rears and then scorches. Extremes are alone
logical, but they are always absurd; the mean is illogical, but an illogical mean is better than the sheer absurdity of an extreme. There are
no follies and no unreasonablenesses so great as those which can apparently be irrefragably defended by reason itself, and there is hardly
an error into which men may not easily be led if they base their conduct upon reason only.

Reason might very possibly abolish the double currency; it might
even attack the personality of Hope and Justice. Besides, people have
such a strong natural bias towards it that they will seek it for themselves and act upon it quite as much as or more than is good for them;
there is no need of encouraging reason. With unreason the case is different. She is the natural complement of reason without whose existence reason itself were non-existence. (*Erewhon*, 1872)

Or we can see what is in a way the triumph of this manner in Shaw:

At last it was alleged by the most evangelical of the disputants that
Charles Bradlaugh, the most formidable atheist on the Secularist platform, had taken out his watch publicly and challenged the Almighty to
strike him dead in five minutes if he really existed and disapproved of
atheism. The leader of the cavillers, with great heat, repudiated this as
a gross calumny, declaring that Bradlaugh had repeatedly and in-
dignantly contradicted it, and implying that the atheist champion was
far too pious a man to commit such a blasphemy. This exquisite confusion of ideas roused my sense of comedy. It was clear to me that the
challenge attributed to Charles Bradlaugh was a scientific experiment
of a quite simple, straighforward, and proper kind to ascertain
whether the expression of atheistic opinions really did involve any personal risk. It was certainly the method taught in the Bible, Elijah having confuted the prophets of Baal in precisely that way, with every circumstance of bitter mockery of their god when he failed to send down
fire from heaven. Accordingly I said that if the question at issue were
whether the penalty of questioning the theology of Messrs Moody and
Sankey was to be struck dead on the spot by an incensed deity, nothing
could effect a more convincing settlement of it than the very obvious
experiment attributed to Mr Bradlaugh, and that consequently if he
had not tried it, he ought to have tried it. The omission, I added, was
one which could easily be remedied there and then, as I happened to
share Mr Bradlaugh's views as to the absurdity of the belief in these
violent interferences with the order of nature by a short-tempered and
thin-skinned supernatural deity. Therefore—and at that point I took
out my watch.

The effect was electrical. Neither sceptics nor devotees were
prepared to abide the result of the experiment. In vain did I urge the

pious to trust in the accuracy of their deity's aim with a thunderbolt, and the justice of his discrimination between the innocent and the guilty. In vain did I appeal to the sceptics to accept the logical outcome of their scepticism: it soon appeared that when thunderbolts were in question there were no sceptics. Our host, seeing that his guests would vanish precipitately if the impious challenge were uttered, leaving him alone with a solitary infidel under sentence of extermination in five minutes, interposed and forbade the experiment, pleading at the same time for a change of subject. ('Preface' to *Back to Methuselah*, 1921)

Here the confident lucidity is genuinely remarkable, the prose in its own terms so excellent an instrument, and yet the selected occasions for the use of intelligence come to seem, after a while, so narrow a world. The bright, entertaining and useful challenge, as in the extract, comes not only to harden into a party trick, but takes over, as a whole way of experiencing others and the world, in which people and objects shrink to fixed appearances, and nothing is left but, playing entertainingly over them, a single confident voice.

Already in Victorian England the novel had ceased to be, in any simple sense, a form, and had become, in effect, a whole literature. It is hardly necessary to stress the advantages of this development; we have only to instance such radically different works as *Wuthering Heights* and *Dombey and Son* and *Mary Barton* appearing within months of each other: deep variations of experience and convention, finding their own forms. The strength of this diversity has never since been absent: Joyce and Lawrence and Forster, to take only three very obvious examples, could differ radically, in a single generation, and yet find novels a natural medium: *Ulysses, Women in Love, A Passage to India:* radically different works, but with a unity in each, of a particular experience and a particular form. Just as we saw a necessary range in discursive prose, so we can see this imaginative range as a vitality and a strength. But of course it is always possible to see the range as a miscellaneity; to deplore the absence of a central and dominating tradition; to conclude that since this or that creative generation, the form, the prose has disintegrated.

There are problems now, certainly. For some considerable time the journal or memoir has been overlapping with the novel, and there has been a further overlap between fiction and argument, fiction and organized observation. It is easy, for example, to see the influence of the novel behind Beatrice Webb's account of her family, her father, and her acquisition of a voice that could give orders.

> This ignorance about the world of labour, did it imply class consciousness, the feeling of belonging to a superior caste? A frank answer seems worth giving. There was no consciousness of superior riches: on the contrary, owing to my mother's utilitarian expenditure (a discriminating penuriousness which I think was traditional in families rising to industrial power during the Napoleonic wars) the Potter girls were brought up to 'feel poor'. 'You girls', grumbled a brother-in-law, as he glanced from a not too luxurious breakfast table at the unexpectedly large credit in his bank-book, 'have neither the habit nor the desire for comfortable expenditure.' The consciousness that was present, I speak for my own analytic mind, was the consciousness of superior power. As life unfolded itself I became aware that I belonged to a class of persons who habitually gave orders, but who seldom, if ever, executed the orders of other people. My mother sat in her boudoir and gave orders—orders that brooked neither delay nor evasion. My father, by temperament the least autocratic and most accommodating of men, spent his whole life giving orders. (*My Apprenticeship*, 1926)

Again, Wells's account of the burning of an old world is technically fiction, but is close in feeling and method to many of his explicit arguments:

> Endless were the things we had to destroy in those great purgings. First, there were nearly all the houses and buildings of the old time. In the end we did not save in England one building in five thousand that were standing when the comet came. Year by year, as we made our homes afresh in accordance with the saner needs of our new social families, we swept away more and more of those horrible structures, the ancient residential houses, hastily built, without imagination, without beauty, without common honesty, without even comfort or convenience, in which the early twentieth century had sheltered until scarcely one remained; we saved nothing but what was beautiful or interesting out of all their gaunt and melancholy abundance. The actual houses, of course, we could not drag to our fires, but we brought all their ill-fitting deal doors, their dreadful window-sashes, their servant-tormenting staircases, their dank, dark cupboards, the verminous papers from their scaly walls, their dust and dirt-sodden carpets, their ill-designed and yet pretentious tables and chairs, sideboards and chests of drawers, the old dirt-saturated books, their ornaments—their dirty, decayed, and altogether painful ornaments—amidst which I remember there were sometimes even *stuffed dead birds*!—we burned them all. (*In the Days of the Comet*, 1906)

It would then be possible to separate a particular class of imaginative writing: that of Virginia Woolf, say.

> For now had come that moment, that hesitation when dawn trembles and night pauses, when if a feather alight in the scale it will be weighed down. One feather, and the house, sinking, falling, would have turned and pitched downwards to the depths of darkness. In the ruined room, picknickers would have lit their kettles; lovers sought shelter there, lying on the bare boards; and the shepherd stored his dinner on the bricks, and the tramp slept with his coat round him to ward off the cold. Then the roof would have fallen; briars and hemlocks would have blotted out path, step, and window; would have grown, unequally but lustily over the mound, until some trespasser, losing his way, could have told only by a red-hot poker among the nettles, or a scrap of china in the hemlock, that here once some one had lived; there had been a house.
>
> If the feather had fallen, if it had tipped the scale downwards, the whole house would have plunged to the depths to lie upon the sands of oblivion. But there was a force working; something not highly conscious; something that leered, something that lurched; something not inspired to go about its work with dignified ritual or solemn chanting. Mrs McNab groaned; Mrs Bast creaked. They were old; they were stiff; their legs ached. They came with their brooms and pails at last; they got to work. All of a sudden, would Mrs McNab see that the house was ready, one of the young ladies wrote: would she get this done; would she get that done; all in a hurry. They might be coming for the summer; had left everything to the last; expected to find things as they had left them. Slowly and painfully, with broom and pail, mopping, scouring, Mrs McNab, Mrs Bast stayed the corruption and the rot; rescued from the pool of Time that was fast closing over them now a basin, now a cupboard; fetched up from oblivion all the Waverley novels and a tea-set one morning; in the afternoon restored to sun and air a brass fender and a set of steel fire-irons. George, Mrs Bast's son, caught the rats, and cut the grass. They had the builders. Attended with the creaking of hinges and the screeching of bolts, the slamming and banging of damp-swollen woodwork, some rusty laborious birth seemed to be taking place, as the women, stooping, rising, groaning, singing, slapped and slammed, upstairs now, now down in the cellars. Oh, they said, the work! (*To the Lighthouse,* 1927)

We could argue that here the facts of an observable world and of common experience have been properly subordinated to an imaginative flow and recreation. But though the subordination will not be doubted, the problem of value cannot be settled *a priori*. What is quite evident in Virginia Woolf's prose is a particular relation to objects and people (the people, below a certain class line, not really very different from objects) which makes any simple abstraction of 'imagination' impossible. This is a way of seeing the world from a precise social position: the rhythms and the language follow from what is really an uncertainty, a wonder, that depends on quite other certainties and in particular the writer's isolation from the very general natural and human processes which must then be not so much described as evoked. I do not say this is an unfruitful situation. We can see how a very similar isolation, in Joyce, leads first to a use of language to describe, in almost tactile ways, a confusion which is a convincing consciousness, as in the following passage from *Ulysses*; and, second, to what is in effect a remaking of language to dissolve all reference points (those obstinate, isolated sights, sounds and smells in Bloom's mind) into a flow of lament for what is literally a dissolving world, as in the following passage from *Finnegan's Wake*.

> His hand took his hat from the peg over his initialled heavy overcoat, and his lost property office secondhand waterproof. Stamps: sticky-back pictures. Daresay lots of officers are in the swim too. Course they do. The sweated legend in the crown of his hat told him mutely: Plasto's high grade ha. He peeped quickly inside the leather headband. White slip of paper. Quite safe.
>
> On the doorstep he felt in his hip pocket for the latchkey. Not there. In the trousers I left off. Must get it. Potato I have. Creaky wardrobe. No use disturbing her. She turned over sleepily that time. He pulled the halldoor to after him very quietly, more, till the footleaf dropped gently over the threshold, a limp lid. Looked shut. All right till I come back anyhow. (*Ulysses*, 1914–21)
>
> O bitter ending! I'll slip away before they're up. They'll never see. Nor know. Nor miss me. And it's old and old it's sad and old it's sad and weary I go back to you, my cold father, my cold mad father, my cold mad feary father, till the near sight of the mere size of him, the moyles and moyles of it moananoaning, makes me seasilt saltsick and I rush, my only, into your arms. I see them rising! Save me from those therrble prongs! Two more. Onetwo moremens more. So. Avelaval. My leaves have drifted from me. All. But one clings still. I'll bear it on me. To remind me of. Lff! (*Finnegan's Wake*, 1939)

But what we cannot then say is that this is uniquely the modern literary imagination. It is the necessary and convincing prose of a particular phase of consciousness, in which the temporary relation of a writer and his world is the principle of organization, to be confirmed by the paradoxical community (the remaining relation between a writer and his readers) of a shared isolation. A critic who belongs to this community will claim, understandably, a total significance for literature of this kind. The novel as a whole, under the suggestively ratifying label of 'modern', will be re-defined in its terms. But what we have really to see is a representative significance, in altering real relations.

When we have seen this, we can look again at those different writers who are attempting, in what is really a connected process of observation and imagination, to find a prose which is capable of including a more common experience: in which the writer is still certainly the imaginative recorder, the observing creator, but where there is no *necessary* separation between his prose and his world. The altering relations, in the history of the novel, between reporting, analysis, and imaginative shaping, are of course still altering. The emergence of a number of writers from social groups with no immediate literary tradition has been very complicated, in practice. They have been affected, inevitably, by the major prose of an immediately preceding generation, but in what they are writing about, in new physical and social landscapes, they draw just as evidently on a nineteenth-century tradition in which a certain confidence of description—indeed a confidence of a knowable world—was based on an actual community between writer and subject, and thence an attainable public relation between writer and reader: a prose directly related to the ordinary language of the world.

It is as yet too early to know how these relations will develop. But we can say with some confidence that the particular achievements of Joyce and Virginia Woolf are as historical, in every real sense, as the achievements of Dickens and George Eliot. 'Modern', as what seems an endlessly persistent adjective, gives quite the wrong lead. The development we traced through Hardy and Lawrence, in which the whole problem was the relation between a received method and a changing society, is of course still active. It seems at times so difficult that it is merely exploited: in an edgy comedy or in a noisy opportunism. But here and there it is being faced, in its real significance, and new prose, new ideas, new feelings, are coming steadily through.

The point of this argument is not a sudden climax. Real development is only rarely of that kind. But we set out to consider whether the question of good prose, of what is called style, can be abstracted from the whole experience of these years in which a land and a people have been transformed. My point was to suggest, with some examples, that good prose and style are not things but relationships; that questions of method, subject and quality cannot be separated from the changing relations of men which are evident elsewhere in changing institutions and in a changing language; and that to see English prose since 1780 as this real history is to make new emphases, ask different questions, and see the present as well as the past in new ways.

3

David Hume:
Reasoning and Experience

In the republic of letters a man can live as himself, but in the bureaucracy of letters he must continually declare his style and department,
and submit to an examination of his purpose and credentials at the
frontier of every field. The influence of bureaucracy even extends to
his readers, nervous under the stare of critics who are conducting
what looks like a census of occupations. Is David Hume (1711–1776)
moralist, logician, historian, essayist? Under which of these
categories are you proposing to read him? Remember, before
answering, the serious penalties involved, if you get on the wrong
side of any one of these lines.

A certain boldness, and even rashness, is necessary now, if we are
to maintain the republic. It is true that we can gather some shreds of
authority, reminding our interrogators that in 1762 Boswell called
Hume, quite simply, 'the greatest Writer in Britain', and that in *My
Own Life* Hume described his 'Love of literary Fame' as 'my ruling
Passion'.[1] We can quote his most recent and best biographer, Ernest
Mossner, for the opinion that from the beginning Hume 'regarded
philosophy as part-and-parcel of literature. To be a philosopher is to
be a man of letters: the proposition was received by Hume and the
eighteenth century as axiomatic' (p. 63). Yet the republic of letters
cannot depend on this kind of authority or precedent. Its laws are
immediate and substantial, in the writing and reading of literature,
or they are nothing. The proof that now matters is that we can read
Hume, sensibly and centrally, as a writer, and that this literary em-

1. Boswell, *Private Papers*, ed. Geoffrey Scott and Frederick A. Pottle, vol. 1, New
   York 1928, p. 130; Ernest C. Mossner, *The Life of Hume*, Edinburgh 1954,
   Appendix A.

phasis not only does not weaken his importance as philosopher, but is even fundamental to it. We can distinguish two elements of this proof: first; his close and lifelong preoccupation with the *writing* of his philosophy; second, his fundamental interest in the relations between reasoning and experience. Though these questions can properly be separated, for discussion, they are not finally distinct. The first is a matter of style, but it is more, finally (even against some of Hume's ways of putting the question), than the simple delivery of something already complete. The second is a matter of philosophy, but again it is in the end much more than a formal argument, for the relation between reasoning and experience is explored as much in problems of structure and style as in heads and proofs immediately recognizable as such. These related questions, that is to say, come together in the question of the nature of literature, as Hume understood and wrote it.

Two pieces engage our first attention: the autobiographical letter of 1734[2], and the similarly personal but more public analysis—a piece that deserves classic status—at the end of the first book of A *Treatise of Human Nature* (1739–40) (i, iv, vii). In each of them Hume is engaged in a kind of self-questioning which has general importance just because it is personal: the relation between reasoning and experience is being touched at the root.

> I was after that left to my own Choice in my Reading, and found it encline me almost equally to Books of Reasoning and Philosophy, and to Poetry and the polite Authors. Every one, who is acquainted either with the Philosophers or Critics, knows that ther is nothing yet establisht in either of these two Sciences, and that they contain little more than endless Disputes even in the most fundamental Articles. Upon Examination of these I found a certain Boldness of Temper growing in me, which was not enclin'd to submit to any Authority in these Subjects but led me to seek out some new Medium by which Truth might be establisht. After much Study and Reflection on this, at last, when I was about 18 Years of Age, there seemed to be open'd up to me a new Scene of Thought, which transported me beyond Measure, and made me, wyth an Ardor natural to young men, throw up every other Pleasure or Business to apply entirely to it. (1734)

The new 'medium', the new 'scene of thought', has all the quality of

---

2. *Letters*, ed. J.Y.T. Greig, vol. 1, Oxford 1932, p. 13.

an experience—a dimension rather than a doctrine—reached, however, by 'study and reflection'. We can describe it in retrospect and
abstraction as an option for empiricism:

> I found that the moral Philosophy transmitted to us by Antiquity,
> labor'd under the same Inconvenience that has been found in their
> natural Philosophy, of being entirely Hypothetical, and depending
> more upon Invention than Experience. Every one consulted his Fancy
> in erecting Schemes of Virtue and of Happiness, without regarding
> Human Nature, upon which every moral Conclusion must depend.
> This therefore I resolved to make my principal Study, and the Source
> from which I wou'd derive every Truth in Criticism as well as Morality.
> (1734)

Yet this option is not in any narrow sense intellectual; it is clearly a
decision of the whole being, as indeed the consequences showed. The
easy way to connect Hume the thinker with Hume the writer is to illustrate the difficulties of translating the new 'scene of thought' into
words:

> When one must bring the Idea he comprehended in gross, nearer to
> him, so as to contemplate its minutest Parts, and keep it steddily in his
> Eye, so as to copy these Parts in Order, this I found impracticable for
> me, nor were my Spirits equal to so severe an Employment. Here lay
> my greatest Calamity. I had no Hopes of delivering my Opinions with
> such Elegance and Neatness, as to draw to me the Attention of the
> World, and I wou'd rather live and dye in Obscurity than produce
> them maim'd and imperfect. (1734)

This is a normal and general difficulty, expressed in the terms of his
century: the search for 'such Elegance and Neatness, as to draw to
me the Attention of the World' is what the literary pursuit was often
and is still often understood to be. Yet something else was happening, in this first creative struggle, and it is Hume's distinction, inquir-
ing into the relation between reasoning and experience at much more
than a formal level, to bring it to notice:

> I have notic'd in the Writings of the French Mysticks, and in those of
> our Fanaticks here, that, when they give a History of the Situation of
> their Souls, they mention a Coldness and Desertion of the Spirit,
> which frequently returns, and some of them, at the beginning, have
> been tormented with it many Years. As this kind of Devotion depends
> entirely on the Force of Passion, and consequently of the Animal
> Spirits, I have often thought that their Case and mine were pretty par-
> ralel, and that their rapturous Admirations might discompose the

Fabric of the Nerves and Brain, as much as profound Reflections, and that warmth or Enthusiasm which is inseparable from them. (1734)

We hardly need further witness of the kind of passionate inquiry which Hume's thinking was; yet at once, in this letter, we become aware of a tension which is more acute, because more local, than the natural strain on any profound and passionate thinker. It is surely surprising, alike to our preconceptions about Hume's empiricism and to our ordinary sense of his mature style, for which 'coolness' continually suggests itself as a description, to read of that inseparable 'warmth or Enthusiasm' and of that surprising 'parralel Case'. There is a subtlety of reference not wholly separable from confusion, in what is still an unfinished movement of mind: the others are 'Fanatics', and yet 'pretty parralel'. While the phrases hang in the mind, one is reminded of Hume's defence of the third book of the *Treatise*, 'Of Morals', against Hutcheson's criticism that 'there wants a certain Warmth in the Cause of Virtue':

> I must own, this has not happen'd by Chance, but is the Effect of a Reasoning either good or bad. . . Any warm Sentiment of Morals, I am afraid, wou'd have the Air of Declama·ion amidst abstract Reasonings, and wou'd be esteem'd contrary to good Taste. And tho'd I am much more ambitious of being esteem'd a Friend to Virtue, than a Writer of Taste; yet I must always carry the latter in my Eye, otherwise I must despair of ever being serviceable to Virtue. I hope these Reasons will satisfy you; tho at the same time, I intend to make a new Tryal, if it be possible to make the Moralist and Metaphysician agree a little better.[3]

Behind the ordinary dilemma of a philosophical style, itself complicated by an anxious consciousness of contemporary canons of taste, something fundamental to the inquiry itself is here being skirted. It is interesting that in this letter to Hutcheson, Hume uses the analogy with which he ends the *Treatise*: the distinction between the anatomist and the painter. At first glance the distinction is commonplace: the anatomist dissects, accurately, to discover the 'most secret Springs and Principles'; the painter describes 'the grace and beauty' of actions; the two functions are different, and must not be confused, though the anatomist can give 'very good advice' to the

3. Mossner, p. 134.

painter, as can the dissecting metaphysician to the engaging moralist. Yet when we read this analogy, as it is written in the *Treatise*, we can see in the language the tension within which Hume was working. He has reached, by argument, the conclusion that 'sympathy is the chief source of moral distinctions,' and now adds, nervously and hopefully:

> Were it proper in such a subject to bribe the readers assent, or employ any thing but solid argument, we are here abundantly supplied with topics to engage the affections. All lovers of virtue (and such we all are in speculation, however we may degenerate in practice) must certainly be pleas'd to see moral distinctions deriv'd from so noble a source. . .
> (III, iii, vi)

After the heaviness of 'bribe', the tone becomes closer and warmer, as if in oversight, yet the whole movement is conscious, reaching its climax in the moving rhetorical questions: 'Who indeed does not feel an accession of alacrity... ?', 'And who can think any advantages of fortune a sufficient compensation for the last breach...?' When the caution returns, it is already partly discounted:

> But I forbear insisting on this subject. Such reflexions require a work apart, very different from the genius of the present. The anatomist ought never to emulate the painter: nor in his accurate dissections and portraitures of the smaller parts of the human body, pretend to give his figures any graceful and engaging attitude or expression. There is even something hideous, or at least minute, in the views of things which he presents; and 'tis necessary the objects shou'd be set more at a distance, and be more cover'd up from sight, to make them engaging to the eye and imagination. An anatomist, however, is admirably fitted to give advice to a painter...

The real question being argued, being *written*, here is the question of what it is to be a moralist. In the letter to Hutcheson, the metaphysician had been the anatomist, and the moralist the painter. But if the end of all the dissection is the discovery of a human body (to which alone appeal can be made, not merely to have effect but to make sense, for it is there that the source of morality resides) then the attention of the anatomist is the intention of the painter, though the detailed work of the anatomist seems, while it is being done, 'hideous or at least minute'. Hume is not departing from analysis, but reconstituting it, when he moves from 'argument' to 'declamation'. The end of the detailed moral inquiry is properly the moralist actively engaging human sympathy, yet the tension is still there, from that first and natural fear of 'consulting his Fancy in erecting Schemes of Virtue and Happiness'; and Hume must forbear insisting, renounce any pretension to the 'graceful and engaging', even while he engages and insists. In this tension, a whole movement of thought—in effect the transformation of empiricism—is being slowly and unevenly brought to light. The moralist must be an anatomist, however unwillingly, because he would be a painter, but a good painter.

The central document of this tension is, of course, the concluding chapter of the first book of the *Treatise*. Parts of this chapter have been widely quoted, but the movement of mind there is so close and subtle that incidental quotation tends to misrepresent. What is at first surprising, in a work in many ways so rigorous, is the note of personal confession. It is tempting to write this down as simple weakness (the young author's itch to be at himself) or, when we have read more widely in Hume, and stumbled over his many ironies, to take it as rhetoric of a subtle kind: the confession of incapacity which in polite studies is the only authorized way to claim capacity; the forbearing to insist as the only polite tone of insistence. But these elements are at best minor. The confession, in a vital sense, is the argument, only it is an argument of a new kind.

Thus the language Hume uses to describe the social sense, which in abstraction one writes down so easily as the basis of his morals, is immediately arresting. He is 'affrighted and confounded' by the 'forelorn solitude' into which his line of reasoning has led him, and can fancy himself 'some strange uncouth monster, who not being able to mingle and unite in society, has been expell'd from human commerce, and left utterly abandon'd and disconsolate. Fain wou'd I run into the crowd for shelter and warmth; but cannot prevail with myself to mix with such deformity.' Between the uncouth and the deformed, what? For 'such is my weakness, that I feel all my opinions loosen and fall of themselves, when unsupported by the approbation of others.' It is just this weakness that, as a reasoner, he has to face: 'After the most accurate and exact of my reasonings, I can give no reason why I shou'd assent to it; and feel nothing but a *strong* propensity to consider objects *strongly* in that view, under which they appear to me.' Assent comes from experience and habit, which he shares with others, but then this weakness is a general weakness; the apparent assent of reason is no more than an illusion in common. The question then is, 'how far we ought to yield to these illusions?' Imagination is dangerous to reason, even when it has become common and conventional, but if we reject it where we can distinguish it as such, and limit ourselves to the understanding, we shall find that we are left without any evidence or certainty at all. The contradictions of all reasoning are then so deep that reasoning itself seems useless, and the '*intense* view of these manifold contradictions and imperfections' leads again to that 'Coldness and Desertion of the Spirit', 'inviron'd with the deepest darkness and utterly depriv'd of the use of every member and faculty'. At this point, Hume instances what has often been taken as his way out of this darkness:

> I dine, I play a game of back-gammon, I converse, and am merry with my friends; and when after three or four hours' amusement, I wou'd return to these speculations, they appear so cold, and strain'd, and ridiculous, that I cannot find in my heart to enter into them any farther.

The sceptic, yielding to fatigue and the demands of his senses, confirms his scepticism, but this is not at all (as Hume's enemies would have it) the relapse into philistinism to be expected from one holding the 'low view' of man. On the contrary, it is characteristic of Hume, in his long dalogue between reasoning and experience, to feel and think even when in apparent flight. His 'animal spirits and passions' have reduced him to 'this indolent belief in the general maxims of the world' but the sentiments are recognized as those of 'spleen and indolence' and the way is prepared for the return to reasoning, when 'I feel my mind all collected within itself.' Curiosity and ambition give energy again, but behind them there is a more decisive realization: if the questions are indeed cold and strained and ridiculous, there is no final alternative but to go on into them, except the relapse to superstition. The declaration that mattered in Hume's life is then almost casually made: 'Generally speaking, the errors in religion are dangerous; those in philosophy only ridiculous.' Contradiction can be lived with; false belief can not. And the conviction of falseness there is, we notice, assumed. All the arguments on it will come later. The sceptic has arrived at a way of living with his scepticism, and this way, paradoxically, is one of affirmation. For 'a true sceptic will be diffident of his philosophical doubts, as well as of his philosophical conviction'. It is in this way that Hume's essential tension is, if not resolved, negotiated. Here, decisively, is the discovery of how to write. The inquiry will continue, searching always farther into the contradictions and imperfections of reasoning. But the anatomist has now most decisively instructed the painter: an engaged, ironic and warily moving painter. For

> we shou'd yield to that propensity, which inclines us to be positive and certain in *particular points*, according to the light, in which we survey them in any *particular instant*.... On such an occasion we are apt not only to forget our scepticism, but even our modesty too; and make use of such terms as these, *'tis evident*, *'tis certain*, *'tis undeniable*; which a due deference to the public ought, perhaps, to prevent. I may have fallen into this fault after the example of others; but I here enter a *caveat* against any objections, which may be offer'd on that head; and declare that such expressions were extorted from me by the present view of the object, and imply no dogmatical spirit, nor conceited idea of my own judgement, which are sentiments that I am sensible can become no body, and a sceptic still less than any other.

The philosophical decision is here, substantially, a choice of style. Of the connexion between style and belief, Hume was formally as well as substantially aware:

> There are certain sects, which secretly form themselves in the learned world, as well as factions in the political; and though sometimes they come not to an open rupture, they give a different turn to the ways of thinking of those who have taken part on either side. The most remarkable of this kind are the sects founded on the different sentiments with regard to the *dignity of human nature*; which is a point that seems to have divided philosophers and poets, as well as divines, from the beginning of the world to this day. Some exalt our species to the skies, and represent man as a kind of human demigod, who derives his origin from heaven, and retains evident marks of his lineage and descent. Others insist upon the blind sides of human nature, and can discover nothing, except vanity, in which man surpasses the other animals, whom he affects so much to despise. If an author possess the talent of rhetoric and declamation, he commonly takes part with the former: If his turn lie towards irony and ridicule, he naturally throws himself into the other extreme.[4]

But this way of putting the matter seems absurdly simple, when we

---

4. *Essays Moral and Political*, London 1742, 'Of the Dignity or Meanness of Human Nature'.

look at Hume's own practice. In the received account of him, the 'turn ... towards irony and ridicule' is predominant, yet in this matter of the dignity or meanness of human nature, Hume's place is clearly with the former option, though he brings it sharply down to earth. The apparent paradox indicates a more real paradox, which is central to Hume's particular character as a moralist. I have described this as the sceptic who finds a way of affirming, but the point that has now to be taken is that this is more than a marginal outlet—the agreed lapse into particular and local affirmations—and is indeed, in his moral writings, his distinctive kind of achievement.

We should perhaps make here the necessary critical distinction between scepticism and cynicism. Again and again we find Hume's power of argument probing, with a sharpness that can properly be associated with scepticism, a particular kind of idea. But it is remarkable how often this very idea is attacked because it appears to degrade human dignity or capacity. There is a good example in the essay from which I have just quoted:

> Now this being a point, in which all the world is agreed, that human understanding falls infinitely short of perfect wisdom; it is proper we should know when this comparison takes place, that we may not dispute where there is no real difference in our sentiments. Man falls much more short of perfect wisdom, than animals do of man; yet the latter difference is so considerable, that nothing but a comparison with the former can make it appear of little moment.
>
> It is also usual to *compare* one man with another; and finding very few whom we can call *wise* or *virtuous*, we are apt to entertain a contemptible notion of our species in general. That we may be sensible of the fallacy of this way of reasoning, we may observe that the honourable appellations of wise and virtuous, are not annexed to any particular degree of those qualities of *wisdom* and *virtue*; but arise altogether from the comparison we make between one man and another. When we find a man, who arrives at such a pitch of wisdom as is very uncommon, we pronounce him a wise man: So that to say, there are few wise men in the world, is really to say nothing; since it is only by their scarcity that they merit that appellation.

The difference between scepticism and cynicism could hardly be more marked; indeed Hume's writing is the outstanding instance, in English, where this critical distinction can be read. Those enemies of Hume who have relied on a kind of free association between sceptical thinking and the denial of value, have succeeded only in muddling an experience of genuine complexity. The sceptical character of his theory of human understanding is of course very evident, but the conclusions he consequently drew, on the relations between reasoning and experience, and between fact and value, are, precisely, the theoretical basis of that movement of mind which I have described as the sceptic who learns how to affirm. To rely on the necessary avowals of scepticism (indeed to reduce these calm and deliberate avowals to what can be called 'admissions'), while ignoring the *consequently* firm assertions of value, is simply to dismember the Humean experience.

The complicating difficulty, undoubtedly, has been Hume's attitude to religion, for here (we have still to observe, in twentieth-century England as well as in eighteenth-century Calvinist Scotland) an obstinate kind of questioning, a scepticism, can lead, suddenly, to a cry of fire. Angry prejudices can be released, only to turn suddenly and assume the name and body of love. Yet the major effect of Hume's religious scepticism is surely the abolition of the argument from design, and this enterprise seems expressly conceived as a way of affirming both reason and the limits of reason in our experience of the human condition. I do not know who would now want to identify 'the religious sense' with the (in many ways irreligious) argument from design, but of course the argument presses further: a moral questioning of the consequences of religion as Hume saw it practised and expounded. Here again we have the sceptical thinker arguing against the intolerance which seems to follow from a unitary explanation of life; against the punishment of body and spirit by the kind of self-abasement which seems to follow from the distance of a perfect God; against the hypocrisy which can fill the gap between actual and aspiring belief; against the corruption of philosophy which can follow from its reservation to deductive reasoning from a principle asserted to be beyond reason. In abstraction even, but much more in the body of the writing, this opposition to negations, this denial of the necessity of particular denials, composes itself into a very positive moral account, which the tone most notably confirms. We can certainly instance Hume's penetration and wit in the *Dialogues concerning Natural Religion* (1779)—notably the brilliant part VI ('the world, therefore, I infer, is an animal')—but we can also instance, from the same dialogues, his deeper achievement: the humanity of the extension of scepticism to scepticism itself; the bold and yet intricate imaginative confidence (at first sight so surprising in a moralist, though it would not be surprising in a dramatist or novelist) which allows and controls the award of victory to the defeated Cleanthes. The simple opposition to scepticism hardly knows, in Hume, with what manner of man it has to deal.

The problem, that is to say, emerges again and again as one of *reading* Hume: reading in a wholly literary sense. This is certainly the case, though a very particular case, with *An Enquiry concerning the Principles of Morals* (1751), 'of all my writings, historical, philosophical, or literary, incomparably the best'. All students of Hume will know the kind of summary that can be given of Hume's doctrines in the *Enquiry*, but, without questioning its usefulness, it can still reasonably be asked whether the main purpose of writing or reading the *Enquiry* is to arrive at that kind of summary of conclusions. The unfinished (and also, in some important respects, unstarted) argument between the 'literary' and the 'philosophical' reader of moral essays, might well now be directed towards just this question. It can be put in one way as the familiar critical question of the relation between content and form. The general intricacy of this relation is especially marked in moral writing. The very terms of definition—'moral doctrine', 'moral writing'—contain, if we would look at them, some of the major difficulties. We do not ordinarily believe, in the reading of literature, that the content of a work can, in any adequate way, be represented by summary; or rather, it can be so *represented*, for the agreed and limited purposes of particular discussions, but can only be *found* in a particular structure and sequence of words. The urgency of abstract inquiry, and indeed of doctrine, is certainly such that we have to use representations. But what can then happen, as the representation becomes by habit the content, is that we can find ourselves working with very feeble versions of both doctrine and style. Thus 'doctrine', commonly, is 'conclusion', although that very word ought to remind us of what, from all antecedent stages, has been lost. And 'style', commonly, is reserved to 'expression', all its deep connexions with a process of experience quite lost or forgotten: style indeed as 'such Elegance and Neatness, as to draw to me the Attention of the World', or worse (since the 'attention of the world' is a complicated connexion), style as that which is not there (its presence indicating the taint of literature), or which interferes as little as possible with the expression of doctrine.

No simple description of Hume's style in the *Enquiry* is likely to be adequate. Indeed the fact of variation, in ways of writing as in ways of thinking, seems essential to any full understanding of it. In one sense, the drive of the argument, of the proof, is very certain and even at times overbearing; but equally there are many signs of uncertainty, hesitation, even reverie, and these are gathered up rather than resolved in the final rhetoric of conviction. Thus the austere firmness of the opening, so confident in the clarity of its antitheses and in its promised penetration and synthesis, stands virtually alone in the work, except perhaps for the first appendix, 'Concerning Moral Sentiment'. This is the boldness of conception and proposition, and it is interesting that it is from this opening and appendix that most of the sentences definitive of Hume's doctrines are taken. Yet when he passes to the substance of proof, more of the mind is at once and, as it were, involuntarily engaged. The 'experimental method ... deducing general maxims from a comparison of particular instances' is in general followed, and has an important effect on the *general* structure of the essay. But in fact, as soon as he begins collecting instances, he touches a different string: he is concerned not only to deduce but to persuade. Consider how early, in the section 'Of Benevolence', he gives the anecdote of the dying Pericles, and not only as an instance in argument but as an instance for the communication of feeling: '*You forget*, cries the dying hero who had heard all....' Whenever this kind of instance occurs to him, Hume's instinct is to make his own feeling about it the proof, and only then to recall and appear to excuse himself—the movement of mind we have seen before:

> But I forget that it is not my present business to recommend generosity or benevolence, or to paint in their true colours all the genuine charms of the social virtues. These, indeed, sufficiently engage every heart, on the first apprehension of them; and it is difficult to abstain from some sally or panegyric, as often as they occur in discourse or reasoning. But our object here....

And it is significant that what immediately follows this recall is not a return to deduction, but a reassertion of the immediacy and communication of feelings of just this kind. The argument that our approbation of the social virtues is due at least in part to their utility is introduced, characteristically, with the suasive question—'may it not thence be concluded?'—following a panegyric on 'any humane beneficent man' which ends: 'Like the sun, an inferior minister of Providence, he cheers, invigorates and sustains the surrounding world.' It is difficult to feel that the scrappy assertions which follow the question carry anything more than a small part of the burden of proof, by comparison with the demonstration of Hume's actual range of feelings of this kind: 'The eye is pleased with the prospect of cornfields and loaded vineyards, horses grazing, and flocks pasturing; but flies the view of briars and brambles affording shelter to wolves and serpents.' The very element of convention, in this kind of description of feeling, is, as it were, folded into the proof. Or again: 'Can anything stronger be said in praise of a profession, such as merchandise or manufacture, than to observe the advantages which it procures to society? And is not a monk and inquisitor enraged when we treat his order as useless or pernicious to mankind?' The shift there, from 'society' to 'mankind', is a shift within a unity of feeling which, if it is not wholly communicated, will quickly reveal itself, in the light of deduction, as a bundle of propensities and prejudices. It is again wholly characteristic that when he passes to the summary of his argument on benevolence—'upon the whole, then, it seems undeniable...'—he moves into a kind of language which is not neutrally descriptive but conventionally communicative:

> The social virtues are never regarded without their beneficial tendencies, *nor viewed as barren and unfruitful.* The happiness of mankind, the order of society, the harmony of families, the mutual support of friends are always considered as the result *of the gentle dominion over the breasts of men.*

To read these sentences without the phrases I have italicized is to see very clearly, by contrast, how Hume is writing and thinking. For these phrases are clearly not emotional intensifications of the argument. Without them, the argument is not really there. The supposed alternative to benefit, as an explanation of approval, is at once suppressed and swollen, until the phrase serves really to confirm, in feeling, the idea of benefit. The powerful normative and appealing clauses of the second sentence move rhythmically to a result which has already, in effect, been assumed, so that in a way no definition of cause is needed; the sentence, by that stage, has done its work. Yet since definition, clearly, for Hume, is not enough, all the feeling of this part of the inquiry is concentrated into the association of 'dominion' with 'gentle' and 'breasts'.

This is to take only one section of the whole work. There are, as we shall, see, further variations. Yet what we can learn here is perhaps decisive. For the point of my observations is not at all to convict Hume of being a thinker who lapses into what is called 'emotive' language. Indeed the assumptions about language which led to the separation of an 'emotive' category seem to me profoundly distorting in any study of communication. Behind them lies that learned and willed separation of writer and reader which itself produces a particular style: in argument, especially, the style that wishes to be no style, or, at second thought, to be elegant. What matters about Hume is that his argument, his doctrine, depends on the same assumptions that we have seen at work in the writing: the shared conventions of humane feeling; the certainty that these are embodied in the common language of approval and disapproval; the conviction that moral activity is the use of this language, and that reasoning is necessary mainly to confirm this use and to expose the inadequacy of other definitions of morals. It is difficult to see how he could have completely established these convictions without embodying them, in practice, in his writing.

That he tried, however, to get outside the assumptions, or rather to demonstrate them by a different kind of writing and thinking, is equally important in any final assessment. The close and strenuous distinction between a mistake of *fact* and one of *right*, in the appendix 'Concerning Moral Sentiment', is only one of many possible examples of the kind of reasoning we can properly call impersonal, and in which Hume's capacity is so evidently of the highest order that it compels respect even in disagreement. Or again he can, even within the drive of his demonstration of moral conventions, pause and reflect with a sudden flexibility of intelligence which is the more remarkable when it has been seen how strong the conventions and the feelings are. A good example of this is the seventh note in section VI, 'Of Qualities Useful to Ourselves', when after a confident account of our sentiments towards rich and poor, as conformable with his theory of moral distinctions, he adds, hesitantly but convincingly, the complexities of these sentiments which in fact confuse the demonstration. In the two final paragraphs of the same section, he introduces, first, an alternative moral dimension, and, second, a sudden relation of conventional regard to different types of society, and each point serves only to disturb what had seemed a too simple and indeed overbearing demonstration; yet if it had indeed been overbearing, the recognitions would not have come. The mood of reverie which comes when contradictions, not so much of propositions as of feelings, are recognized, is always impressive. Near the climax of his argument, in part i of section IX, there is the old tension: 'I must confess that this enumeration puts the matter in so strong a light that I cannot, *at present*, be more assured of any truth which I learn from reasoning and argument....' Yet if the matter is as clear as that, and still men dispute, 'when I reflect on this, I say, I fall back into diffidence and scepticism, and suspect that an hypothesis so obvious, had it been a true one, would long ere now have been received by the unanimous suffrage and consent of mankind'. But what is equally characteristic, in this whole movement of mind, is the brisk resumption, in part ii, of what remains the most difficult part of his proof—the movement from 'approbation' to 'interested obligation'. Even here, however, he slides from a statement of the problem to a rhapsodical solution of it, quickly corrected to more detailed and incisive argument, and then, at the point of final difficulty, the kind of engagement (which is not only persuasive rhetoric) that we have already examined:

> Treating vice with the greatest candour and making it all possible concessions....
> That *honesty is the best policy* may be a good general rule, but is liable to many exceptions. And he, it may perhaps be thought, conducts himself with most wisdom who observes the general rule and takes advantage of all the exceptions. I must confess that if a man think that this reasoning much requires an answer, it will be a little difficult to find any which will to him appear satisfactory and convincing. If his heart rebel not against such pernicious maxims, if he feel no reluctance to the thoughts of villany or baseness, he has indeed lost a considerable motive to virtue; and we may expect that his practice will be answerable to his speculation.

As he considers and rejects the 'secret and successful' breaker of moral laws, the mind of the reader may return uneasily to the simple panegyric on success in part ii of section VI, and to the two inclusions of secrecy in his listing of the social virtues. These lists, throughout, break into many kinds of consideration. It is, then, difficult indeed to emerge from our reading and be satisfied with the more easily abstracted definitions. Indeed, to read for these definitions is to mistake Hume: the 'definitions' depend, empirically, on all the instances and on all the apparent synonyms.[5] Or, to put it another way, the substance of Hume's inquiry is in the whole body of the writing: in the variations, hesitations and contradictions as deeply as in the lines and heads of proof.

In his account of moral activity, which in its main directions is deeply positive and affirmative, Hume seeks to embody two principles: the communication of feeling, which is sympathy, and the engagement of feeling, which is the necessary involvement of man with mankind. A position of this kind inevitably emphasizes conventions: not only is the common language the moral consensus, but also there is a practical equivalence between humanity and society. This element of convention, not only in Hume but in eighteenth-century culture generally, raises certain important critical questions.

It has been suggested, for example, that in his reliance on approval and disapproval as moral criteria, he is opening the way for, and indeed participating in, the degeneration of social morals to the trivial and external concerns of Lord Chesterfield. It is, I think, true that when he is affirming certain kinds of convention, in the language of his period, an evident blandness of tone can take temporary charge: 'He must be unhappy indeed, either in his own temper, or in his situation and company, who has never perceived the charms of a facetious wit or flowing affability, of a delicate modesty or decent genteelness of address and manner.'[6] Certain words in that sentence, 'facetious', 'affability', 'genteelness', are now so heavily compromised that conviction of Hume is almost too easy. Yet a certain smoothing complacency is undoubtedly present: most often, I think, when he feels he is going against the grain of his time, and seeks anxiously to appease it. I find it necessary to remember, when Hume purrs in this way, that in fact, through most of his life, he was challenging some of the central beliefs of his time: indeed, became notorious, lost jobs through prejudice, had his very tomb guarded

5. Cf. C.W. Hendel's introduction to his edition of the *Enquiry*, New York 1957, pp. xxvi-xxvii.
6. *Enquiries*, ed. L.A. Selby-Bigge, Oxford 1894, enlarged 1902, IX, i, 226. Future references are to this edition.

against desecration. I cannot myself associate a man like that with Chesterfield, though the literary fact remains clear, that at times he sounds so bland and comfortable that he is now paradoxically exposed to a different kind of enemy.

And then, quite apart from this occasional blandness, we have certainly to note a limitation of his mind by temporary social assumptions. It is significant that when in his discussion of benevolence (*Enquiry*, II, ii) he introduces instances of moral feelings modified by 'further experience and sounder reasoning', three out of the four (on charity, tyrannicide, and luxury) seem now profoundly ambiguous. Indeed the reduction of charity to a weakness has the real complacency which in subsequent Poor Law legislation became inhuman and terrible. Much of Hume's political writing is marred in this way, by a too easy acceptance of convention at those points where society was not, after all, equivalent with humanity.

Again, we must certainly remark a limitation of kinds of feeling: the prudential exclusion of intensity and passion; the limitation of responses to suffering; the too easy sneer at enthusiasm: 'A gloomy, hair-brained enthusiast, after his death, may have a place in the calendar; but will scarcely ever be admitted, when alive, into intimacy and society, except by those who are as delirious and dismal as himself' (IX, i, 219). His attack on the 'monkish virtues'—'celibacy, fasting, penance, mortification, self-denial, humility, silence, solitude' (IX, i, 219)—has the disability of so many of his lists: that it is not really discriminating, and that the often bad is confounded with the often good. His argument against them is similarly mixed: that they disqualify from fortune and society, which is simple complacency; and that they 'stupefy the understanding and harden the heart', which is at least arguable of part of the list, and indeed seems to me true.

Yet we must not surrender to an opposite but equal limitation. The social feelings are real, are not merely Chesterfield, and Hume's range, here, is both wide and deep:

> Let us consider what we call vicious luxury. No gratification, however sensual, can of itself be esteemed vicious. A gratification is only vicious, when it engrosses all a man's expence, and leaves no ability for such acts of duty and generosity as are required by his situation and fortune. Suppose that he correct the vice, and employ part of his expence in the education of his children, in the support of his friends,

and in relieving the poor: would any prejudice result to society? On the contrary, the same consumption would arise; and the labour, which, at present, is employed only in producing a slender gratification to one man, would relieve the necessitous, and bestow satisfaction on hundreds. The same care and toil that raise a dish of peas at Christmas, would give bread to a whole family during six months. To say, that, without a vicious luxury, the labour would not have been employed at all, is only to say, that there is some other defect in human nature, such as indolence, selfishness, inattention to others, for which luxury, in some measure, provides a remedy; as one poison may be an antidote to another. But virtue, like wholesome food, is better than poisons, however corrected.[7]

This is the best of Hume, and it has been too little emphasized.

Nor can we finally say that, in his attention to social approbation and disapprobation, Hume neglects the self-approval of individual conscience. Indeed, on the very last page of the *Enquiry* he writes: 'Inward peace of mind, consciousness of integrity, a satisfactory review of our own conduct; these are circumstances very requisite to happiness, and will be cherished and cultivated by every honest man who feels the importance of them' (IX, ii, 233). And in his final paragraph, contrasting the pleasures of virtue with the 'empty amusements of luxury and expense', he writes of 'the unbought satisfaction of conversation, society, study, even health and the common beauties of nature, but above all the peaceful reflection on one's own conduct' (XX, ii, 233). The unity of these points of reference is indeed Hume's whole moral appeal.

Yet was this unity possible? Is the unity not merely conventional? In answering these questions, we must first take account of one fact, that Hume quite often enters, in his moral and political writings, a distinct kind of social relativism, which of all ways of thinking can be the most dangerous to the simple reliance on convention. At a formal level, the matter can be easily settled. Nobody who has read such essays as 'Of National Characters', 'The Rise of Arts and Sciences', 'Of Commerce', and 'Of Refinement in the Arts', would wish to accuse Hume of confusing a local and temporary society with universal and historical humanity. On the contrary, he is sometimes a remarkably original contributor to new kinds of relative historical analysis.

7. 'Of Refinement in the Arts', in *Essays*.

> In countries where men pass most of their time in conversation and
> visits and assemblies, these *companionable* qualities, so to speak, are
> of high estimation and form a chief part of personal merit. In coun-
> tries where men live a more domestic life and either are employed in
> business or amuse themselves in a narrower circle of acquaintance, the
> more solid qualities are chiefly regarded. (VII, 212)

And he goes on to a comparison of England and France. The
distinguishing word here is 'companionable', and indeed, just before
this passage he has written:

> As the mutual shocks in *society*, and the oppositions of interest and
> self-love, have constrained mankind to establish the laws of
> *justice*....:in like manner, the eternal contrarieties, in *company*, of
> men's pride and self-conceit, have introduced the rules of *Good Man-
> ners* or *Politeness*.... (VIII, 211)

This distinction between 'society' and 'company' seems simple
enough to maintain, especially to the modern reader. We are used to
'society' as a general description of the system of common life, and
indeed to the abstraction from descriptions of particular systems or
societies to a general condition of 'society' as such. But the earliest
meaning of 'society' had been 'the company of one's fellows': a
description of an immediate relationship between persons. The complexities in the development of 'society' as a word reflect general
complexities in actual social development and social philosophy;
they are by no means particular to Hume. But because of the nature
of his moral thinking, Hume was especially exposed to these complexities and their consequent confusions. For example, when he is
discussing 'social virtues'—'humanity, benevolence, lenity, generosi-
ty, gratitude, moderation, tenderness, friendship' (IX, i, 226)—he
runs together qualities which cover the whole range from directly
personal behaviour to public standards. It is not that he fails to
recognize the kind of distinction that we would now make, but that,
usually, 'society' is for him both the common system of life and the
activity of a particular class of persons—in fact a ruling class. His
beneficent man is also quite naturally master and employer; in that
limited position, social and personal virtues can be seen as often co-
incident. But this has the disadvantage that his kind of thinking
about social values tacitly excludes the experience of those who are
not a ruling class, and this is profoundly disabling in a system of
morals which depends so fundamentally on *universal* approbation.

Further, the comparisons he can make between the moral systems of different societies are not easily extended to comparisons of moral systems within a particular society: the practical point at which his assumption of a moral consensus breaks down. It is interesting that Adam Smith went on to just this question, distinguishing 'two different schemes or systems of morality current at the same time' in 'every society where the distinction of rank has once been completely established'.[8] Hume, unconsciously assimilating 'society', at many points, to a sense not far from the class-based 'company of his fellows', misses what seems to me the central difficulty in his whole argument from consensus. I have made a rough count in the *Enquiry*, and taking 'company of his fellows' as sense *A*, and 'system of common life' as sense *B*, find twenty-five uses of *A* as against 110 uses of *B*, but also, at some critical points in the argument, sixteen uses which are really *A/B*. His further uses of 'political society' (four), 'civil society' (three), 'human society' (nine), 'general society' (one), 'family society' (one), add further complications. The truth is that Hume is trying to generalize and even universalize, in the matter of virtue and society, while retaining within this crucial term not only an unconscious particularity but also, largely unanalysed, the essential complexities of the operative and connecting word.

This point affects, finally, the question of Hume's reference to 'utility' and to the utilitarian tradition. It is clear that he uses the principle of utility as a foundation of morals, and it is in fact the case, against some accounts of him, that he uses, in the *Enquiry*, such characteristic phrases as 'just calculation' and 'the greater happiness' (IX, ii). But it is also clear that his 'utility' is based, not exclusively or even primarily on the separate calculating individual, but essentially on what he took to be general and objective social experience. Further, through the complexity and confusion of 'society' that we have noted, he was able to identify this with general human experience. The 'calculation', that is to say, is made identical, or nearly so, with the actual social process; or, to put it another way, the process of living in society is the calculation, which needs no other and separate principles to determine it. I do not think it is fanciful to see this identification of society with a contained and self-

8. *The Wealth of Nations*, London 1776, vol. 2, pp. 378-9.

regulating calculation as the reflexion of a particular stage of bourgeois society in which the relation between the market (the obvious model for this process) and the society as a whole could be seen as organic. By derivation, the relationship between personal moral decision and the social process could also be seen as organic. When this identification between the market and the whole society visibly failed to hold, as in the shocks of change immediately after Hume's life, the market element, in the calculation of utility, became abstracted, and society, for the utilitarian moralist, was only the aggregate of abstract individual calculations. From that kind of utilitarianism Hume is quite distinct.

On the other hand, the emphasis on separate individual moral calculation had appeared long before Hume, and was an object of his conscious attack. There is, surely, in a thinker of Hume's quality, never only reflexion. His whole enterprise can be seen as an attempt to restore the identity of social and personal virtues, at a time when the tensions of change had forced and were forcing these apart. That he failed was inevitable; he could only succeed, in his own clear sight, by a unconscious limitation of what was relevant social experience. Yet the enterprise, like Burke's enterprise in the emphasis of community, passed into the stream of thought, beyond its local failure. The complexity, both of Hume and of his actual influence, must surely be seen in this way. As the last great voice of a mature but narrowly based culture, on the edge of transformation by profound social change, the sceptic who wished to affirm, who in his own writing learned how to affirm, succeeded in articulating modes of scepticism and modes of affirmation which could work and move even when the living basis of his own difficult resolution had passed away with his generation and his society.

The Fiction of Reform

Between the early 1770s and the late 1830s there is an apparent absence of definition in the development of the English novel. Most maps of the period show little more than the isolated peaks of Jane Austen and Walter Scott and the similarly isolated but smaller features of Fanny Burney, Maria Edgeworth and Thomas Love Peacock. This contrasts sharply with the preceding and succeeding periods, in which the outlines of what is at once a generation and a form can be quite confidently drawn. The question which then arises is whether this contrast is a matter of the terrain or of the cartography. For the literary historian the problem is often masked by the fact that the period which is so ill defined in the novel is so well defined in poetry: the two Romantic generations and their original, influential forms. For the cultural historian the problem is more difficult, not only because (as might be abstractly inferred) this is a period of major social and cultural change—indeed in the industrial revolution and in the struggle for parliamentary democracy one of the two most significant in all modern English history—but also because, in spite of the map, this is a period of remarkable expansion in the novel, notably from the 1780s: an expansion which it is too easy to dismiss as merely quantitative.

On some of the most recent maps a particular contour has in fact been influentially traced: the Gothic novel, which has experienced a significant rise in popularity. It is an authentic feature, from *The Castle of Otranto* through *The Mysteries of Udolpho* to *The Monk*. The difficulty comes when its defining elements, of the supernatural and of terror, are used to override or assimilate novels of a quite different kind, for example Mary Shelley's *Frankenstein*. This happens either when the Gothic novel is treated as simply a literary fashion, or when it is seen, as André Breton argued, as a pathological symptom of 'the social turmoils which agitated the whole of Europe towards the end of the eighteenth century'. For it is an ignorant reduction of the cultural responses of this period, and specifically of these responses in English novels, to suppose that widespread conflict and terror produced no more than their displaced symptoms, or no more than an emotional disturbance which was assuaged by exercises in sensation. On the contrary we have to recognize an at least equally significant development, in which the conflict and the terror were, in specific ways, directly confronted, and an attempt made to follow them through to their social causes. Gary Kelly's hypothesis of the *English Jacobin Novel* (1976) is an important contribution to this necessary recognition and redress.

The term 'Jacobin', as Kelly begins by recognizing, has its difficulties. Indeed they are more severe than even he allows. John Thelwall noted that the title 'Jacobin' was 'fixed upon us, as a stigma, by our enemies'; the parallel with some modern uses of 'Communist' or 'Bolshevik' or 'Marxist' is quite close. Prejudice both against the French Revolution itself, and against the years of revolutionary terror, was quite consciously invoked. Yet the English novelists in question, though all supporters of the French Revolution, were based in a native formation which, politically and philosophically, preceded 1789. The nearest things to terror which occurred in England were the 'Church and King' riot which destroyed Priestley's laboratory and manuscripts, the prosecution of *The Rights of Man*, the State Trials of 1793 and 1794, the suspension of Habeas Corpus and the 'Twin Acts' against 'treasonable practices' and 'seditious meetings' (read liberties of opinion and association). This conscious repression had direct effects on the novelists, and in the case of the most remarkable novel of the period—William Godwin's *Things As They Are*—a literary effect of the most significant and interesting kind.

Kelly's selection of novelists can be questioned. He concentrates on four: Robert Bage, Elizabeth Inchbald, Thomas Holcroft and Godwin. All four are relevant, but it is difficult to sustain a case for excluding Charlotte Smith, especially in *Desmond* (1792), Mary Hays, in *Emma Courtney* (1796), and Mary Wollstonecraft, in the unfinished and posthumously published *The Wrongs of Woman* (1798). Each of these is more overtly radical than any of the other works selected, and *Desmond*, including scenes of the revolution in France, is nearer any reasonable association with Jacobinism in its strict sense. Indeed, by selection and exclusion, Kelly weakens one element of his hypothesis, while at the same time, in a different direction, strengthening it. What is seen as common to Bage, Inchbald, Holcroft and Godwin is, if a French analogy is required, and as he himself points out, more Girondin than Jacobin, but more than either it is a specific complex within an English tradition of social dissent and humanitarian reform. This is especially evident in Bage and in the early novels of Inchbald and Holcroft. It is at its most significant in its collision and interaction with the revolutionary events in France and with the English repression which sought, arbitrarily, to prevent revolution and to destroy reform in a single blackening campaign.

The central tenets of this position are, first, that characters are formed by circumstances, education and training, and, second, that candid explanation, rational inquiry and consequent reform can overcome what are always not vices but errors. It is easy to see how this position relates to the spirit of the Enlightenment, and how it provides a confident basis for schemes of social and moral reform. What has not been so easy to see is that the position also provides a basis for a new kind of integration in the form of the novel. The most significant achievement of Kelly's book is his discussion and demonstration of this important development, which has more bearing on the subsequent development of the nineteenth century than has been at all commonly argued. At one level he makes a convincing case, and the strongest examples seem to be Bage's *Man As He Is* (1792), Inchbald's *A Simple Story* (1791) and Holcroft's *Anna St Ives* (1792). Yet, while the changes are evident, the integration provided by these versions of cause, consequence and change is still, in general, of the material of personal relationships in the tradition of Richardson.

Two problems stood in the way of the next stage of development: first, that corruption, while of course neither metaphysical nor innate, might prove, by the extension of rational inquiry, to be systematic; and, second, that if it were systematic it might resist or even overwhelm the most candid and rational attempts to reform it. The first problem bore more directly on the actual composition of novels. A typically virtuous or vicious character, with his appropriate circumstances and education, could already be written, by known means. The whole moral and secular tradition of individual characterization supported it, and to our own day has not lost its hold, being used again and again even to define what the novel can or must do. To view the matter otherwise, beginning from general circumstances—a condition of society—and seeing characters as produced and reproduced within them, is not only a break from tradition; it is an immediate break from method and poses the most serious problems of actual writing, if the general condition is to be substantially rather than summarily present and if it is to be seen as not merely circumstantial but formative. Some of these novelists—Holcroft and notably Godwin, and also, in one intense case, Mary Wollstonecraft—made serious attempts to explore this new fictional world, and the tendency indeed can be generally observed. The deliberately generalizing titles—*Man As He Is, Things as They Are, Nature and Art, The Wrongs of Woman*—confirm the tendency. Meanwhile, however, the second problem, that a systematic corruption might not only resist but overwhelm its candid and rational would-be reformers, was being directly experienced, not in the search for new fictional forms, but in mounting prosecution and repression. To write a novel with such a theme, even without direct reference (which was usually anxiously avoided) to the cleansing of corruption by the revolution in France, was indeed to risk your liberty, in the crucial years between 1791 and 1798. It is hardly surprising that the search for new forms, in itself so difficult yet already so clear as a tendency, was confused, dispersed and in effect, within that tradition, halted.

But there remains one cardinal case: the best novel and, if we can read it, the best record of that time: Godwin's *Things As They Are*, the original title which Kelly convincingly prefers to the original subtitle which is now so much better known: *The Adventures of Caleb Williams*. Indeed the change of emphasis in the title (made by Godwin in 1831) is part of the history, including Godwin's subsequent history: a change from the attempted embodiment of a systematic corruption to the individualized history of what can be seen either as a singular adventure or as a psychological case. Kelly has many useful things to say about the novel and he provides us with much valuable information. But since in general I disagree with his reading, I would like, in response to the stimulus of his work, to sketch an alternative account and to connect it with his more general themes.

Godwin's *Enquiry Concerning Political Justice*, published in 1793, is a landmark in the tradition of philosophical reform which we have seen as underlying the new novels of the 1790s. As soon as it was published, and so widely recognized and acclaimed, he turned again to fiction, being 'now unwilling to stoop to what was insignificant'. He wanted to write a novel not 'for temporary effect' but to be 'incorporated with the very fibres of the soul'. By his own later account, and most significantly in terms of the tradition and situation already discussed, he began with the powerful image of a man pursued and hunted down, and then worked back from this to devise circumstances which would provoke the pursuit.

This is, I believe, a genuine mutation in the doctrine that characters are formed by circumstances: not in the simple sense of denial, for the circumstances are studiedly reconstructed and the original doctrine is in this sense still apparent, but in the more complex sense of a sentence from his original preface: 'it is now known to philosophers that the spirit and character of the government intrudes itself into every rank of society'. What we then have is not, or not only, a world of moral conflict in which vice and benevolence, or reason and ignorance, contend. What is newly present is the sense of a system—political but then also inevitably moral—which, as 'government', *intrudes itself*. This is not only the recognition of immediate pressures, which in fact led him to suppress the preface in the first edition, because, as he put it later, 'terror was the order of the day; and it was feared that even the humble novelist might be shown to be constructively a traitor'. It is also, as I understand it, a deeper recognition, of what we might now call hegemony; or, in Godwin's terms, not merely the formation but the corruption of character by a systematic political order. And the point of this recognition, in terms of fictional method—in fact at a point of transition from the 'circumstanced character'—is, first, a version of social relations as dependence, pressure and pursuit, and second, a transcendence of moral contrast by a new process in which both hunter and hunted, persecutor and persecuted, are dynamically though of course differentially formed and impelled by a general condition which is common to both.

Thus, on an immediately preceding model, Godwin could have

made Falkland, the pursuer, vicious by upbringing and circumstance, and Caleb, the pursued, contrastingly virtuous. In fact this contrast is limited to the initial situation, in the conflict between the noble Falkland and the vicious Tyrrel. When Falkland murders Tyrrel and not only denies his crime but lets an honest man be executed for it, he moves into a connecting relationship with his secretary Caleb who by rational inquiry, which can also be called 'curiosity', discovers the crime and is then pressured, slandered and at last hunted down to prevent his disclosure of it. This is an action which has gone beyond 'circumstances'; it is at once a dynamic and a reciprocal conflict, or, as Godwin eventually saw it, a mutual corruption, within pressures which come through as terrifying just because they are so general, so 'intruding' and so pervasive.

The intuitive depth and the imaginative power which Godwin brought to this recognition have been sufficiently recognized by generations of readers. But there remain two problems in analysis. First, the novel has been reduced, often plausibly, to the different concept of 'psychological realism', which is of course fully present but which is altered if it is construed within a timeless, ungrounded 'psychology'. The novel has been interpreted, within a dominant tendency, in a range from a study of neurosis to an allegory of Godwin's neurosis. The pressures of a time and a condition, which Godwin repeatedly invokes at every level, from Tyrrel's arrogant landlordism to Captain Raymond's once virtuous outlaws, are then seen as mere projections or indeed as 'circumstances'. Within this fashion, even the radical politics of the 1790s are seen as a neurosis. But the case is important precisely because Godwin seeks to show not so much the interaction of those abstracted entities, 'the individual' and 'society', as their integration at a depth which fuses the deepest personal fears and impulses and the most pressing general forms of domination and injustice. It is in this sense that *Things As They Are* is an indispensable novel of a major English tradition: a tradition that is clearest in Hardy, whose *Tess* and *Jude* may indeed be directly compared with it.

Yet within this achievement there is a specific and significant problem: that of the novel's alternative endings. This is a case comparable in general importance, as a matter of imaginative consciousness in process, with Elizabeth Gaskell's alteration of *John Barton*, and the evidence, in Godwin's case, happens to be more direct and accessible, though still difficult to read. Godwin began the novel in February 1793. From January 1794, with the writing well advanced, Godwin began visiting Joseph Gerrald, who had been convicted of sedition. It was an intensely observed case. Coleridge wrote of Gerrald, in terms that irresistibly remind us of *Things As They Are*:

> Withering in the sickly and tainted gales of a prison, his healthful soul looks down from the citadel of his integrity on his impotent persecutors.

On 29 April 1794 Godwin took leave of Gerrald in Newgate. On the following day he finished his novel. Caleb's last attempt to establish the truth of Falkland's crime is dismissed by the magistrates; his mind breaks under the strain of this final rejection of his integrity. Then, on 4 May, Godwin wrote the conclusion again, in the form that was eventually published. Caleb accuses Falkland, while also accusing himself of a shameless pertinacity. Falkland, moved by the appeal, confesses and shortly dies. Caleb finds himself also guilty, 'in the corrupt wilderness of human society' which has poisoned them both.

It is possible to prefer one ending or the other; most readers who have known of both have preferred the second. But the real significance, it seems to me, is that both endings were written; that both, in that sense, were possible. Nor was this an abstracted process; the figure of Joseph Gerrald was obviously close at hand. What Coleridge had said of Gerrald was true, but it did not save him; he was transported and died, at thirty-three. It is then understandable to feel angry at what would be a contrived fictional ending, in which earnest moral appeal, aided by self-accusation of rashness and thoughtlessness, persuades a guilty criminal to confession and reform. Godwin's own much later reference to Gerrald, reading the published novel in prison, staying awake to finish it quickly when it had cost the author so much more time to write, but then crying, refreshed, 'Tomorrow to fresh woods and pastures new', is indeed almost incredibly insensitive and offensive. The confession of guilt in an inquiry for the truth is at least, for the date, convenient.

There is a sentence in the first ending which is imaginatively crucial. 'Alas! Alas! it too plainly appears in my history that persecution and tyranny can never die'. But then what, at this date, was the lesson of Gerrald? It is an unanswerable question: in the systematic hardness of a tyranny which denied his integrity and destroyed him; in the moral example of a courageous resister, who thus reaches beyond himself. At the time of writing the latter might seem the truer answer, but what is significant is that Godwin, after writing the first ending to agree with the first answer, did not change it to agree with the second. He changed it, accepting defeat in a more profound sense, to a bitter recognition of mutual destruction, within an over-powering general condition: persecutor and persecuted corrupted together, but with the whole truth told so that it could be fully understood.

It is a tragic if temporary, even provisional, ending to the fiction of reform.

Forms of English Fiction
in 1848

There are many reasons for remembering 1848, and among them the fact that the first bookstalls were opened on the new British railway system: one might say by a man called W. H. Smith, but in fact by a firm with a title that reminds us of one of the most famous novels published in that year—W. H. Smith *and Son*. Son, as it happened, was eventually to be defeated by, and then to defeat, in the Conservative interest, a writer called John Stuart Mill, in the constituency of Westminster. This empirical reminder of W. H. Smith—and Son—in an analysis of the world-historical year of 1848 could well seem an impertinence. Indeed it is an item of vulgar capitalist enterprise which can seem to stand between us and the more attractive uplands of high bourgeois ideology. Yet any historical analysis, when it centres on a date, has to begin by recognizing that though all dates are fixed, all time is in movement. At any particular point there are complex relations between what can be called dominant, residual, and emergent institutions and practices. Then the key to an analysis is investigation and identification of the specific places these occupy within an always dynamic field.

Thus, in terms of capitalist book–selling, Smith's bookstalls and the associated Parlour and Railway Libraries, cheap reprints of popular novels, are emergent. But in terms of emergent *production* we must look quite elsewhere. Between production and bookselling, there are those other social relations indicated by what was actually, in majority, being read, and here W.H. Smith—and Son—are again relevant, since they recorded their 'top ten' authors. An interesting list: Bulmer Lytton, Captain Marryat, G. P. R. James, James Grant, Catherine Sinclair, the Canadian Thomas Haliburton, Mrs. Frances Trollope, the Irishman Charles Lever, Mrs Elizabeth Gaskell, and

Jane Austen. I would imagine that most students and teachers of literature would be relieved when they came towards the end of the list and found people they'd been reading in the last two months. Again, if one looks at the titles, asking what they were reading in 1848, we find that at the top of the list were: *Agincourt, The Romance of War, The Last Days of Pompeii, Midshipman Easy, Tower of London, The Heiress of Bruges, Stories from Waterloo, Scalphunters, Rody the Rover, Pride and Prejudice,* and *The Little Wife*.

A theoretical problem is at once evident. In one now familiar mode we can move from the characterization of bourgeois society in that epoch to a characteristic bourgeois ideology and then its appropriate fictional form. I have indeed heard it said that 1848, that remarkable year for new major novels, is the moment of the initiation in fiction of a characteristic bourgeois realism. There are then two immediate problems: first, that what the bourgeoisie was reading was on the whole not bourgeois fiction, in any of its ordinary senses; second, that the new major novels, from *Vanity Fair* to *Dombey and Son* and from *Mary Barton* to *Wuthering Heights*, can be characterized as bourgeois realism only by an extraordinary flattening, a mutual composition which succeeds in hiding the actual and effective process, the complex formation of the real forms.

In an alternative mode of historical as distinct from epochal analysis, the problems are still there but may be more specifically negotiable. For we have to begin by recognizing the very complex interlock in politics and culture of dominant and residual forms, and the even more complex process, in relation to that interlock, of specific and still-forming modes of emergence. In fiction especially, this is clearly the true shape, the moving shape, of the year 1848. Thus, in the titles mentioned just now, and in the majority of the authors, one can identify two popular 'forms' in the loose literary-historical sense of form, as primarily determined by content but carrying its own formal consequences: the *historical romance*, which is virtually dominant, particularly when it is a historical romance associated with war; and the *consciously exotic*, itself often significantly associated with the new epoch of colonization.

The historical romances, one should observe in passing, are different from those of the period of Scott, although that is how in the text books they tend to turn up. They have much less real historical content; the distinction we make between historical and costume novels or drama is appropriate to many of them. A place, a setting of a colourful kind, is there, but the historical movement, the historical tension within the period, is subordinate to the sense of historical spectacle. The same is true of the exotic. It is not, needless to say, the story of the colonial wars: it is the adventure story extracted from that whole experience.

But these, I would argue, are in 1848 residual forms, in the sense that while they still command a majority readership among a given formed public, they are beginning to be written less.

Through the 1840s there is a distinct decline in the production of both, and the beginning of other kinds. Nevertheless, this residual element is a crucial part of that complex interlock, central to English culture in the forties, between what (in shorthand) are aristocratic and bourgeois views of life and value systems. The bourgeoisie, that is to say, is in these terms reading predominantly aristocratic fiction, with that kind of social universe assumed. And what is coming through in its own forms is at a lower level of development, in the first instance. The interlock between the residual and what in the course of the forties was becoming a dominant bourgeois culture, is negotiated not through the residual forms, but through new kinds of consciously class-directed fiction. Here we must begin to make some distinctions within the dominant.

It is fairly easy to find bourgeois fiction in the 1840s which quite directly corresponds to the explicit values and interests of the bourgeoisie—stories which are transferring their interest from birth to wealth, from inherited position to self-made position. As recently as the 1830s it had often been doubted whether the middle class were sufficiently interesting to have novels written about them—a doubt that has since occurred to others. But within the forties the aristocrat who had seemed the natural figure for romance was beginning to be affected, in a certain category of fiction, by the new bourgeois ethic of self-making and self-help. Indeed a strong emphasis on work, as distinct from play, carried with it, actually as one of the main incentives of this class of fiction, a clear diagnosis of poverty directly related to lack of personal effort or indeed to some positive vice. Thus those explicit, conscious bourgeois values which were the formal social character of the class in that period got into fiction, but not, as a matter of fact, into any very important fiction. Hence the stereotyped terms 'bourgeois fiction', 'bourgeois realism' don't work as if they were simple formulas. You can find that straight ideology in a lot of the new magazine fiction, the family-magazine serial fiction of the 1840s; you can find it in the tracts addressed to particular sectors of the working class with the aim of either religious conversion or conversion to temperance. These were put into fictional forms, stories of how people could succeed by temperance and effort, or fail by drunkenness, weakness and vice, but with a directly attached moral that you must not blame your poverty on others or expect others to relieve it; it is a matter of your own effort and your own sobriety. In the tracts and in the magazine fiction, then, you find the straight ideology; in fact in a range from those who present it in a nasty manner, to push the social problems away, through to very convinced, sympathetic people who have nevertheless made this interpretation of the poverty and suffering of their decade. But none of it builds towards a major form. At its best, I would have thought, the work of Mary Howitt is exemplary, and she is not far from Mrs Gaskell if you are simply picking up a range of social and moral attitudes. However, in the fiction it is a very long way from one to the other.

Now, alongside that dominant, specifically *bourgeois* fiction—the association of self-making ways of wealth and virtue; poverty as a moral fault; emphasis on the sanctity of marriage; manipulation of plots to punish sexual offenders quickly—you find something which is not residual, except perhaps in one area, but is equally not emergent. There is a subordinate and there is a repressed culture, and each has its appropriate fictional forms within the specific interlock. The *subordinate* culture is of course that of the working class, which, at the level of politics, at the level of social and industrial organization, was already in the first phase of its maturity as a class, but which culturally was still in very marked ways subordinate. If there are elements of emergence—the discovery of new forms in which the experience of a different class can be expressed—they are right at the edges, often significantly near to the personal voice, in autobiography, or else in certain kinds of poem. In the working-class fiction and much of the popular verse of the time, poets and novelists quite closely associated with the working-class political movement carry out an extraordinary reproduction of bourgeois forms, though sometimes with the moral turned the other way. But much more

often, in the complex interlock of the period, there is an identification of the *aristocracy* (of the landlords specifically) as the class
enemy. The developing working-class perception of the industrial
bourgeoisie as the class enemy was crucial to the politics of the
period. But within the culture—and this encouraged many quite
powerful forms—the old aristocracy, the landlords, were much more
commonly so perceived. They, at any event, are the butt of most of
the 'radical melodrama' and associated fiction. And this is after a
period in which, in the real history, the landowning classes and the
industrial bourgeoisie had begun to make their decisive social composition. Much of the working-class fiction and poetry therefore
reproduces what are in fact dominant bourgeois forms. It doesn't do
so entirely, but when it moves into anything new it often moves
towards something which overlaps with that other element I have
termed the *repressed* culture.

The repressed culture is that consequence of the bourgeois failure
to recognize even the facts of its own experience and, above all, its
sexuality. A huge trade in pornography was a classic feature of
book-selling from the late 1820s right through to the mid-Victorian
period—actually not with much newly produced pornography, but
mainly with reprints and adaptations of eighteenth-century work or
translations. That area is there, and curiously there is an area of the
subordinate fiction, very popular among working-class readers,
which is not too far from it, although not pornographic in a strict
sense. But it is scandal: scandal about the court and about the aristocracy; not about the bourgeoisie or the working class themselves. If
you look at Reynolds's *Mysteries of the Court of London*, directly
imitating a French form in Sue, or if you look at Reed's *History of a
Royal Rake*, you will find the sort of thing which had a distinct place
in the social perspective of working-class readers because it told them
that the highest people in society were, in fact, behaving scandalous-
ly. And the terms of this judgement were terms which that part of the
working class shared with the newly self-organizing and consciously
moral bourgeoisie. That Reynolds could move from speaking at a
Chartist meeting in Trafalgar Square to writing the *Mysteries of the
Court of London* shows how opposition and the experience of subordination were being expressed at different levels which do not
cohere. And, while this was so, the emergence of anything which
could be properly called a proletarian fiction is not really to be look-

ed for. You get some adaptation of residual forms: the popular series of historical novels about Wat Tyler or Jack Cade; versions of the Civil War written from the radical side, which fiction hadn't normally done; romances of the radical melodrama kind in which a poor girl is seduced and abandoned (but here again the seducer is a fairly regular social figure, aristocrat or officer, and not yet typically the manufacturer or the commercially rich man). So it is right, I think—with great respect to Samuel Bamford, to Ebenezer Elliot (who, among those popular writers of the forties, perhaps comes nearest to finding an authentic voice), to Thomas Cooper and to the many hundreds of others who tried—right to see it as a subordinate culture, though with significant links to what is actually crucial about the dominant culture in the long run, that it included a large repressed area where it could not admit what it was reading and could not admit experiences which it nevertheless craved.

I have said that it is in relation to the complex interlock of classes that you have to diagnose the problem of emergence. If you read back to what was emerging at the time, either from your own later historical oᵢ theoretical understanding of what should have been said—which is a natural temptation—or even from your calculation of the probabilities of what might have been said, you may be looking in the wrong place and you make yoke together things which were in fact emerging in significantly different ways. The changes can be better appreciated if we look at the matter in terms of the problem of form.

In formal terms seven novels written around this year—*Jane Eyre, The Tenant of Wildfell Hall, Wuthering Heights, Vanity Fair, Shirley, Mary Barton* and *Dombey and Son*—suggest a generalized diagnosis of the emergence of a conscious, incorporating bourgeois culture with its appropriate fictional form, which is realism. One can fairly easily flatten these novels into that, at too early a level, though the real question is whether or not one can eventually group them significantly. Take first the easiest thing to say about *Jane Eyre, Tenant of Wildfell Hall,* and *Wuthering Heights*: that they introduce a new stress on the imperatives of intense personal experience, or indeed, as all the introductions put it, on passion. It is not that this isn't a perfectly reasonable general description, but when you look at it in terms of form there are immediately some interesting problems.

Jane Eyre seems the simplest case because it is called an autobiography, edited, you remember, by Currer Bell—and with that characteristic distancing of the identity of the actual author in the pseudonym: 'an autobiography edited by...'. But this is at the level of the most external form of presentation, because the voice that takes over within the actual writing totally controls the narration and the observation, and it is throughout a personal voice of a kind which is differently located, within the different kinds of discourse, from conventional personal-centred fiction. The difference is most obvious in the common problem of reading Charlotte Brontë aloud. There is a radical difference when you read her aloud and when you read her silently as a private reader, which is clearly what the voice is arranged for. For there are *secrets*, to put it at its plainest, that you and Charlotte Brontë are meant to share, as if you were on your own; tones which are not so easily accessible if other people are listening. That very particular personal voice—the direct 'Reader, I married him'—is, with a necessary kind of intensity, making the direct invitation: 'Put yourself in my place, feel with *me*.'

That particular note is very distinct even from *The Tenant of Wildfell Hall*, because if you look at that in terms of form you find a *double* personal narrative. What you have is a male narrator enclosing the diary of a woman, and that diary is the means of disclosure of the misunderstanding of a relationship which has troubled the narrator in the whole of the previous period. To complicate matters still further, the narrator is writing in the form of a very long letter to a friend. Chapters I to XV comprise this letter and XVI to XXXXIV the private diary, while chapter XXXXV resumes the male narrative. Already this deliberate dispersal of points of view introduces a certain difference, a certain distinction, into what is otherwise flattened into the notion of an autobiographical subjective intensity. Indeed, it is much more significantly related to a more familiar form which is that of the misunderstood relationship—and here a word can be said on a more general problem. The most familiar fictional device within the terms of bourgeois fiction for blocked intense sexual feeling was the discovery...Well, let me put it another way. Two people who, within the terms of this culture, cannot be in love and relate, find themselves doing so. What is in the way, normally, is not just the institution of marriage, but the actual existence of sometimes the husband but usually the wife. The characteristic device which allows an escape without breaching the morality, is that the wife turns out to be insane, alcoholic or indeed deeply vicious. The tied partner displays extraordinary heroism in tending the alcoholism, the insanity or what may be, thus proving that self-sacrifice produces virtue. But there's a built-in moment at the end when, having proved your virtue, and of course waited, you find that the relation can happen. This is not just something that happened in the magazine fiction; it happens in Jane Eyre. Actually *The Tenant of Wildfell Hall* has a more interesting relation to another facet of the culture than to this fairly deliberate device for admitting relationships outside marriage without questioning marriage as such. And this is that, particularly in the tracts and in the magazine fiction, there was a negotiation of the man/woman relationship in terms of the ideality of the brother/sister relationship, sharing everything that a man and woman could properly share, or needed to share. There is no hint, at least not at a conscious level, of incest or anything of that kind. It is simply that they are good friends, they share experiences, they help each other, they support each other. Therefore the brother/sister is, in a sense, an ideal sort of relationship.

It is very interesting that what is seen as a guilty relationship (in the terms of *The Tenant of Wildfell Hall*) turns out to be a brother/sister relationship, which can therefore be properly a substitute for a marriage relationship. Again, of course, there is the prolonged test of suffering, which in fact has occurred before the time of the narration but which, within the time of the text, occurs in the middle, where the diary goes back over it. So that by the time that point is reached the long suffering has happened. What has been perceived as a guilty relationship then becomes the ideal brother/sister relationship, and they can move on from it. This would not be possible without that specific form which modifies autobiography, in allowing the two points of view on a relationship which can be misunderstood.

Or—if one can risk saying anything so brief about *Wuthering Heights*—look at the fact that again there is double narration, but significantly by persons who, both off-centre from the material of the narrative, have an attendant and in time differentiated relationship to the primary events. This has moved to a multi-centred objective viewpoint, both in time and narration, onto a series of events—themselves placed through generations—which can be *summarized* as an assertion of absolute primary intensity. One can hardly read *Wuthering Heights* at all unless one recognizes *that* as the value at its centre. But it is very consciously placed within a structure which the most careful analysis discovers to be even more complex than had been initially noticed—a structure of time, of inter-relation of modes of observation and stages of the primary relationship. If you look at the sequences through Lockwood and Nelly Dean, if you look at the constantly open relations between the modes of observation that Lockwood and Nelly Dean as narrators can command, and then the modes of experience that those they are observing are structurally involved with, directly and through the generations, you find something very much more complex in form and therefore in the whole structure of the experience than can possibly be represented by the singular expression of intense subjectivity. Indeed, we find both the subjectivity and a process of its displacement, and one must not take them, in my view, as constituting a value from either side. When Cathy has said 'If all else perished and he remained, I should still continue to be', she has made one of the classic assertions of a sense of identity and of a sense of relationship (identity in relationship), and this, I believe, is one of the most profound responses to the actual culture of the 1840s, although it is not at any overt level political or social: 'If all else perished and he remained, I should still continue to be.' And yet it is precisely in direct relationship to this that Nellie Dean can say: 'I was out of patience with her folly'. At that point, within a deliberate form, you have to consider the possibility of the truth of that observation; not that it is folly to believe it, but that it is folly to assume it, as Cathy is doing at that point in the action. She assumes that because she has a necessary relationship, it is therefore a permanent relationship. What I mean is that within a structure of this kind you are not asked, as in the ordinary account of bourgeois realistic fiction you are supposed to be asked, to identify with a single point of view on the experience. The opportunities for very complex seeing, both within a given situation and within time through a developing situation, are built into the form of the novel. And this is only taking an example within what is otherwise an easily associated trio of subjectivist novels.

If you look at *Vanity Fair*, you see at once how very distinct these emerging forms are. Powerful as it is, the novel adopts an older, much more available stance in its narration. The prefatory notice is by the manager of the performance, and in an important sense this is a placing for the reader. The narrator/manager is able directly to intervene in a variable relationship with the reader. 'As we are to see a great deal of Amelia there's no harm in saying at the outset', he remarks, at once distancing the relationship to the reader. The writing moves narrative and commentary, in and out of scene, towards that final placing of 'Come, children, let us shut up the box and the puppets, for our play is played out.' This is a conscious placing of what is actually a very remarkable social-critical perspective within the half-playful, half-managing tone of an older kind of fictional form. It interests me that the account usually given of nineteenth-century bourgeois realism is of a character who discovers at various points, in a traverse through a range of society, certain unadmitted general facts about the society. This is held to be the perspective of critical realism. The most obvious English novel corresponding to that model is *Vanity Fair*, although when you look into it, you find that it is not really interpretable in terms of that model. The delineation of Becky is not primarily of a society but of a 'character', and that is a very much older fundamental form.

I shall say just a few words about the others, because I want to move on to more general points. In *Shirley* Charlotte Brontë moves towards a more generally emergent social mode. 'If you think... that anything like a romance is preparing for you, reader, you never were more mistaken. Do you anticipate "this and this", do you expect "that and that"? Calm your expectations...something real, cool and solid lies before you.' Now, the 'something real, cool and solid'—not that *Shirley* is very cool—is much nearer the amendment that presages bourgeois realism in a strict sense. Characteristically it is back-dated. 'The story is told. I think I now see the judicious reader putting on his spectacles to look for the moral. It would be an insult to his sagacity to offer directions.' This is a particular consciousness of a relationship to the reader: that the moral is there but it's not for me, the narrator, to draw; the narrator can assume others of good sense and judgement. In this sense it is different from—earlier than—the realist novel, but it has that ambition.

It is *Mary Barton* that is usually taken as a classic example of the objective narrative which occludes the fact of narration. Obviously there are long periods in which this is so, and yet the location of the crucial stance at the beginning is more complex than that. At an important point when the narrator is describing the walk in the fields, she admits her partial knowledge of its reason; whether it is because they were on holiday or, in effect, 'I don't know whether it was some other reason'. This close but limited information is actually the crucial formal relation of the narrative. There is a deliberately close but limited access to the writing that was actually being done by the class that Mrs Gaskell was writing about, as in her close reliance on Bamford, or in the inclusion of dialect in that deliberately associating and yet outwardly explanatory way. I remember the first thing that struck me about *Mary Barton* was that as early as page two a piece of carefully reproduced dialect is footnoted and explained. It is at once, of course, the formal and the social relationship. She is determined not to misrepresent the lives, the speech of those she is writing about; she is not going to assimilate them to some other model; this is the crucial Gaskell emphasis. At the same time, in attempting this emphasis within a culture as deeply divided into classes, especially on this issue of literacy and book-learning, as that one was, she knows that the readers will be in majority of another kind. Therefore, she has to annotate the internally reproduced life. This paradox at a formal level can in turn be related to the well-known history of the transition from the initially conceived *John Barton*—an imaginative adherence—to the eventual *Mary Barton*, close but then profoundly qualified.

In *Dombey and Son* there is a general and even a commanding narrator. And yet the more I think about Dickens, the less I think that 'narrative', in the ordinary sense, is a good way of describing his mode. The word that insistently suggests itself is 'presentation'. For there is an unusual *mobility* in this narrator. He moves from place to place and from the point of view of one character to another, with much more diversity than any other novelist of his time. He moves from style to style with the same mobile assurance: that he can establish at a break a new mode. There is nothing of the uniformity of narrative of the classic realist text. And there is something else which I don't know if we have the terms for, but I would like to consider it because it introduces a crucial variable in the question of realist fiction and especially of its function in this year of 1848. One can say that much of the narrative mode of the emergent novel-form was predominantly *indicative*. It was, or offered to be, an account of what had happened and what was happening. If one takes 'indicative' as that description, then one can—the term is obviously not fully satisfactory—talk of an element of Dickens's writing which is *subjunctive*, which is clearly 'what if' or 'would that' or 'let us suppose that'. In other words, he introduces a perspective which is not socially or politically available. It is a hypothesis of a perspective, a feeling, a force, which he knows not to be in the existing balance of forces that was there to be observed. The notion of the subjunctive within the generally realist novel is one which I think could do with more thinking about. The realist perspective is commonly held to exclude the possibility of an alteration of forces. The classic complaint against naturalism is that it simply reproduces the forces which are known to be operative and leaves us with greater knowledge but no more capacity for action. The subjunctive mode within that kind of realist narrative, always difficult to extend and sustain, is often found in the ends of novels. There is a good example at the end of *Dombey*. It is present also in those characteristic interventions when Dickens invokes, beyond the terms of the realist text, the notion of a quite different but attainable perspective, in which we could see all the forces and relationships differently; in *Dombey* in the famous Chapter 47. The presence of that kind of subjunctive mode seems to me crucial; it is precisely the sense in which Dickens was connecting things that lay far ahead of him.

I have so far been taking instances at the most simple level of form as stance, or form as mode. But it is possible to enquire whether there are not, below these differences, deep forms which could be identified as deep ideological forms. I've already mentioned one in passing. It is the classic Lukacsian diagnosis of the nineteenth-century hero as the man who wishes to live a fuller life but who discovers, in experience, the limitations of his society: not only the blockage of his own fullness but a general limit which is then capable of being an alternative social perspective. He discovers, at the point where he cannot fully realize his own life, the objective social limits which prevent everyone fulfilling their own lives. But this is a model derived primarily from French and Russian fiction, which is indeed full of examples of it. I think there are not many examples in England which are properly that, and in any case the question that needs to be put to it—it's a question that bears evidently on *Jane*

Eyre, *Wuthering Heights* and, in a way, on the whole of Dickens—is that everything depends on something which that description of the deep form blurs. This is the question of value at the point of the discovery of limits. To take an example which, though just outside our period, happens to be theoretically much clearer, one might assimilate *Felix Holt* and *Jude the Obscure* to the Lukacsian formula of the discovery of objective limits, that discovery being general. But one would be very foolish to stop at that point because the culmination of *Felix Holt* is precisely the discovery of limits in a *resigned* mode, the discovery of certain 'true' limits on the human capacity to understand and to act, whereas in *Jude the Obscure* the discovery of limits—although so much more destructive that there seems absolutely nothing left—is profoundly subversive of the limiting structure which has blocked the key figure. This difference of weighting is structural. It is not simply what is said at the end. It is something which you can trace right back in the whole organization.

Now, if you think back in those terms to what can be called a subjectivist intensity, which is undoubtedly a characteristic of the new novels of 1848 in one of their groupings, you can move quite quickly to discovering what the 'limits' are. We have seen that there are structural limits in the established relationship which have to be circumvented before the intensity can be fully expressed or realized. There is also, in a sense qualifying the challenge of this new subjectivism, the possibility of subjectivism in quite another mode. The introduction by Charlotte Brontë of that mode in which it is very difficult to consider the feelings of any other character, or even the situation of any other character, except through the dominant terms of the feelings of the narrator, becomes in the end what I have called the fiction of special pleading. At a certain point subjectivism in that sense becomes a project of the elimination of other beings, except as they relate to the intensity of one's own (narrated) perceived needs. That limit often expresses itself in sentimentality and in certain kinds of evasion. One sees those limits, but they don't seem to me to be limits of the kind that Lukács and others in that Marxist tradition are talking about. For although there are undoubtedly major factors in the social structure which are barring intense experience, which are certainly barring self-images of autonomy of being and feeling, as distinct from the social role and the social function, although such barriers are easily discoverable, the level of the most authentic protest seems separable from those more local historical structures. They lie very deep within the whole cast of the civilization which is, for its own deepest reasons and often while denying that is doing so, repressing intensely realized experiences of any kind.

It is then very difficult when you are looking at these works—this is the point which comes out with the other deep form—to distinguish between what is really the pressure of ideological limits and the widening area of actual social limits. Moreover, we have to distinguish between limits of these kinds and what is really an unfinished impulse towards something which, by definition, within those structures and forms, cannot be finished, but where *the move towards expressing it* is of major value.

Let me give another example of a deep form and how it both indicates and in a sense betrays some of this fiction. It is identifiable as a new fact of the fiction of the 1840s, and very marked in 1848 itself, that it admits class relations, including class conflict, as the conscious material of fiction. In this sense it is, although not unprecedented, very new in its emphasis. It has that direct relation to a period of intense, overt class consciousness. Now, according to the deep forms that some have then perceived, the conflict is admitted precisely so that it can be reconciled or evaded. This is becoming, I think, a popular analysis, to judge from the times I've heard it. And the example everyone goes to is *North and South*, on which I would say that it is not an inaccurate diagnosis; the conflict of *North and South is* set up to be reconciled. I mean, from the beginning it is so. The reconciliation is carried out in terms of one of the deep evasions of the nature of the conflict, characteristic of much of the fiction of that time: that when humanity and the necessity of profit collide, fiction moves to the fortunate legacy. There has to be a surplus of an external kind to finance the humanity within the terms of trade. This recourse to the legacy to solve the socially and economically impossible is, of course, widespread throughout the fiction around 1848; just as recourse to the Empire as a source of fortunes or as a place to hide from the conflicts of the society is deeply characteristic. But it seems wrong to apply that back to *Mary Barton* or to Dickens, in simple ideological ways. Of course, one sees that the notion of reconciliation is there, but one then has to distinguish very sharply between the types of reconciliation envisaged. There is the type of reconciliation which Dickens so often projects, of people having changed heart and realized their relations to one another in a different spirit. Or there is the kind of reconciliation which Disraeli projected, that the people and the aristocracy can unite against the industrial bourgeoisie and thus solve the class conflict by winning it— when Sybil is not only the Chartist but the dispossessed aristocrat, and marries an aristocrat. Their common union—'Chartist marries aristocrat against the industrial bourgeoisie'—reconciles the class conflict by uniting against it and superseding it.

But then there is the type of reconciliation which, it seems to me, is deep in *Mary Barton*. This is intended to be the consequence of experiencing directly what you had only abstractly conceived: the death of a son, actual losses in the family. Certainly there is a sickliness in the Barton house, and a negotiation over the dead, as it were; but this does not seem at all to be of the same kind as the *North and South* reconciliation or the Disraeli political fantasy. In other words the suggested deep form—that the conflict is introduced because it has to be and because it can then be evaded in false reconciliation— this I think is wrong. One could argue that it is wrong by quoting Marx, but this doesn't seem particularly conclusive. He did describe a 'splendid brotherhood of fiction writers', who were Dickens, Thackeray, Charlotte Brontë, Mrs Gaskell, who issued 'more political and social truths than all the politicians, publicists and novelists put together'; in particular because they had accurately diagnosed every sector of the middle class. But this doesn't settle the matter at all, because Marx is always as likely to be 'off' as 'on' in literary terms. Yet there is a sense, which is peculiarly inaccessible to a non-historical imagination, that in failing to distinguish between the *kinds* of subjective impulse and the *kinds* of reconciliation, the shallowest conventional forms are discovered to be the deep ideological forms, while works written within a tension between conventional forms, deep forms and serious attempts to move beyond both are simply degraded and collapsed.

The theoretical issues involved in this are central to the whole problem of production and reproduction. Clearly at a certain level the emergent fiction must be sharply distinguished—which is why I started with W.H. Smith and Son—from what the middle class were mostly producing and reading: the true reproduction of conscious bourgeois positions. And distinguished not only as a higher and more sophisticated form of the same thing. This is true even when we see that it has crucial features in common with it, so that it would be wrong not to consider it in relation to that dominant form, not to consider the very large elements of simple reproduction in these new novels. But what in my view would be as wrong and much more damaging, would be to fail to recognize the significant openness of certain of the new impulses; of the inclusion of certain realities of the class situation and of class conflict; the pushing through to certain intensities however difficult they then were. For these, as new content and as new forms of the content, are genuinely emergent elements: production, significant production, attempting to lift certand at the same time, in a fully extended production, bearing the full weight of the pressures and limits, in ways which the simple forms, the simple contents, of mere ideological reproduction never achieve. Of course we now know more than these writers of 1848 about the pressures and limits—the deep and decisive social relations and conflicts—of what for us is now a period, a date. But to the extent that we know these substantially—not indifferently, not as mere 'knowing'—we have to recognize that a significant part of this understanding is that we know *them*; know what in struggle, and partially, then began to come through.

The Reader in
Hard Times

What are we to say of a powerful and persuasive novel which, in striking its 'key-note', makes a general statement which is then contradicted by its own mode of characterization and its own mode of narration? The general statement, in *Hard Times*, occurs in the memorable description of Coketown, in the chapter entitled 'The Key-Note' (I,V):

> It contained several large streets all very like one another, and many small streets still more like one another, *inhabited by people equally like one another*, who all went in and out at the same hours, with the same sound upon the same pavements, to do the same work, and to whom every day was the same as yesterday and tomorrow, *and every year the counterpart of the last and the next*.

I have emphasized the clauses that are subsequently contradicted. What is being generally described is the uniformity and monotony of the new kind of nineteenth-century industrial town and of the new kind of systematic labour process which it embodied. That delineation persists, as a major theme of the novel. But the inhabitants of Coketown, 'people equally like one another': Stephen Blackpool and the fellow workmen with whom he cannot agree about joining the union; Stephen Blackpool's drunken wife and the devoted Rachael; Louisa Gradgrind, Tom Gradgrind and Bitzer; Thomas Gradgrind and Josiah Bounderby; or the outer circles of Harthouse and Mrs Sparsit, Slackbridge, Mrs Pegler, Sissy Jupe and Mr Sleary? As almost always in Dickens's fiction, these characters are shown to be very unlike one another. The different characters of the outer circle can be said to impinge on Coketown, or to be drawn into it from other social spheres. But the characters inside the system are equally unlike one another : in terms of social class, as most broadly between Bounderby and Blackpool; but also, and very deliberately, within classes, where differences of character are shown as the origins, or the partial origins, of different personal histories and different moral responses. Indeed, this explicit differentiation is one of the main modes of the novel.

And if the uniformity indicated by the 'key-note' is contradicted by the deliberately individualizing and contrasting characterization, the monotony and repetitive continuity—'every year the counterpart of the last and the next'—is similarly and equally deliberately contradicted by the actual narrative. The novel recounts a whole series of radical changes in individual lives, and the relationships of the end are very different from those at the beginning. Dickens directs attention to one obvious source of these changes:

> Time went on in Coketown like its own machinery; so much material wrought up, so much fuel consumed, so many powers worn out, so much money made. But, less inexorable than iron, steel and brass, it brought its varying seasons even into that wilderness of smoke and brick, and made the only stand that ever *was* made against its direful uniformity.
>
> (I,XIV).

This is 'Time' as the natural turning of seasons, but it introduces another aspect of 'Time', that of human growth: 'Time...presently turned out young Thomas a foot taller'. Each is contrasted with the imposed 'Time' of Coketown: a system of regulated and measured production. But there is yet another 'Time', which is crucial to the actual narrative: time as sequence and consequence—the stages and effects of personal actions; the complex interactions, pressures and disturbances, of an active social history. The reality of time in this sense—narrated time—is decisive in the novel, and the last chapter—further sequences and consequences—is characteristically extrapolated into 'futurity'.

What then are we to say when we observe a specific and deliberate mode of characterization and a specific and deliberate mode of narrative contradicting what has been so deliberately offered as the 'key-note'? We might be tempted to turn the question round. This kind of individualizing and contrasting characterization, this kind of sequential and consequential narrative, are so normal in fiction that it might seem simpler to isolate the 'key-note' as contradictory. Is it the case, perhaps, that once launched on his spectacular presentation of Coketown—'a town of unnatural red and black like the painted face of a savage'—Dickens was drawn along, by the force of his rhetoric, to these falsely generalizing assertions about the people and the years? That might be a response within orthodox literary criticism, which might also analyse, in a similarly local way, the tensions between the imagery of 'interminable serpents of smoke', 'the head of an elephant in a state of melancholy madness', 'the painted face of a savage' and the discursive descriptions 'a triumph of fact' and 'nothing...but what was severely workful'. These are passages, within a single generalizing description, between a sustained imagery of the exotic and a sustained assertion of the exclusion of 'fancy' by 'fact'. It is indeed not easy to disentangle the assertion of a severely limited and uniform system from the presenter's responses to that system, in the exotic imagery which makes that 'rational' system seem 'savage' yet which is still part of its direct physical presentation. But literary criticism, annotating these questions, assembling their instances, evaluating their effect by some imputed criterion of 'successful writing', soon reaches its limits, and with *Hard Times* especially soon. For it becomes clear, in these questions and instances, and in the broader case of the contradiction between the 'key-note' and the general characterization and narrative, that we have to move, to find answers, to a much deeper and more formative level.

It is tempting to call this level 'ideological'. For there are indeed ideological novels, in which the fiction is more or less coherently directed by an underlying systematic view of men and the world. And there is at first no great problem in calling *Hard Times* an ideological novel. It offers a generalizing interpretation of a particular way of life, in terms of deliberately contrasted values. It privileges the voice of the narrator, to direct this interpretation, and indeed ends with specific ideological address, going deliberately beyond the text.

> Dear reader! It rests with you and me, whether, in our two fields of action, similar things shall be or not. (III, IX).

One of these 'fields of action' is clearly that of the writer, in composing this kind of text, with this kind of purpose. It would then not be a case of violating the integrity of the text with some *external* consideration.

Yet it soon becomes clear that 'ideology', in its ordinary sense—an underlying systematic view of men and the world—is an improbable way of negotiating a text in which some of the problems have defined themselves as contradictions and tensions. It is true that 'ideology', while always systematic, need not be singular. Indeed it is a feature of some ideologies that they are precisely designed to reconcile or override real and immovable tensions and contradictions. Yet, when they are so designed, they are, in their own terms at least, relatively coherent. The great interest of *Hard Times*, over and above its readily recognized and deliberately offered ideological elements, is that at its deepest level it is not coherent, and that much of its interest—its general interest, but also its specific relations with many of its readers—arises from this fact.

For at its deepest, most formative level, *Hard Times* is composed from two incompatible ideological positions, which are unevenly held both by Dickens and by many of his intended readers. Put broadly, these positions are: first, that environment influences and in some sense determines character; second, that some virtues and vices are original and both triumph over and in some cases can change any environment. In their extreme forms these positions are quite distinct. In English thought, Godwin and Owen argued the former; many Christians the latter. The intellectual problems of either position are severe, and it cannot now be a question of introducing some other position which supersedes them. For what is immediately relevant to nineteenth-century fiction is that each ideological position corresponds to powerful formative and interpretative modes. The assumption of original virtues and vices, or more generally of inherent differential moral character, is of course much older in literature; it is deeply related to several systems of religious thought. The proposition that environment can come near to determining character is more consciously modern, and as a fictional mode is perhaps not earlier in English than Godwin, Bage, Inchbald, Holcroft—the 'Jacobin' novelists of the 1790s. 'Environment', there, is still essentially defined as moral institutions and the consequent moral education. It is not yet 'environment' in the sense of the fully naturalist novel, in which a whole social, material and physical world is seen as primarily influential or determining. The fictional modes that follow from these versions of 'environment' are equally distinct. The earliest mode is the fiction of moral education: embodiments of the formation of character, good and bad, by the nature of an immediate (family and educational) environment, and of the reform or corruption of character by willed changes in this environment. The naturalist mode, by contrast, in its final development, represents a set of social, material and physical circumstances which form and deform characters in specific and indeed systematic ways. Willed changes in family and education are not excluded, but family and education are themselves seen as influenced or determined by the moral general environment, which must then, if at all, be much more generally changed. In actual fictions, either mode can be modified by elements of the quite alternative position: that though 'circumstances' may affect, even radically affect, the *history* of a character, his or her true formation lies elsewhere, and the capacity for change, whether in an individual or in the general 'circumstances', is similarly rooted in primary personal qualities, often of course related to some wider, usually religious, source. At the most explicit ideological levels, these different positions are often flatly stated as the contrast between believing that educational and social reform are necessary to produce better individuals, and believing that individuals must first change (the 'change of heart') before any other reforms are possible. In most novels, however, where the underlying positions are often not fully conscious, the positions are more modulated and more qualified, as well as more implicit, though the deep formative effect (choosing to begin, for example, from an individualized characterization, *or* from a shaping family and education, *or* from a decisive social and material situation) is usually quite evident.

What is then remarkable about *Hard Times* is that we find something more than this normal modulation or qualification of one or the other formative positions. What we actually find, simultaneously though unevenly, is the powerful presence of *each* of these positions. The Godwinian version of a shaping environment, in family and very specifically in education, is there from the beginning in the Gradgrind philosophy and M'Choakumchild's school. Another version of shaping environment, intellectually close to the naturalist position though relying on generalized presentation rather than the full naturalist mode of close working detail, is powerfully evident in the description of Coketown and its system. It is this version which allows the transition we noted, from the streets 'all very like one another' to the people 'equally like one another'. But at the same time, simple cases of the quite alternative position—primary characters not determined, in a way not even influenced, by their systematic environment, though of course suffering and enduring it—are at least equally important: most obviously, Stephen and Rachael.

What then are we to say? Can we simply say, with Stephen Blackpool, that it's 'aw a muddle'? Or can we settle for saying—it is a familiar and comforting conclusion—that this is 'life', contradictory and paradoxical 'life', which of course escapes all simplifying ideologies? Not quite, or indeed not at all. For the ideologies in question are not all, are not even primarily, those which are introduced (like Gradgrind's philosophy), satirically interpreted and shown as refuted by experience. The ideological positions that matter are those that shape the novel: the demonstrated effects of an educational environment and a social environment; the counter-movement of some original virtues and vices. Great stress is laid on both ways out of the situation: the loving way of Sissy Jupe, the way reached by Louisa and even, in part, by Gradgrind, the way in suffering of Rachael—'heart' and the 'change of heart'; but also the way of a reformed educational system, teaching 'fancy' as well as 'fact', and of a reformed economic and social system, moving beyond self-interest to mutual duty and community. This highly specific composition, holding these positions and indeed precepts in its own very particular relations, is not to be reduced to some undifferentiated concept of 'life'.

The question of 'muddle' is more taxing. There is a mode of exegetic and analytic reduction which depends on an assumption of simple and coherent structures: ideologies or forms. It is often a powerful mode, but it is most at risk when it discovers what may be either incoherence or complexity. It relies on a classicist model of whole forms and, by extension, whole ideologies. It then cannot treat those many works which are either radically disturbed by the simultaneous if uneven presence of incompatible positions and modes (there are many such cases in English nineteenth-century fiction; George Eliot is an outstanding example) or (which at once distances the cases) made radically incoherent by them. The consequent distinction between complexity and incoherence is, however, far from straightforward in particular examples. Moreover, there is some danger in any choice of 'complexity', since in its merely laudatory sense it can spirit away the difficulties.

Hard Times, as I have said, is not coherent, but equally it is not 'aw a muddle'. The resigned passivity of Blackpool's conclusion on the social system is as far as could well be from the urgent, at times breathless involvement of Dickens. But this involvement, just because it is involvement, cannot be fully described in literary-critical terms. The privileged authorial voice, directing its reader's views and responses; the deliberate plot, mingling consequence and coincidence to insist on full revelation; the broad and overt emotional tones, from scorn and mockery to pathos and reverence: all these are identifiable in the text. But it is their *composition* that (only just) controls them. In formal terms they are difficult to *compose*, to make cohere, as has often been noted of Dickens. This has led to descriptions of his writing as opportunism, using any and every mode for merely local effect, or, more favourably, as simple entertainment, unworried by deeper problems of coherence. In the latter judgment, *Hard Times* is one of the less regarded novels; it is too 'earnest' or 'diagramatic'. In the former, opportunism is a harsher version of 'muddle', and can be rejected, in terms, for the same general reason: whatever Dickens may be doing in *Hard Times* he is clearly not just looking for a series of local effects; he is looking for a general effect.

But then what general effect, given the unmistakeable contradictions and incompatibilities? This question takes us from the text beyond the text: not so much into the general social context or background, though in reading *Hard Times*, especially, much can be learned from that kind of sociological inquiry; but into the social relations of its specific composition. We can see what this means by an analogy. Dickens, as we saw, described Coketown systematically, and then described its inhabitants—'equally like one another'—in its terms. There is thus, so to say, a 'Coketowner', who is ideally present before the effective individual variations are introduced. Reflecting on this, seeing its partial but imperfect truth, may we find ourselves also reflecting on another ideal presence, equally related to a system, who has at least as much to do with the text though he is only present in address? 'Dear reader! It rests with you and me, whether, in our two fields of action, similar things shall be or not.'

'Similar things': narrated events and consequences like these. 'Our two fields of action': not our separate and variable, thus multiple, fields, but *two* fields, of which only one, the writer's, is fully defined. For it is surely not as 'reader', reader only, that such responsibility can be exercised. Or is it? This is the real question behind the ideal presence. While the second field is only that of the 'reader', a certain coherence is assured. The writer has written; the reader has only to read, for then the thing is done. But at the same time the reference is deliberately outward: not this fiction but these realities; whether similar realities 'shall be or not'. And at this point, of course, the ideal 'reader' dissolves, or is in danger of dissolving. Any actual reader, among readers contemporary with the text, might be the real-life counterpart of Stephen Blackpool or Thomas Gradgrind, Louisa or Rachael, Sissy Jupe or Mr Sleary.... But is the list quite endless? In the abstract possibilities of readership, evidently so. The novel might be read by a capitalist manufacturer, a member of parliament, a working man or woman, a wife, a trade unionist, a conservative, a radical... That list is both endless and unpredictable, and it is at once evident that the will and capacity, to say nothing of the means and resources, of these highly varied individuals to decide whether 'similar things shall be or not' are highly differential. But then these inevitable differentials, of human desire and social intention, quite as much as of capacity, are *textually* overridden and composed. A necessary 'dear reader', composed in specific ways, is implicit in and completes the text; is indeed, by a whole strategy of composition, *produced by*, intended to be produced by, the text.

This may then be the key to the contradictions and incompatibilities: the production of a general reader who is also a generalized response. Not *any* general reader. Sympathy, indignation, concern: all these are written into this reader's characterization. Socially he must be diverse, though not universal; organized institutions—parliament, trade unions, even chapels and schools, are mocked or distanced, for this reader is, above all, an individual. All the fundamental economic and political conflicts are then mediated in a specific mode. Capitalist employer confronts worker, but as a particularized Bounderby (from whom many employers could distance themselves) against the humble Blackpool, himself distanced from the anonymous workers led (misled) by Slackbridge. Capitalist economics is attacked, but in so close an association with philosophical radicalism that what is left to oppose it (given the other general exclusions) is not easily generally identified, in ways that might divide the composed ideal reader. Its most positive statements are linguistically qualified, by the awkwardness of dialect orthography (Blackpool in II, V) or by a lisp (Sleary in III, VIII). Thus the reader can move, at many critical points, *within* the composed general response of indignation and sympathy. What he should do, to decide whether 'similar things shall be or not', is left undefined, within the composed response, since specifications would fracture his ideal composition.

Hard Times is then a moment, an ideal moment, of a generalized unease. By its specific mode, it catches up wide and diverse feelings of shock and concern, in a particular and complex historical situation. It energizes attention to them, enforces recognition, touches hope and despair. It is an unusually precise expression, not of an ideology, but of a structure of feeling: the most generous, the most indignant, but because of these very qualities the most anxious, the most uncertain, of its divided time.

Cambridge English,
Past and Present

Was there ever in fact a 'Cambridge English'? Not as in 'Oxford English', which in its most general use is a manner of speaking, but in the received sense of a distinctive and coherent course and method of study. There has been an English Tripos in Cambridge since 1917, and an independent Tripos and Faculty since 1926 ('Tripos' is the Cambridge term for an honours degree course). I realized recently, looking at these dates, that I had been in contact with English at Cambridge for two thirds of this history, since I came as an undergraduate in 1939. Moreover for the last twenty years or so I have, in some problematic ways, been near the centre of its affairs. It is then at first sight curious that I still look at what is called 'Cambridge English' as a historical phenomenon: as something happening, throughout, at a certain distance. One reason is easy to find. Through some accident of time or temperament I always arrive rather late for Golden Ages. One of the first things I was told in Cambridge, having grown up in what seemed to me a significant rural culture, was that significant rural culture had disappeared a few years before I was born. Again the heroic or infamous period of Cambridge Communism, in the 1930s, was when I arrived just disappearing into the altered circumstances of the war. Similarly with Cambridge English. What Basil Willey, supported by Muriel Bradbrook and others, has called its Heroic or Golden Age ran from 1928 to somewhere in the 30s. Tillyard saw narrowing and decline from about 1930. F.R. Leavis, in 1943, offered a sketch for an English School, to realize the essential values of the Cambridge English initiative, by way of explicit contrast with most of what was actually happening. From these authorities, who knew in direct ways the first third of the history, it is easy to get a sense that Cambridge English is a matter either of the past or of the future: in any case not something you can walk round a windy corner and actually find.

At the beginning this did not worry me. Indeed I was largely unaware, between 1939 and 1941 when I left for the army, that I was following, or might rather earlier have been following, or with some necessary redirection might still follow a distinctive and innovating course. Part One of the Tripos was a broadly unsurprising extension and consolidation of the work already done in a small rural Welsh grammar school. It was only when I came back, in 1945, not only to read Part Two but also to hear all around me the controversies about Leavis and the conflicting accounts of that tangled earlier history, that I became conscious of the disputed idea of 'Cambridge English' and at the same time aware of new kinds of work and challenge in what had seemed, at a respectful distance, a relatively straightforward academic course, which occupied only a limited part of one's life and interests. When I returned in 1961, as a Lecturer, the general situation was remarkably similar: as disputed, as tangled, as problematic and as unresolved.

In fact, since 1946, at a good distance from Cambridge, I had been trying to find my own way through the questions defined by that post-war experience. The specific outcome was *Culture and Society*, which was also, I suppose, the occasion for my return. But I don't now want to follow that line; it has been closely discussed elsewhere. I want rather, from both a later and an earlier position, to look again at the general idea of 'Cambridge English': at what it actually was and was not, at what forces shaped and moved through it, at what happened in different phases and is still happening. It is then a sign of a certain dislocation—a differently experienced dislocation—that I begin with the unfamiliar and distanced question: was there ever, in fact, a Cambridge English?

One of the few certainties is that it was late. Cambridge was one of the last British universities to make any proper provision for English studies. That should not surprise us. Like Oxford but in this even more rigidly, it had steadily resisted the introduction of virtually everything beyond the received Classics and Mathematics. In the late nineteenth century, among the eventual newer Triposes, Natural Science and History were among the least esteemed. A conventional majority could usually be mobilized for the status quo by one after another established and prejudiced authority. The first limited introduction of English was, ironically, by way of Old English, and later of philology. Yet, out of business, so to say, and then as a part of the new Modern and Medieval Languages Tripos, actual work began to build up. In this relatively unprovided period there was the *Cambridge History of English Literature* and there were college lectures on writers by a range of men with other formal commitments. The small course, however, even after various amendments, tied the study of some English literature to a main body of work in language and philology.

The principal innovation of the phase from 1917 can then be as well negatively as positively stated. Through a series of changes it became the first course to allow a practical separation between literary and linguistic studies. This has been described so often as a liberation, an emancipation, an unchaining, that it will seem lacking in piety to pause and inspect it. Certainly the available accounts of the linguistic work being done, in comparative philology and morphology, indicate good reasons for impatience. Yet looking back at the break from the present situation, in which the distance of literary from linguistic studies is a central problem—and in which, incidentally, modern linguistics has been given only a marginal position in Cambridge—there are serious questions to ask.

Of course it was absurd that there should be no organized study of English writing in its most general respects. The drive towards English studies, though always flanked by philology and by some nineteenth-century Anglo-Saxonism of a nationalist kind, had been in general broad and humane. The interests that came to be defined as aesthetic and cultural, or earlier as spiritual and historical, turned readily to so much available and valuable work. It was indeed these interests which produced the new nineteenth-century sense of Literature, as a body of imaginative writing which represented these most general human qualities. Behind that again was the late eighteenth-century sense of *English* Literature, a *national* literature, as distinct from the earlier classical and European emphases. English studies in the schools, in the nineteenth century, included the history and geography as well as the literature and the language of this self-conscious and consciously taught *nation*.

In the universities the major humane interests were still offered to be satisfied in Classics, which had also its own strict linguistic disciplines running through from the private schools. English, in that university context, could at first be most easily acknowledged by a linguistic discipline of the same kind, in Old English and its relations. But the emphasis on Literature, and the demand for it, were building up in other parts of the society. Newer universities were tentatively admitting it, but there were also two now often disregarded social forces: in the new adult education movement, and among women. English Literature was asked for everywhere in the new university extension classes, and people with a different kind of education—as Churton Collins argued at Oxford: Collins whose *Study of English Literature* was described by Tillyard[1] as a text for the principles on which the Cambridge English Tripos was founded in 1917—were needed to teach them. There was also a major interest in this kind of literary study by women: a direct interest; a special interest, among teachers of English studies in the schools; but also an interest defined from the excluded position of women in that phase of the culture, an exclusion most frequently overcome precisely in the making and reading of literature. Thus when we read of the insufficient 'rigour' of English studies—as one among many masculine terms—or of English as 'the women's subject' we should at last call this bluff. It was in areas of active and frustrated intelligence, outside the narrow class-based and sex-discriminatory culture of the nineteenth-century university, that these new forms of learning were first sought and found. It may be significant that it was only after the war that young men, back from the trenches, could fight an enclosed pedantry with a full heart and vigour. They could even, like Tillyard, in the significant and contradictory language of the exclusion, talk of 'the right to sport in every glade and green pasture': at once the new assertion of *rights* and a context of loose Edwardian pastoralism.

It was in this spirit that what has been called 'Cambridge English' arrived. Yet it then almost inevitably bore the marks of the experience of exclusion. It was in effect accidental that it was so quickly separated from language studies. The Professor of Anglo-Saxon, who had begun as a Classic, thought modern English would and even should become the new centre of humane education, and so did not oppose the ending of compulsory Old English. The six philologists, meanwhile, included two Germans and three women: an improbable

---

1. E.M.W. Tillyard, *The Muse Unchained*, Cambridge 1958, p. 32.

phalanx, at that date, against the new campaign. Indeed the prejudice with which Tillyard writes of the Germans and the women is even now astonishing. But what was coming in carried its own cultural freight, in the difficult concepts of Literature and of Englishness. There had been an Anglo-Saxonist nationalism, and one man had significantly described it as 'reversing the Renaissance'. What now happened, in very complex ways, was a redefinition of 'true English', partly behind the cover of the separation from philology. The English ruling class had long traced its real ancestry to the classical world and especially to Rome, as distinct from its actual physical ancestors. Culturally—and with many evident reasons—a comparable real ancestry was now defined. It was made easier by the fact that between 1917 and 1926 English was mainly intended as a Part Two, usually after a Classics Part One. But there were secular as well as conjunctural reasons. Tragedy—which, incidentally, had been taught, from Aeschylus to Ibsen, as a university course in Leeds in 1907—made sense as a subject in Cambridge because it could move from Greek and Roman drama to Shakespeare. The eventual English moralists were headed by Plato, Aristotle, Paul and Augustine.

What was being traced, of course, was a genuine ancestry of thought and form, with the linguistic connections assumed from the habits of the private schools. It is not so much this cultural *connection* that counts; it is the long gap, in the culture, history and languages of these islands, across which this persuasive formulation simply jumped. 'We should know the poets of our own land', but then not Taliesin or Dafydd ap Gwilym. 'Of our own people', but then not the author of *Beowulf*. It is a complex matter just because, in restoring classical and European emphases, as in its vigorous inclusion of comparative literature and especially French and Italian, the Cambridge course was indeed avoiding what by this time was being called a 'provincial' limitation. Yet its own province, rich as it was in resources, was defined in ways that were bound to prejudice the culture and history of its own land and peoples. The carriers of a literate tradition, now fully acknowledged as autonomous in modern English, were in this very function at a deliberate distance from their whole actual and differentially literate culture. If all that was being excluded was a narrow morphology, the case would be different, but in the eventual definition of Cambridge English as the carrier of a

consciously minority culture there is something much more important than Beowulf's revenge; there is the seed, within the liberation,
of most of the subsequent and now notorious conflicts.

We often fail to see this, in its connection with the subsequent
distance from full linguistic and cultural studies, because in the experimental and innovative twenties two significant initiatives were
made and were very widely influential. These are, first, what
amounted to a redefinition of criticism, and, second, a new and
vigorous emphasis on what, within the new autonomous province,
was defined as 'life and thought'. That formulation, incidentally,
derives from the Modern Language papers, though there were variations, as in 1917: 'Literature, Life and Thought' for the Renaissance:
'Life, Literature and Thought' for the Middle Ages. Each tendency
was so strong, and produced such notable work, that it seems easy to
give a positive definition of Cambridge English from them. Yet eventually what was to matter was the relations between these two
tendencies: a history of hoped-for unification and actual and at times
bitter conflict.

It is ironic that the redefinition of criticism happened mainly
because of the intervention—again, in local terms, almost accidental—of a quite different kind of thinking, drawn from philosophy,
psychology and physiology. Without Richards, and with the quite
different exception of Leavis, there is little evidence to suppose that
the new school would have been more than an extension of the
humane and scholarly appreciation which was already growing in
English studies everywhere. There would have been the usual
changes of interest and tone and vocabulary that occur between
generations, but even after Richards and Leavis—and it usually
seems a very long way after them—it is not clear that the majority
work of the Cambridge English School, in its virtues as much in anything else, is radically discontinuous with the humane scholars and
critics who worked elsewhere and before 1917. Yet, for a while
decisively, Richards was there. His central achievement, I still
believe, was to see the element of collusion in just this tradition of
appreciation: the informed, assured and familiarized discourse of
people talking among themselves about works which from a shared
social position they had been privileged to know. There is an element
of brutality in Richards's famous protocols, in which an assured
taste and competence were challenged by the absence of the inform-

ing signs and tips. And it does say a lot for that generation who shared the experiments with him that the devastating actual results were accepted, learned from and drawn on to stimulate a new emphasis on close and precise and specifically challengeable reading. That remarkable emphasis is by any standards a major educational contribution.

Yet it was called Practical Criticism, and there are then two problems. Practical, to begin with, because there was also Theory: the two, in Richards's work, not only connected but inseparable. As it happens there are good reasons for rejecting Richards's actual theories, but then theoretically, rather than in a slide away to 'practical' as not only self-sufficient but educationally and even morally superior. Over the years this slide has happened, and this, even more than the fact that some of the work was reduced to school routines, explains the dissatisfaction since the sixties with what is still, in its best terms, the most important element of the Cambridge English course. The consequent resumption of theory, on Richards's scale—that is to say, not only theory of literature or of criticism but of fundamental processes of language, meaning, composition and communication—was greeted in its own backyard with cries of 'alien', 'extra-literary, 'metacritical', 'sociological', 'Marxist', 'structuralist' and God knows what. These were the sort of shouts that Cambridge English, in the twenties, heard from elsewhere and for a time rejected. The theory and the practice, working together, were providing powerful examples of the reading that was necessary if Literature—the assumed common point of reference—was to come through at last as itself.

But it was that innocent formulation—'coming through as itself'—which concealed more fundamental problems and tendencies. The description 'practical criticism' concealed—and continues to conceal—two very different methods and intentions. These were, as Richards formally recognized, first the analysis of a work to discover its actual verbal organization—a process of reading—and second what was called the 'evaluation' of a work—a discovery of what was usually called its 'merit'. It is now clear that Richards's real contribution was in the first of these—analysis—and that it is in this sense that he connects with later work of a different kind in linguistics and in communication theory. Indeed, this was his own real trajectory, for what he founded in Cambridge he also decided to leave: 'decided', as he put it, 'to back out of literature, as a subject, completely'.[2] But meanwhile, invoking the methods of analysis but linking them with its own version of evaluation, there was the confusion of 'criticism'.

It is easy to see how the two were originally thought to cohere. Richards's theory of language and of reading was based on a notion of trainable individual competence which had the desirable effect of ordering and harmonizing mental impulses. Meanwhile, the version of Literature which he shared with others was in terms not only of a 'storehouse of recorded values' but of these as especially indicating 'when habitual narrowness of interests or confused bewilderment are replaced by an intricately wrought composure'. It could then be believed that analysis of the 'intricately wrought' was necessarily integrated with that clarification of response which was 'composure', which in turn was at the centre of a theory of value.

This is a plausible kind of liberal rationalism, deployed specifically in an acknowledged crisis of culture and belief and offering 'the values of Literature' as, literally, the way to save us. Ironically, however, what then came through was not, except intermittently and selectively, Literature, but Criticism. For to read actual works of literature is to find many things other than 'intricately wrought composure'; indeed to find, in terms of either inherent or of transferable values, in effect every kind of position and valuation, of belief and disbelief, of resolution and disturbance and settlement and conflict and disorder. As 'itself', that is, but of course that was what the singular formulation was for: to disguise the real diversity in the interest of a new secular absolute. There was more possibility of a single position in criticism, but only if the corresponding abstraction of the 'trained and discriminating reader' was moved and taught into place: the developed individual who had moved beyond all other conditions and experiences to this achieved and saving clarity and composure.

Obviously this could not last, though the pretension lasted. The virtues of a genuinely enlightening kind of analysis were confused and often overborne by a new stance in which literary criticism was offered as—and very locally believed to be—the central activity in all

2. *I.A. Richards, Essays in His Honour*, New York 1973, p. 29.

human judgment. That is why there was so much resistance, later, to work which was showing the diversity and conflicts of the social conditions of both writing and reading, and to work which was questioning, from linguistics, the simple autonomy of the text and, from psychology, the settled subjectivity of the individual reader. On the other hand, with this clear role defined by the supposed unity of analysis and evaluation—now not only literary but the most general kind of discovery of values—it is not surprising that one man of great capacity and conviction assumed it, though in doing so he precipitated the long overt crisis of Cambridge English. Leavis really believed, in ways that made him break with Richards at just this crucial point, that close reading and analysis of literature was the discovery and animation of the most central human values, and from that position he developed not an 'intricately wrought composure' but at once a drastic discrimination and a militant assault in the whole field of culture and society. That he could do this only by converting the 'storehouse of values' to a highly selective 'great tradition', with Literature thus further specialized, adamantly refusing literary works which did not serve these purposes, is clear. But what was so bad about the Cambridge opposition to him was that, if still in his own very specific ways, he was taking the original proposition with a seriousness and commitment which had always been formally claimed, but which when it was seen in action—when it was clearly and fully spelled out—was evidently disruptive of the milder habits of quietly precise reading and solitary or intimately shared composure which were always the more likely academic outcome.

Could it really amount to that: that to learn to read literary works by close analysis involved you in an assault on a whole system of social and cultural and academic values? Of course not, most of Cambridge concluded, and indirectly they were right. But with the supposed unity of analysis and evaluation under the title of Practical Criticism now so roughly demonstrated by an obviously otherwise conditioned and powerful critic, they could, for intellectual adequacy, only either go on to some new position or go back and disentangle the knot so strongly tied in the twenties. Some attempts were made, but the Golden Age—the age of that illusory identity—had in any case gone, and what succeeded it, in majority, was at once more consolidated and more modest: the filling out of a relatively orthodox course in the history and criticism of English literature, supported by a new professionalism of critical commentary and scholarship. On these reduced terms it was agreed to produce sound and reputable and respectable work. It continued to attract and to educate large numbers of able students. Indeed its preoccupying problem, from the thirties to the seventies, was the coexistence of this steady and reasonable success with the severe internal dissensions and the continuing public rows which were residual from the unresolved problems and challenging initiatives of its experimental period, and which were quite enough, when added to old suspicions of the subject, to allow the university to limit its teaching resources for the large actual body of work it was doing. It is then no surprise to find a locally justifiable preoccupation with problems of administration and resources dominating the period in which, at a deeper level, it was fundamental intellectual problems which really needed attention.

In fact what first attracted the next stage of controversy was not a matter of the initiative in analysis and criticism, but of the equally early initiative in what was called 'life and thought'. It can be seen that in the twenties, in the supposedly straightforward transition from competent analysis to clear minds and humane values, this raised few contemporary problems. Richards, though he chose his examples from a wide historical range, was always essentially synchronic in his methods: clear reading and clear writing were absolute supra-historical values, as in his eventual version of Platonism. At the same time, since there had been no source of professional English lecturers, historians as well as classics were teaching the subject and with their colleagues were putting the history alongside the literature in straightforward empirical ways. There was a notable development of intellectual history, by Willey, in work which retains its full value but which needs two things saying about it. First, that it stabilized, in its very titles, a weak version of the complex and dynamic relations actually involved in any full commitment to 'literature, life and thought'. What was now increasingly called 'Background' sat unproblematically, and with its own kinds of enlightenment, with what 'Literature' was practically taken to mean: the 'storehouse of values', and now the philosophical alongside the literary: modestly alongside, indeed backgrounded whenever, in the emphases of the School, 'literature as such' was foregrounded. Then second, that it very significantly halted, in those terms, at the nineteenth century: at the period which quite openly connected with the social and cultural and intellectual formations which were active and contentious in a contemporary urban, industrial and in some ways democratic society. Willey took his own deep religious and related interests into the nineteenth century, in a continuation of the kind of attention he had given to the earlier periods. But the full evident life and thought of the period after the Industrial Revolution was in a different dimension, and it was here that the crisis of the formulation began.

In the twenties there had been another apparently simple version of the formulation. Much of the critical work was in close relation to a new modernism in contemporary writing and especially to a cultural and pseudo-historical version of this in Eliot: the 'dissociation of sensibility' and the consequent fall from the seventeenth century. In the dominant critical practice a new literary history, from the metaphysicals to the modernists, was powerfully argued, the more so because the selection answered so well to the more teasing kinds of reading and analysis. A cultural history followed, which in either its weak general versions or its strong particular version in Leavis ratified the position of the school: the best literature of the past *against* a disordered and destructive present; thus a literary-critical school assuming a necessary minority status but carrying the values of the past and of a possibly emergent present in its role as guardians and witnesses of the significant literature. In its weak version this has gone on, intellectually untroubled because in any case, until very recent times, this specific role fitted so well into the idea of a necessary and privileged humane university: an idea which, seeing dangers only from radicals and levellers, was eventually to find its assumption of privilege within a traditional social order undercut by the real social order that had come through not so much from the seventeenth as from the nineteenth century: a world of the open struggle of classes, including in education, and of the fierce priorities of industrial capitalism, with its very different ideas of what universities are for.

Thus the 'life and thought' formulation came in practice to depend on very simple and transient positions: the stabilities implied in the idea of 'background', with ideas and for that matter social orders fairly placidly succeeding each other and writers doing the really important work, making literature from them; and the conviction of being a virtuous minority, against commercialism—the preferred word for capitalism—but also against 'popular taste' and what Richards, in those early days, called 'the more sinister potentialities of the cinema and the loud-speaker'.[3] Actual history impinged less and less. The most identifiable Cambridge positions became, as in both F.R. and Q.D. Leavis, a kind of cultural history which traced the long fall and ratified the new minority—a persuasive and eventually popular doctrine, but also one which initiated kinds of analysis of contemporary culture which were eventually to be developed in quite different directions. Increasingly however, as an active position, it came to seem to the majority to have little to do with the actual study of literature. The general position could be assumed, but the real work was to get on with the directly literary studies.

Except that there, still, in those received regulations, was the direction to 'life and thought'. How could you do it, students and others asked, when you already had more than enough authors to work on, whether or not at one a week. It was all so vague anyway. Thought, perhaps—that would be in texts: but Life?

There was indeed no way through these questions from the position which Literature, in its now specialized sense, had been assigned. For this was where the long separation from language studies had its most serious effects. Theoretically and practically it is clear that it is in language that the decisive practices and relations which are projected as 'literature', 'life' and 'thought' are real and discoverable. On the other hand, if you start from the projections, you get either the artificial concept of 'literary language', or simply the forms of thinking about 'life and thought' or about 'society', which develop when the full practice of language and its active composition have been reduced to a representational or a marginal aesthetic status.

There had been work in Cambridge which pointed in more active directions. Leavis, by contrast with Richards, had extended—to be sure in his own way—the analysis of examples of writing to a historical dimension: the practice that became known as 'dating', when it was set as an exercise, but that was described by one very senior member as a parlour game and, significantly, was eventually generally dropped from practical criticism. It is not the only way, but

3. *Principles of Literary Criticism* (1926), p. 36.

its emphasis was entirely right. Again, Muriel Bradbrook's work on the conventions and institutions of English Renaissance drama provided a base for a genuinely historical and linguistic analysis of the deep composition of the plays: a different kind of reading of these oral and multivocal forms, of their linguistic diversity and yet their shaping and changing rules, which is now again being developed. From either of these initiatives there were ways through to the full and informed inquiry which the 'literature, life and thought' formulation required and challenged. But both the distance from modern linguistic studies, which were beginning to offer some more precise and varied forms of analysis, and the theoretical block represented by a conception of literature as a series of authors to whom there must, *must*, be 'personal evaluative response' or its available facsimile, shut off or at best postponed bodies of knowledge and ways of seeing and thinking which could at last fully substantiate *English* studies, in a reach much wider and deeper—at once better informed and closer to more real interests—than the now largely reproductive professional routines of an old literary criticism and literary history.

Language in history: that full field. But even within a more specialized emphasis, language produced in works through conventions and institutions which, properly examined, are the really active society. Not a background to be produced for annotation where on a private reading—naked reader before naked text—it appears to be relevant and required. Instead the kind of reading in which the conditions of production, in the fullest sense, can be understood in relation to both writer and reader, actual writing and actual reading. A newly active social sense of writing and reading, through the social and material historical realities of language, in a world in which it is closely and precisely known, in every act of writing and reading, that these practices connect with, are inseparable from, the whole set of social practices and relationships which define writers and readers as active human beings, as distinct from the idealized and projected 'authors' and 'trained readers' who are assumed to float, on a guarded privilege, above the rough, divisive and diverse world of which yet, by some alchemy, they possess the essential secret.

I can see, looking back, that challenging that notion of the essential secret, insisting that even the best orthodox professional routines were reducing or obscuring the many significances of this active

language which was always so much more than a specialized
Literature, was at best likely to be misunderstood, marked for early
export to Sociology or History or even hotter regions; at worst seen
as a threat, a barbarism—and indeed it was another language that
was being spoken. What now most encourages me is that in spite of
the comminations, so much of this different kind of work began to
get done, much of it in fact in Cambridge and in people moving out
from Cambridge, and moreover done in interestingly varied and
contending ways. Rejecting, as it did, many of the particular positions of Cambridge English of the twenties—and understandably, in
turn, rejected by them—it was nevertheless, I continue to believe, a
response in its spirit and in its large experimental intentions. The real
problem is not there but in the fact that the two most important
original initiatives—close analysis and 'life and thought'—not only
reached blocks on their own further development but could not, for
this and other reasons, be brought into coherent relation with each
other, which indeed would mean changing and strengthening both.
Thus there could be many initiatives of valuable particular work, and
even within the precarious compromises—so repeatedly breaking
down and being fought out yet again—there was some real openness
and diversity, as the hard-fought-for student dissertations eventually
demonstrated in the most practical way. Even at graduate level, until
quite recently, this was so, though the whole rule-bound and
isolating research system was always more likely to limit it.

What there was not, however, because in any fully worked-out
sense there never had been, was a 'Cambridge English': a distinctive
and coherent course and method of study. The Golden Age was
golden only in its beginnings, its searchings, its open and freespeak-
ing and for some years tolerant experimentation and inquiry. My
own social and intellectual distance from it should not need emphasis. Indeed many friends have told me that I have never distanced
myself enough, but they are wrong. The distance is entire, the intellectual conflicts absolute. My only community and inheritance in
Cambridge is with some of the questions then posed and with the
campaigning energy and seriousness that were brought to them. As
these are now pushed away, disregarded even where they are
nominally honoured, their largeness of spirit is indeed worth recalling. And I recall alongside this the eminent interventions, from the
English Association, from Oxford, to try to stop the brawling infant

in its tracks. It would be doing no honour to those who attempted a serious 'Cambridge English' to have to settle to saying that these authorities need not have worried; that the infant would, after all, grow up to be remarkably like them. But then this, properly taken, is not the last word.

Crisis in English Studies

Recent events in Cambridge, of which some of you may have heard, have persuaded me to bring forward some material which I was preparing for a course of lectures in the autumn. Because the material was originally conceived on that scale, the prospect for this crowded hour can be considered daunting. But it seems important to try to set out a general position now, rather than leave so many of these issues in the air until they can be more fully examined. My main purpose is one of identifying and briefly explaining some currently controversial positions beyond the labels which are being so loosely attached, but I have a quite different argument to put in front of that, which seems to me to go to the centre of the controversy. Within both Marxism and structuralism there are diverse tendencies, and there is further diversity in other tendencies in part influenced by them. Several of these tendencies are in sharp opposition to each other. This has to be emphasized not only to prevent reductive labelling but for a more positive reason, that some of these tendencies are compatible with the existing dominant paradigm of literary studies while others are incompatible and have for some years been challenging the dominant paradigm—and thus its profession. I am using 'paradigm' broadly in Kuhn's sense of a working definition of a perceived field of knowledge, indeed of an *object of knowledge*, based on certain fundamental hypotheses, which carries with it definitions of appropriate methods of discovering and establishing such knowledge. Now the case of Literature seems to me exactly such a paradigm. Moreover, as Kuhn argued, such paradigms are never simply abandoned. Rather they accumulate anomalies until there is eventually a breaking point, and attempts are made to shift and replace the fundamental hypothesis, its definitions and what are by this stage the established professional standards and methods of enquiry. That evidently is a moment of crisis. I think it is where we now are, although at a relatively very early stage, in literary studies in Cambridge.

Of course the definition of an object of knowledge that is perceived in certain ways becomes hopelessly confused within any dominant paradigm with the object about which the knowledge is to be gained. This is clear now in some uses of the term 'Literature', which is, after all, in its most common general sense, not often *produced* by literary departments but is still held in some way to be possessed and defended by them. This takes variable forms. Thus it is said that it is our business to teach 'the canon of English literature'. This use of 'canon', borrowed from Biblical studies, where it meant a list of sacred writings accepted as authentic, is significant. For of course the 'canon of English Literature' is not given; it is produced. It is highly selected and in practice reselected. In its simplest version it was decisively challenged by Richards in his experiments in practical criticism. He showed that even highly trained students could be taught the canon but could not in majority produce for themselves its implicit valuations. Indeed, they often preferred writing which was well outside the canon. These findings forced the most effective modern redefinition of the paradigm, though it did not replace it. In this redefinition, Literature came to be paired with Criticism. For since, by contrast with Biblical studies, scholarship could not itself *establish* the literary canon (though it could do local verification inside it), a new process—critical judgement—had to be taught as the condition of retaining the defining idea of Literature.

Literature had once meant, at least until the early nineteenth century, a body of printed writings; indeed that neutral sense survives in such contexts as 'literary supplement' or 'literature stall'. This use, obviously, had the effect of a specialization to print, and this was quite generally appropriate to the period between the seventeenth and the early twentieth centuries, but then with certain anomalies. There was drama, which was writing not to be read but to be performed. There was what was called, from earlier periods, 'oral literature'—a strange and often misleading classification. There was eventually the problematic status of writing in modern forms such as broadcasting, film and revived oral production. But then increasingly through the nineteenth century there was further specialization of the term, based on what are now evidently anomalous categories. Literature came predominantly to mean 'imaginative writing' of novels and poems, in a difficult distinction from 'factual' or 'discursive' writing. It was not only that this tended to conceal the element of *writing*, the linguistic composition of facts and arguments, in the excluded ('discursive' or 'factual') areas; it was also that the relations assumed between 'imagination' and 'facts' for the other 'literary' cases were, while at times obvious, in many cases the very problem that had to be construed. That would have been difficult enough. But there was then a further specialization in which, so to speak, the category of 'Literature' censored itself. Not all literature—novels, poems, and plays—was Literature in that capital-letter category. An actual majority of novels, poems and plays were seen as not belonging to Literature, which was now in practice the selective category, and thus the received 'canon' established by criticism.

So, if someone now says: 'Literature is more important than all the isms', it can seem a persuasive idea when the *isms* are, for example, those strangers: Marxism and structuralism. But one *ism* does not so often get mentioned: *criticism*, which is now, by this redefinition of the paradigm, actually incorporated in 'Literature' itself (is indeed what defines it and can even come to dominate it). There is often then the paradox that what most people are actually doing in literary departments is criticism or critical scholarship, and that this is seen as a proper literary activity, though it is so unlike what others—writers of novels, poems, plays—are doing, always elsewhere.

So you have in sequence, first, a restriction to printed texts, then a narrowing to what are called 'imaginative' works, and then finally a circumscription to a critically established minority of 'canonical' texts. But also growing alongside this there is another and often more potent specialization: not just Literature, but English Literature. This is itself historically a late construction, since for medieval writing, at least to the seventeeth century, it is obviously uncertain. Is 'English' then the language or the country? If it is the language, there are also fifteen centuries of native writing in other languages: Latin, Welsh, Irish, Old English, Norman French. If it is not the language but the country, is that only 'England' or is it now also Ireland, Wales, Scotland, North America, Old and New 'Commonwealths'?

The idea of a 'national literature' is a historical production of great importance for a certain period. The term *Nationalliteratur* began in Germany in the 1780s, and histories of 'national literatures', with quite new perspectives and emphases from older and more general ideas of 'humane letters', were being written in German, French and English from the same period, in which there was a major change in ideas both of 'the nation' and of 'cultural nationality'. Subsequent historical developments, especially in our own century, have made these 'national' specializations uncertain, and have created anomalies which have to be temporarily regulated year by year by examination rubrics and so on. 'For the purposes of this paper, *English* should be taken to mean...' In fact this is a very potent anomaly, since the question of 'Englishness', so often adduced in English literary studies, is now for obvious social and political reasons very critical, full of tense and often highly emotional problems of traditional identity and contemporary threat. Consider some current attitudes to some recent new work as 'French' or as 'Paris fashion'. These are not just descriptive terms but are used deliberately in a marking-off sense. What is often being defended, it seems, is not just a body of writing but a major projection from this, in which the actually very diverse works of writers in English are composed into a national identity—the more potent because it is largely from the past—in which a mood, a temper, a style, or a set of immediate 'principles' (which can be contrasted not only with 'theory' but with all other forms of reasoning) are being celebrated, taught and—where possible—administratively imposed. This is a long way from literature in the sense of active and diverse writing. Rather it is a stand, a last redoubt, from which much more general notions of Englishness, of values, of tradition are defended against all comers; until even native dissidents (to say nothing of all those foreigners) are seen not merely as different but as alien— speaking not our language but some incomprehensible jargon. It is not, so far as all the English are concerned, how most of them actually feel and think in the face of related problems of identity, stress and change. But among what can be called, with precision, traditional English literary intellectuals, it is not just a profession; it is and has sounded like a calling and a campaign. In its own field it is congruent with much more general reflexes and campaigns of the English ruling class as a whole, whose talk and propagation of 'heritage' have increased in proportion with their practical present failures.

Now, for various reasons, both Marxism and structuralism, in their different ways, have impinged directly on the paradigm and on its anomalies. Indeed the surprising thing is that in so many of their actual tendencies they have been accommodated, or have accommodated themselves, *within* the paradigm, where they can be seen as simply diverse approaches to the same object of knowledge. They can then be taken as the guests, however occasionally untidy or unruly, of a decent pluralism. However, certain other tendencies are not so assimilable and are indeed quite incongruent with the received definition. It is these that are involved, not without dust and heat, in the current crisis. For this crisis is, above all, a crisis of the dominant paradigm and of its established professional standards and methods. Yet for the reasons just given, this acquires a resonance well beyond the terms of a professional dispute. It is, in the fullest sense, one of the key areas in which a very general cultural crisis is being defined and fought out.

I will now go on to describe, briefly, the main and very diverse tendencies in Marxism, formalism and structuralism, as they bear on what by received habit we call literary studies. To know any of these properly needs much further study, but I want at least to identify them, and then briefly indicate, because this is now the crucial point, which of these tendencies are compatible with the paradigm—and thus with established professional arrangements—and which in my view are not.

In Marxism the first area to explore is that which is centred on the idea of 'reflection', in itself a very complex notion and used differentially within the Marxist tradition. It does historically represent the earliest application of Marxism to literary studies, but in three interestingly different ways.

First, there is that most general proposition in Marxism: that the whole movement of society is governed by certain dispositions of the means of production and that when these dispositions—forces and relations in a mode of production as a whole—change through the operation of their own laws and tendencies, then forms of consciousness and forms of intellectual and artistic production (forms which have their place in orthodox Marxist definition as a 'superstructure') change also. Some shift in relatively direct ways, like politics and law; some in distant and often indirect ways—the traditional examples are religion, philosophy and aesthetics. According to this Marxist version of the history of art and thought, changes at the most basic levels of the social order resonate in the most distant areas as people become conscious of these conflicts and in various ways fight them out.

This proposition has been endlessly argued about, most of all within the Marxist tradition itself. But in its relation to literary studies we can distinguish two versions: one rather crude, though it is still widely known (and often all that is known) as Marxism in literary studies; the other a good deal more sophisticated or appearing to be more sophisticated. The first crude version is this: if it is true that literary and intellectual production is, in the broadest sense, a reflection of fundamental conflicts in the social order, then the business of Marxists engaged in such studies is to identify the conflicting forces and then to distinguish (as was commonly done in the thirties) progressive kinds of writing and reactionary kinds of writing, to take positions about these, and, above all (for the emphasis was always more on production than on criticism), to find ways of producing new kinds of writing which correspond to the needs of the fundamental conflict.

This is—and not only in caricature—a very simple position. At its weakest it amounts to branding certain kinds of literature as good or bad according to their presumed political or historical tendency. More generally the literary argument is seen as dependent on an assumed total position or class world-view. These general truths, moreover, are conceived as coming first, and then being demonstrated and illustrated in literature. Not surprisingly, when this variant of Marxist interpretation encountered a much closer kind of literary analysis in the thirties, for example in Leavis (himself engaged and embroiled in moral and cultural discriminations within literature), it suffered a rather decisive defeat. It was seen as crude and reductionist, or as at best dogmatically selective.

And yet it has still to be said that no Marxist, however he/she redefines the terms of this general proposition of social determination, can wholly give it up without abandoning the Marxist tradition. The more modern forms of this argument in fact dispense with the idea of reflection. For even after it had been allowed that there are distances, that there are lags in time and so on, it is clear that too close and direct an a priori correspondence had been assumed between those things which could be historically identified as happening elsewhere in the social order, and actual literary production. So, instead of looking for those direct and obvious connections which could support the simple labelling of works as politically good or bad, or as representing this or that tendency or class, the general position was retained but with a radical redefinition of what the variable literary and aesthetic processes actually are. Eventually that became, at a later stage, a quite complex position; but I have mentioned the older version first, both because it is the most widely known and because, existing in crude as well as some more refined forms, it is at once challenging and difficult.

Now the second position which was constructed around the idea of reflection was really very much simpler. This turns out to be one of the wholly compatible tendencies, drawing on a very long tradition in literary thought, of the general idea of reflection, and indeed of the broader and more passive version of mimesis. (There is a quite different, active sense of *mimesis*, which is not reflection at all but a process of grasping, interpreting and changing.) This tendency defines valuable literature as that which reflects social reality, and its preferred method is realism: judging works of art by their fidelity to or illumination of otherwise observable social reality. And if this is the criterion, then there must be no external labelling of progessive and reactionary works. As Marx observed of Balzac (a man at the opposite political extreme from himself): precisely because Balzac represents the realities of French society he is important. He would have been a much inferior writer if he had attempted to turn this realistic representation towards what both Marx and Engels continuously attacked as 'tendency literature', in which instead of reflecting reality you to try to turn it in the direction of some political presupposition of your own. It was thus crucial in this tendency that the work reflected reality—reality as it was, however unwelcome.

But we have to allow something, perhaps a lot, for the fact that Marxism, as a general position, claims unique insights into the nature of this reality, or rather its fundamental laws. This can be very different, in practice, from the idea of reflecting any 'reality' that happens from time to time to exist. Yet that difference tends to concern primarily questions of *historical* argument. The method of literary analysis—the demonstration of a reflection of a state or process defined as its basis or context or background—usually remains compatible. For this is after all a very familiar position in all literary studies. People again and again actually ask, in more or less sophisticated ways, how this novel or that relates to some otherwise observable reality. Indeed this forms a very large part of the most orthodox research in criticism and scholarship. Thus one kind of 'Marxist' position, defended on its own grounds, is in practice nearly always compatible with much more widely approved and justified methods.

So also, I believe, is the third version of the reflection theory, which becomes particularly apparent in the work of Lukács—the previous phases having been primarily represented by Plekhanov. Lukács argued that we can take a deceptively simple view of the relation between a work of art and reality, because the reflection of reality *in its immediately apprehensible form* may be either insufficient or indeed illusory. Hence that definition of realism which Lukács eventually embraced: a definition harder in some ways to defend theoretically than the previous positions, for it said that the task of the writer is to reflect underlying *movements*. This is where the previous point, about the privileged insights of Marxism, becomes much more salient, for the 'underlying movement' tends to belong to the 'laws', to privileged analysis, and thus looks very different from the citation of empirical detail within a Marxist or any other perspective. Yet it is also an attempt to move beyond these empirical simplicities, in a way related to other attempts to show an indirect or a penetrating or an ideal relation between 'what happened' and what writers 'have made of it'. Hence Lukács' attack on naturalism, which (it was said) simply reflects the appearance of things as they are, the immediately accessible reality. The alternative to naturalism is a *realism* which, while faithful to the contemporary reality which is its subject, is concerned above all to discern the underlying movements in it. Great stress is then put on realism as a *dynamic* rather than a static category. Lukács's accounts of the historical novel or the changing forms of drama are cast in those terms. Yet interestingly, when quite different kinds of writing were developed in the twentieth century to represent, precisely, dynamic movement—as, for example, Brecht—Lukács attacked them: indeed, he tended to remain deeply attached to that older version of realism as reflecting and illuminating a general, and generally knowable, reality.

Now, for a long time the Marxist contribution to literary studies—

at least in work available in English—was represented by reflection theory. But already from the 1920s a very different definition of literary production and its social relations had been developing within Marxism. This was centred not on 'reflection' but on what appears to be the quite different concept of 'mediation.' Actually the first sense of 'mediation' is not much more than a recognition of the more refined senses of 'reflection'. It accepts that it is misleading to look in literature for the 'reflection of reality.' Necessarily, by its construction as literature, reality becomes mediated in certain definite ways. This is again a perfectly familiar and even orthodox proposition within literary studies. It is not far from Eliot's notion of an 'objective correlative', although it starts at the other end of the process. But it is concerned above all to refute the reductive versions of the earlier phases, in which you could look for untransformed content. Significantly the great arguments about 'mediation' took place about Kafka. Because here was a kind of writing which either had to be rejected on the simplest premisses of reflection theory—the 'sick fantasies of a decadent class'; 'pessimistic and subjectivist lucubrations, far removed from the active and vigorous life of the people'—or *interpreted* by different versions of the idea of mediation. I must resist the temptation to give detailed examples of the different readings of Kafka—as the fiction of alienation, of bureaucracy, of declining imperialism, of Jewishness in the diaspora, of the Oedipus complex, of fatal illness, and so on—which came out of these different versions of mediation, but they are in the record. Still, however, the earliest sense of mediation is only a refinement of the idea of reflection, and I must briefly mention three other senses.

First there is the very interesting notion developed by Walter Benjamin in the 1930s: the idea of *correspondences*. This is a decisive shift, because Benjamin does not argue that a work of literature is the literary transformation of some element of reality. Rather, there is an observable 'correspondence' between certain kinds of writing and certain other contemporary social and economic practices. The most famous example is his long analysis of Baudelaire, where he argues that certain new conditions in the city, leading to new forms of the 'crowd' and within these to the redefinition of 'the individual', produced a number of new forms of writing, including Baudelaire's. There the reference is not to an otherwise existing, otherwise observable social reality, which the literature 'reflects' or even 'mediates', but to the fact of an observed correspondence between the nature and form of the literary activity and the nature and form of other contemporary practices of a more general kind.

Benjamin came to be close to the important ideas of the Frankfurt School, though he fell out on just this point with Adorno, who went much further in use of the idea of mediation. Adorno argued that correspondences of *content*, let alone reflections or mediations of content, are basically irrelevant to art. Indeed, the presence of such correspondences or reflections is virtually a guarantee that the art is not authentic. Art is produced—and this was his contribution to the Kafka argument—by a process which he called the discovery of 'dialectical images', which had no possibility of being discovered or expressed in any other form. The 'dialectical image' arose within the processes of art, and when created, although it might by analysis be related to the whole structure within which it was formed, was never overtly or directly related. Indeed the condition of its success as art was that it achieved an *autonomous* existence.

This is a sense of mediation which eventually connects with forms of literary structuralism. Lucien Goldmann, in his studies first of the French classical drama, particularly Racine, and then in work on the nineteenth- and twentieth-century novel, produced a position which still further widened the category of mediation: correspondence was never a relation of content, but always of *form*. He said, further, that it is only in secondary or inferior literature that vulgar sociologists, as he tended to call them, look for and find their simple relations between literature and society or reality. On the contrary, he argued, what is reflected in those works is merely the contradictory and *unachieved* consciousness of the time. The deep consciousness of the time is achieved only in certain major works and is achieved by them in their form and not in their content. This is the whole thrust of the analysis of Racine, although I must say that he does not always keep to his own prescriptions. Nevertheless, the proposition is that the correspondence, the mediation, is entirely a matter of the *form*. A certain disposition of human relationships is always present as the deepest consciousness of a particular epoch, and this disposition is homologous with a specific ordering of the elements of the literary work. Goldmann called this position 'genetic structuralism'. This was a deliberate opposition to orthodox structuralism because he argued that if we are to understand such forms, we must understand them in their processes of building up, stabilizing and breaking down; whereas in other tendencies of structuralism, there was a rejection of any notion of that kind of *historical* genesis and dissolution.

It would now be convenient to pass at once to literary structuralism, but from the real history of the case we have to make a detour through formalism. For there can be no doubt that formalism—both the early work of the Russian formalists as well as the later developments in emigration in the United States and then France—has had a more practical effect on literary studies that are now broadly grouped as 'structuralist' than that more general structuralism which is active in other disciplines, especially in anthropology. Brevity here is especially constraining, but the key demarche of the formalists was a new definition of *literariness*. Indeed they were reacting precisely against the modes of study, or most of the modes of study, that I have previously described. At first, they were reacting within a specifically Russian context, in which these theories, Marxist and related, were very active and current. The formalists said: the crucial omission you are making is that quality which makes a work *literary*. This is not to be found in what you are enquiring into, which is the relation of the work to something else. The central question, necessarily, is what makes this precise work literary. It was thus the formalists who began to use, with a quite new emphasis, the notion of '*literary language*' which one still so often hears.

It doesn't make for clarity that there are of course also much older concepts of 'literary language': either of a kind of language appropriate to the elevated processes of literature, or of a standard of correctness by which all other usage can be judged. Those are old and often now merely conservative positions. Moreover the former, in the fixed modes into which it tended to settle down, was again and again challenged and often effectively overthrown by writers, who in certain periods consciously rejected received 'literary' or 'poetic' diction, and tried to restore ⁻elations with the popular and 'living language'. We have always in practice to look to historical evidence about actual and changing ways of writing, and about its changing social relations, if we are to get very far with the notion of a 'literary language' as distinct from the more general uses of language. It can be the problem of the relations between speech and print, or between elevated and popular forms, or, still, it can be an inherent problem in the modes of any conscious composition.

The formalist emphasis had very little to do with the more familiar positions of conservation or elevation. On the contrary, what they proposed was a revolutionary break, as the condition of any authentic literature (the most influential position) or as a condition necessary in their own time, as 'classical' modes broke down. These two arguments still need to be clearly distinguished, but what the early formalists proposed was a conscious estrangement in language, a deliberate break from ordinary language use. This is what in practice always happens when a work announces itself as literary. Either in its most specific uses of words, or in some break with the conventions and perspectives from which a particular subject matter is ordinarily seen, it makes the jump to literature, to the 'literary'. And then the business of the analyst is to trace precisely those breaks which constitute the literariness of the work.

This position is very productive. The argument between the formalists and more traditional Marxists has been, I believe, very important. Moreover, from about 1925, there is a less well-known development of formalism of a kind which has taken the argument into a quite new stage. Yet compared with people who know formalism as the early work of Eichenbaum, Shklovsky and so on, there are far fewer who are familiar with Volosinov or Bakhtin or Mukarovsky. But it was the work of these later formalists, with their inquiries into general or universal 'literariness', which transformed the whole argument about the study of literature, and in the end, the status of the paradigm itself. This late stage was indeed a social and historical formalism, because it was concerned not only with a general definition of literariness, but with the changing conditions in which 'literariness'—now in its turn a dynamic concept—is achieved by particular writers, as well as with much wider processes of historical and social development.

Consider Volosinov for example. His work remained virtually forgotten for fifty years (he was writing in the late twenties and there are many who believe that he was only ever a pen-name of Bakhtin). Deeply influenced by the new school of structural linguistics and accepting the analysis of language as analysis of a system of signs, Volosinov nevertheless insisted that language is at once a system of signs and a *socially produced* system of signs. He further argued that verbal signs are always 'multi-accentual'. He could thus reject those conceptions of a 'system' that were being offered by structural linguistics—as well as by psychoanalysis—in which certain rules of the system produce meanings and forms. For in real social and historical life there is constant systematic production and yet this is also a constantly open production. It is then possible to place 'literariness' within the open potential of a language, which is both generally and specifically available.

This is a decisive break with earlier formalism. While emphasizing what the formalists indicated as distinctive about literary language, it does not restrict linguistic generation and regeneration to works of literature. The process of language itself is a continual possibility of shift and change and initiation of meanings, and this range of possibility is embedded in the 'rules' of both the linguistic and the social system. The work of Bakhtin himself, especially in his study of Rabelais, had indicated the beginning of a certain new kind of literariness—and thus an *historical* literariness—by observing the interaction and the creative surpassing both of modes of folk literature, which had traditionally been present, and of the polite literature which had come down within a more limited and conservative social tradition. It was precisely in the interaction of those received and different traditions that a new indication of what it was to be literary was formed.

All this is very different from the early formalists with their more local stress on what makes language literary, such as the local use of 'devices'. It is an historical indication of how specific kinds of literariness come into social practice. There is then Mukarovsky, who is perhaps the most serious reviser of the original formalist positions; indeed his work points towards some of the later most incongruent and incompatible kinds of analysis. Mukarovsky argued devastatingly (although in the end not quite carrying the argument through) that aesthetic quality is not even primarily produced *within* a work of art. He thus moved away from aesthetic formalism, which had looked inside the work for indications that it was literary or was intended for aesthetic response. On the contrary, he said, the aesthetic indications, and thus the aesthetic norms and aesthetic values, are themselves always *socially* produced. There are changing indications of what is and is not to be regarded as art and of what is and is not to be regarded as art of a certain kind. Although these indications bear on the internal organization of the work, they are always much more widely operative and have a history.

It is very significant that from the late fifties in the USA and in France, the body of work that was first translated and became influential was the work of the early formalists, and the later more social and historical work was comparatively little known until much later. This had serious effects on the way in which certain formalist positions were developed in literary analysis. The most limited (though in local terms still impressive) kind of formalist analysis became the dominant form which was believed to correspond, in literature, with what was by this time called 'structuralist' methodology in anthropology, in linguistics and in psychoanalysis. This is why it is still difficult to understand the relations between structuralism, in its full general sense, and what are often much more local literary positions. Yet there were of course some connections.

One of the most common tendencies in structuralism, of notable value in anthropology and in linguistics, is that it refuses to interpret an event in its own isolated terms or in its immediate form of presentation. It seeks, rather, to locate an event, a relationship or a sign within a whole signifying system. Such systems are governed by their own *internal* rules: a position initially reached as a creative solution to the problems, in the field, of studying languages organized by quite different notions of syntax from any that were available within the Indo-European tradition. Instead of appropriating the novel event to an already known system, the attempt was made to find its meaning within a specific structural system: in practice by the relations of this unit to other units, and then the discovery of the general internal rules of the specific system.

What would such a procedure involve in literary studies? First, there is the possibility of some direct transfer from structuralist linguistics. Indeed, this has promoted certain refined techniques of analysis which are increasingly being practised, though still looked at with suspicion by the older literary departments. There is stylistics, for example, but much more important is discourse analysis, often at a certain evident distance from the ordinary language of literary analysis but often also commanding a more precise vocabulary in the analysis of syntactic forms, or in the identification of the narrator or the speaker and the relation between speakers. Some of this passed into literary studies a number of years ago and is available, as one technique among others, in fairly ordinary procedures of literary analysis.

More generally, however, the notion of an internal rule-governed system was easily applicable; indeed it was in some ways directly congruent with a position that had already been reached without reference to structuralism within literary studies itself. When this tendency in literary structuralism appeared as an import from France in the sixties, I even risked saying that it seemed strange only because it was a long-lost cousin who had emigrated from Cambridge in the late twenties and early thirties. That was not in fact its only source. Yet there is at least an indirect inheritance from the kind of thinking which Richards had been doing about the isolated internal organization of a poem. And this was especially apparent when you looked at where the cousin had been: in North American New Criticism. What had happened in Cambridge was, by contrast, a confused but striking association of moral and indeed normative judgement with these techniques of isolated internal analysis. This was regarded elsewhere as an unfortunate impurity and a deviation from the only relevant discipline, which was the analysis of a specific verbal organization; indeed the object as in itself it really is, an ironic echo in this context. Either way the local techniques were or could quickly become familiar in literary analysis, where they were directed, constitutionally and very respectably, to analysing the internal organization of *the* text, *the* poem.

This kind of literary structuralism is not only congruent with the paradigm which I began by describing. It is the paradigm itself in its most influential modern form. And indeed whether it is genuinely structuralist is a necessary question. In its usual forms it is so obstinately local and technical, so little concerned with any wide or general systemic properties, that it barely deserves the name. What can much more reasonably be called 'structuralist', in cultural studies, is that work which analyses internal organization not as an end in itself—the acquisition of competence in reading—but as the necessary way of analysing, and thus distinguishing, specific or systemic *forms*. Thus Goldmann's work on dramatic forms, and much current work on narrative forms, are attempts to discover the rules, the structural rules, of specific general forms of drama or fiction. This is very different from the more local technical analysis taken from linguistics. It is an application of the fundamental structuralist idea to problems of form which have indeed been profoundly neglected in literary studies. In Goldmann's case such analysis is at once formal and historical—there are historically changing forms. However, in many more centrally structuralist interventions it has been believed, in ways resembling much older theories of literary genres, that there are discoverable rules of general literary organization: of 'Narrative' as such, 'Drama' as such, and so on. It is an important kind of project, but typically it often unites an extremely local technicism, of internal analysis, with extremely broad categories—deliberately unhistorical and comprising aesthetic or psychological abstractions—as the 'structures' to which all detail relates.

A third kind of 'literary structuralism' is the work influenced by the largely philosophical arguments of Louis Althusser. These came into literary analysis through his pupil Pierre Macherey and are represented in this country by, for example, Terry Eagleton's *Criticism and Ideology*. This is a quite different tendency. It says: certainly society, the social order, is a rule-governed system, but above all it is a system of systems, determined in the last instance by the economy. Within this general determination each practice—such as writing—has an important relative autonomy. Yet it is still a part, and must ultimately be perceived as a part, of a wider system to which it cannot be reduced but to which it must ultimately be related. How in practice is this relation handled and demonstrated? It is through what is seen as the binding force of the whole system: ideology. Ideology is very much more, here, than the ideas and beliefs of particular classes or groups. It is in effect, with only limited exceptions, the condition of all conscious life. Thus the area to which most students of literature normally refer their reading and their judgement, that area summarized in the decisive term 'experience', has in fact to be seen as within the sphere of ideology. Indeed, experience is seen as the most common form of ideology. It is where the deep structures of the society actually reproduce themselves as conscious life. Ideology is indeed so pervasive and so impenetrable, in this account, that you wonder who is ever going to be able to analyse it. But there is a precedent, after all, in the case of the Unconscious, with which it has certain close connections and analogies. There is an absolute unconscious, psychoanalysis says, but there are also discoverable techniques of penetration and understanding. In the case of Althusser, the leading technique of penetration is theory. Only theory can fully escape ideology. But there is also, in the case of literature, a relatively privileged situation. Literature is not just a carrier of ideology, as in most forms of reflection theory. It is inescapably ideological, but its specific relative autonomy is that it is a form of writing, a form of practice, in which ideology both exists and is or can be internally distanced and questioned. Thus the value of literature is precisely that it is one of the areas where the grip of ideology is or can be loosened, because although it cannot escape ideological construction, the point about its literariness is that it is a continual questioning of it internally. So you get readings which are very similar to certain recent semiotic readings, where you construct a text and subtext, where you can say 'this is what is reproduced from the ideology'; but also, 'this is what is incongruously happening in the text which undermines or questions or in certain cases entirely subverts it'. This method has been used in very detailed and interesting analysis.

Then, finally, there is a tendency which undoubtedly has a relation to structuralism, certainly to structural linguistics, yet which—validly in my opinion—denies that it is a structuralism. This is what is now called semiotics. Semiotics in general is, without doubt, a true natural child of structuralism. It is a science of signs and a science of systems of signs (not confined to language). Meanings are construed not by their apparent content but by their relations within a general system of signification. In recent semiotics, this kind of analysis has been vigorously extended to advertising, to film, to photojournalism and in the case of Barthes to fashion. If you have this fundamental procedure of reading a system of signs—of which the meanings do not simply disclose themselves, but have to be constructed by understanding their place in a system which is never itself disclosed, which indeed always has to be *read*—then you have something which although it begins within structuralism can become in some of its later work separable from it. Thus instead of seeing literary works as *produced* by the system of signs, which has been the central emphasis of the most orthodox structuralism, this later semiotics has on the contrary emphasized that productive systems have themselves always to be constituted and reconstituted, and that because of this there is a perpetual battle about the fixed character of the sign and about the systems which we ordinarily bring to production and interpretation. One effect of this shift is a new sense of 'deconstruction': not the technical analysis of an internal organization to show where all the parts, the components, have come from, but a much more open and active process which is continually taking examples apart, as a way of taking their *systems* apart. It is clearly in this sense a much more explosive tendency than any of the other tendencies within structuralism. It is not simply demonstrating the operation of systematic rules in ways which can settle down as competences within the paradigm. On the contrary, whether it is analysing literature or television or physical representation, it is looking not for the academically explanatory system, but for the system as a mode of formation, which as it becomes visible can be put into question or quite practically rejected. In that sense the whole impulse of this radical semiotics is very different from the structuralist version of production and reproduction which has been much more widely influential—and more welcome and at home—in literary studies.

I now want to say that in recent years there has been an observable moving together of two positions which started a long way apart. I can perhaps best illustrate this in my own case. Much of the literary work I have done, with I think two or three exceptions, can be read as compatible with what I called at the beginning the dominant literary paradigm. That is to say, it is work which may be approaching the analysis and judgement of literature with an exceptionally strong consciousness of the social determinants upon it, but the centre of literary attention is still there, and the procedures are judgement, explanation, verification in terms of historical explanation, and so on. One work, however, of which this cannot be true is *The Country and the City*, which is in fact very near that first Marxist position I described, because it sets out to identify certain characteristic forms of writing about the country and the city, and then insists on placing them not only in their historical background—which is within the paradigm—but within an active, conflicting historical process in which the very forms are created by social relations which are sometimes evident and sometimes occluded. So that is in any reading a break.

But of course there was other work, going back especially to *The Long Revolution*, which had not been perceived as within literary studies at all but which can now evidently be seen as a shift of emphasis which would end by rejecting the dominant paradigm. I mean especially the work on the social history of English writers, the social history of dramatic forms, the growth of standard English, and also the new positions on what is necessary in the analysis of culture. A further shift was apparent in the work on communications, on television, on technologies and cultural forms, and on the sociology of culture, although these were again typically seen as a separate interest outside English or literary studies. Now all this came together for me around 1970 and from that time I developed a more explicit theoretical position which I eventually described in *Marxism and Literature* as 'cultural materialism'. This is of course outside the paradigm altogether, but it is not the case that it has moved away from the ultimate common concern, the works about which knowledge is to be gained. It has moved much wider than literature in its paradigmatic sense, but it still centrally includes these major forms of writing, which are now being read, along with other writing, in a different perspective. Cultural materialism is the analysis of all forms of signification, including quite centrally writing, within the actual means and conditions of their production.

It was here, perhaps to our mutual surprise, that my work found new points of contact with certain work in more recent semiotics. There were still radical differences, especially in their reliance on structural linguistics and psychoanalysis, in particular forms; but I remember saying that a fully historical semiotics would be very much the same thing as cultural materialism, and I was glad to see certain tendencies in this direction, as distinct from some of the narrower structuralist displacements of history. I could see also that some of the simpler positions of early structural linguistics could be modified by new emphases on the social and historical production of signifying systems, as in Volosinov and the social formalists. There remained the problem of the bearings of psychoanalysis, where there were still radical differences, but on the other hand I knew that Marxism had been generally weak in this area of the problems of subjectivity, and there might now be a radical new dimension of enquiry, testing evidence and propositions in this area which is so evidently important in the production of meanings and values. Thus in practice two different kinds of work were now in touch with each other and were developing in some cases very constructively. Perhaps we were so involved in this in Cambridge that we forgot that while we pushed on in these ways the older paradigm was still there and was still institutionally powerful, though the anomalies by this time were quite evidently disorganizing it even at the most practical levels. Some new work was being included to cover the anomalies, but the result was then incoherent from most points of view.

So I come back at last to my original argument. Most actual Marxist and structuralist tendencies are and have been, however locally unfamiliar or crudely identifiable as strange and partisan, compatible or even congruent in a broad sense with the orthodox paradigm, especially in its practically loosened and eclectically incoherent form. Certain others, however, are not; and most specifically that first position in Marxism, which instead of privileging a generalized Literature as an independent source of values insists on relating the actual variety of literature to historical processes in which fundamental *conflicts* had necessarily occurred and were still occurring. That was the sense and the challenge of the *The Country and the City*. The other positions that are not compatible with the paradigm and its professional organization are cultural materialism and radical semiotics. For these necessarily include the paradigm itself as a matter for analysis, rather than as a governing definition of the object of knowledge.

It is necessary to insist on these distinctions. What their institutional consequences may be it is much too early to say. In some other universities and in some of the new higher education institutions the shift from the old paradigm has already in whole or in part occurred. Yet it still matters very much what happens in the older, more established institutions. In Cambridge especially we have to ask a hard question: can radically different work still be carried on under a single heading or department when there is not just diversity of approach but more serious and fundamental differences about the object of knowledge (despite overlapping of the actual material of study)? Or must there be some wider reorganization of the received divisions of the humanities, the human sciences, into newly defined and newly collaborative arrangements? This is what now must be faced in what is also, for other reasons, a frozen—indeed a pinched—climate. All that we can be certain that we can and must do is to clarify, very openly, the major underlying intellectual issues.

Beyond Cambridge English

It is often said that there are more than six centuries of English literature. It is not often said that there are less than two centuries of English literacy. Of course 'English', in those two statements, has different meanings. The first refers primarily to the language, the second to the people. But then it is the ordinarily unexamined relation between these meanings that can reveal a central problem in English studies. The idea of literature, throughout, has been so closely connected with the condition of literacy that it can hardly be said that this deeper relationship needs to be forced. Powerful social and cultural conventions control or displace what is otherwise an obvious connection. What then is 'English literacy', for professional students and teachers of English? Is it their own condition and that of people much like them, currently and retrospectively applied? Or is it the diverse and changing conditions of their whole nominal people? To approach two centuries of English literacy means restricting our count to a bare majority. General literacy has a bare century, and within that many are still disadvantaged. In relation to what is seen as 'our' literature, where then do students and teachers of English stand?

I have made my own awkward stand. By my educational history I belong with the literate and the literary. But by inheritance and still by affiliation I belong with an illiterate and relatively illiterate majority. It is said that as the whole society develops, and has for the past century been developing, these inherited problems and contradictions resolve themselves. I do not think so. Beyond our local and diverse histories there are major intellectual issues, of a fully objective kind, which need to be traced to this radical unevenness between literature and general literacy. Underlying them, always, are

the complex general problems of language, and it is in how these problems are dealt with, in the coming years, that the success or failure
of English studies will, in my view, be decided.

It is strange that many people still think that 'language' is self-
evidently a separate 'subject' from 'literature'. There are reasons in
the way 'literature' itself has come to be understood: not so much as
active writing but as a singular body of creative experience or moral
resource or simply human record, which we explore through 'its'
language. But there are as strong reasons in the way 'language' has
been defined and studied. It is interesting that the earliest meaning of
'philology' in English was 'the study of literature'. Both 'grammar'
and 'rhetoric' were originally closely associated with the study of exemplary written texts. It was only much later that philology and
grammar acquired more specialized and autonomous senses, and
were eventually joined by an autonomous 'linguistics'. So far had
this gone, in developments on what could be seen as both sides, that
'Cambridge English' could be described, by Tillyard, as an 'effort to
make philology yield to literature', while Churton Collins argued
that 'literature must be rescued from its present degrading vassalage
to Philology'. That phrase should be remembered when some now
speak of restoring philology or rhetoric to an English course.
Neither, evidently, is an unproblematic subject or method. Yet the
confidence of that talk of 'rescue' and 'yielding' needs to be
remembered even more carefully. What the linguistic specializations
and autonomies relied on was one of the great periods of all human
learning and inquiry: the massive scholarship of historical philology;
the profoundly innovating analyses of linguistics. No serious person
could look at the methods and results of these bodies of work and
suppose that humane education could ignore them. No serious person, that is, unless he was already looking at something else: what
could now be seen as the body of English literature, the plays and
poems and novels which clearly constituted in themselves a major
'subject'. It was then a matter of institutional decisions: of separa-
tions and combinations, of balances and options, and of course of
committees and influence and power. It will doubtless be so again,
but it is the hard intellectual issues, not always (to put it mildly) clear
or even conscious in such proceedings, that have most urgently to be
examined.

I have been engaged in this argument for many years, and it has always been difficult to decide whether to put an emphasis on short-term and local changes, which might be adopted within the broad existing arrangements, or to speak only of the radical reconstruction which is intellectually necessary and then to put oneself—or be effectively put—beyond the boundaries of the existing discourse. In English at Cambridge this has been an especially difficult choice, since there was so much in its early work and aspirations, and still in its surviving formal definitions, to offer grounds for hope. I look back, for example, to F. R. Leavis's sketch for an English School and especially its proposal for a seventeenth-century Part Two, which includes not only his well-known emphasis on practical criticism and his underlying assumption of the nature of the transition or fall from the seventeenth to the twentieth century, but also a proposal for student essays, as an alternative to formal examinations, on topics as diverse as the rise of capitalism, the causes of the civil war and 'the evidence regarding popular culture'. With proposals of that breadth it was difficult to believe that Cambridge English was a lost cause, but though many now speak of that period of literary studies as being dominated by Leavis—and in the broadest cultural sense that is so—he was in practice isolated and defeated in the Faculty, to such an extent that his friends and pupils saw themselves as an alternative faculty, though then over the years with some surprising actual results. One familiar way of evading radical arguments is to personalize them around some discordant individual; the easy habits of a culture steeped in personal disparagement can then be relied on to smother the issues. This happened again in the late sixties and in the late seventies and early eighties, but meanwhile all the real underlying problems remained.

These underlying problems stemmed, even and perhaps especially in Leavis, from the belief that all this necessary work—the collaborative analysis and understanding of a culture—could be done from a central base in literary criticism. Yet it has been clear from the 1930s, and obvious from the late 1950s, that many other kinds of knowledge and analysis have to be drawn on if the work is to be properly done, and that instead of relatively isolated forays from some presumed and then increasingly specialized centre, there has to be a more open and equal-standing convergence of independent disciplines, seeking to make their evidence and their questions come together in a common inquiry. If this change of emphasis is not made—and to make it is to move decisively beyond the short and narrow terms of reference of the existing authorities—what seems in practice to happen, indeed to have been happening at an accelerating pace in the last twenty years, is that the problems and contradictions of the existing formulations are suppressed or at best fossilized, and what is offered instead, now with a whole specialized profession behind it, is not so much an exploratory as an instructing and examining course: necessarily, in view of its rich subject, with much of interest and value, but necessarily also, as can be seen at once when eyes lift, as they must, from the series of texts and essays, failing—deeply failing—to meet the full active interests of students, including those interests which stem from a love of writing and from a human concern with all its conditions and materials and possibilities.

It is from these active interests that a new convergence is being proposed. As early unformed or indeed uninformed questions, they can be easily put down by any academic authority, with the usual remarks about ignorance and the sneers against relevance. But that trick can only be turned in the authority's own ignorance of the work of neighbouring disciplines, where the questions and the evidence that interlock with these questions and this evidence have been made precise and substantial and indeed convergent. I will offer some examples of kinds of work that seem to me to be convergent in this way.

In English studies I would identify two tendencies and a possible third. First, there is that close historical analysis of the language and conventions of plays and poems and novels and arguments, which was once an integral part of what was called 'practical criticism' This was always relatively weak in its analysis of conventions. It was often overridden by the impulse and habit of supra-historical or ahistorical 'evaluation', in the interests of a universalist or subjectivist 'criticism', and in practice often declined to the limited but still useful exercise of 'dating'. But it is still, at its best and potentially, a major and practical form of convergence. Second, there is still much to rely on in the intense practice of close reading and analysis, which has been limited more by its relative isolation from other kinds of enquiry than by anything in its own methods. Indeed the varieties of close reading which are now practised, including those which have reintroduced syntactic analysis, seem to me certain to be indispensable. Moreover, certain methods learned there have been extended and adapted to the now equally necessary analysis of speech and writing with images, in close work on film and television. Here there is a convergence not so much with another subject as with a major part of the practical culture of all contemporary students.

The possible third tendency is one with which, in the past, I have often identified but in fact ended by redefining: that work which is usually described as 'on the reading public'. As empirical work it is still important, but it is characteristically limited by its failure to notice the unevenness of literature and literacy or, worse, by actual rationalization of it. There are several periods, including those most governed by print, in which attention to the 'non-reading public' is equally necessary. Some kinds of writing, and some important forms, need to be understood as much from the limiting relations which the unevenness imposed as from the confirming relations which an actually organized public supported. Moreover, it is always at least as much a matter of 'audiences' as of 'reading publics'. The complex interactions of oral and written and written-for-oral forms which run through our cultural history—central before the seventeenth century, central again in the second half of the twentieth century, significant in their very displacements and difficulties in the intervening centuries of the relative domination, within a limited literacy, of print—cannot be reduced to one privileged form. The conditions and relations of actual production, as these are evident and discoverable in actual plays and poems and novels, ought always to be a major element in English studies. But it is significant that the tolerance accorded, if with an edge of disdain, to 'reading-public' studies is usually not extended to studies of the economics and politics of writing, to comparative analyses of printed and oral (often communal-oral) work, or to work on the material history of writing, printing, book production, theatres, cinemas, broadcasting, within which and often in part changed by which actual composition has been variably done.

The worst thing that now happens in English studies is that sustained work of this last kind is identified for early export to some other department: to history, to sociology, or to that most effective if least funded university department—the voluntary underground. For what has also to be said is that there will have to be equally significant changes in history and sociology and elsewhere if the best possibilities of this work are to be realized. It is true that sociological theory and method can at once improve, often beyond recognition, work on reading publics and cultural institutions. It is true that history offers fuller and more general evidence to what are often the extrapolated or privileged accounts of literary and especially critical history. But the very questions which some kinds of reading of plays and poems and novels suggest are questions which ought also to be central in history and sociology themselves, but which their most orthodox methods have failed to identify. The state of the language at a given time, for example, often indicated but not fully discoverable from its most enduring writing, is clearly a major historical issue. The extraordinary linguistic diversity of English Renaissance drama, so marked by comparison with what preceded and succeeded it, and so intricately connected with shifting social relations and with the interaction between high literacy and an exceptionally developed oral culture, can be discovered in full and complex detail in the plays. But it has then to be related to a whole body of other available evidence, in education and in oral records and in more general social relations. We have already seen enough work to know that this is a fully practical convergence, but there are other areas to which there are still theoretical obstacles.

I have been working for some time on the problems of reported speech in novels, as this is related, in complex ways, both to literary conventions and the diverse actual speech of periods and regions and classes, and to the typically controlling or enclosing language of narrative and analysis. I have found, in this work, some useful contacts with historians, and there is a particularly encouraging development, inside history, of studies of the oral tradition and oral evidence and of hitherto neglected forms such as the unpublished autobiographies of working men and women. But when it is argued, as it must be argued, that an understanding of these matters depends not only on the historical evidence of actual speech but on the quite evident literary conventions of its representation—the assimilation of speech, in polite novels, to the formal language of narrative or analysis; or the gross case of the conventional 'orthography of the uneducated' in which class and regional diversities are represented by errors in spelling, as if English had any such orthodox norm—there is usually a loss of contact, as if either the history or the literary conventions settled the matter. The whole point is their interaction and even their evidence of failure to interact. Again, in sociology, it is at the point of fine detail in the literary representation of social figures and social relations that the convergence with a more general sociology is necessary and desirable but is often theoretically blocked, as if a literary convention were not also an historical and a sociological fact at the same time as, and just because, it is a working literary convention.

Yet it is in the newest area of the general convergence that the problems of significant identification are now most acute. Literary studies have to an extraordinary extent lost contact even with work in empirical history of the language. But the problems of contact with what is newly generalized as linguistics are more subtle if not more pressing. There was a small rush, for local ideological reasons inside literary criticism, to areas of theoretical linguistics which had much to contribute to humane studies but comparatively little to any practical convergence. On the other hand, the genuinely convergent developments—in discourse analysis, in sociolinguistics and even in some stylistics—were often based on very limited grounds. There was analysis of texts composed for analysis, when there was a whole world of real discourse, including literature. There was a limitation to unhistorical assumptions of norms and deviances. There were simplistic assumptions of detachable and identifiable 'style'. Within each of these areas, in increasingly interesting ways, developments are occurring which belong to the convergence, and which are much more likely to belong to it if the questions and the evidence are moving in also from the other direction. For example, we have to run the abstraction of discourse through the specificities of highly variable oral and printed forms. In the concept of dialogue, say, we have an extraordinary range from philosophical dialogue to at least three major kinds of dramatic dialogue, in works which are among the highest peaks of European culture but which, for that very reason, require something more than appreciation or interpretation; they require analysis of their constitutive *forms*, which are at once in the broadest sense social and cultural and yet in the most precise sense capable of being analysed by new kinds of linguistic markers. In sociolinguistics, to set alongside the necessary fieldwork, there is a vast range of oral and written composition over a historical period long enough to suggest questions and answers in some of the most profound social relationships, in the complex and dynamic interactions between what we call everyday language and the many and variable levels of formal composition. Others will have other examples, but what needs to be emphasized is that such work is already practical and indeed in progress, and that as active work, in many societies, it is having to meet, in addition to its own formidable problems, the relatively trivial but in practice equally formidable problems of its relations with existing and vested 'subjects' and institutions.

It happens that I am in touch with this work in many parts of the world, especially in North America and the rest of Western Europe. It is genuinely difficult, with this work all the time on my desk, to look out of the window and suppose, as local pieties would have it, that Cambridge is still some kind of model. Certainly work has been done here that has contributed to the convergence, but the dominant models are very different. For by contrast with what it has done in the natural sciences, on which its modern intellectual reputation primarily depends, Cambridge has not achieved or seriously tried to achieve, in the humanities and in the social sciences, the kind of contact and movement between neighbouring disciplines that are the conditions of any serious convergence. Elsewhere, as here in Natural Sciences, there are Schools and groupings beyond Faculties. There are courses which allow very extensive and variable combinations of work, all done from its own base, which at once meet variable interests and permit, at their best, new developments and interactions of knowledge and inquiry. In its coming difficult years Cambridge needs, above all, a School of Humanities, to which English among others, taking full advantage of the Parts of Triposes and exchanges between them, would have much to contribute. Whether it will get such a School should not be judged only from current positions and reactions. Think of what it must have been like to propose an English Tripos in 1890 or 1910, against as compact and confident a majority. Or is that comparison fair, to the earlier period? There is usually some inertia and apathy, an unwillingness to make any changes. One thing an academic establishment is very good at is precise reproduction, and it has its own—sometimes drastic—ways of controlling and selecting from its genetic pool. Moreover, an increasingly examination-centred university can find great difficulty in recognizing that there can be crucial differences between its familiar internal standards and the standards of the international intellectual community, especially in cases of new kinds of work.

But particularly in English there are other levels of problem. A stress on standards and a concern with order were always central elements of Cambridge English, but they could go either way: to a shared search and discovery—the emphases of Richards and of early *Scrutiny*—or to an appropriation, through practical control, of the body of knowledge. These profoundly alternative directions are still, I believe, a matter of complex dispute. The situation of the whole society, much of it confused or bewildered by the scale and pace of change and decline, is bound to affect even local differences. There is now so strong a push to re-establish forms of order and discipline based on projections of past greatness and specifically of great Englishness that it would be astonishing if certain inherent tendencies in the constitution of English literature as an enclosed subject were not congruent with, even actively recruited and contributing to, this assertion of order through a version of tradition.

Well! When that appears it must, I believe, be fought. In its worst forms it can be readily and confidently fought. But before we can fully understand it, as the dominant and privileged response it is, we have to look also at certain even deeper conditions, often counterposed to so simple a traditionalism. We have to look at the major intellectual formulations through which the unevenness of literacy and of learning has been lived with and either mediated or rationalized: I mean the formulations that are known as modernism.

It is remarkable, when you look into it, how much theory and practice, of both established and innovative kinds, now depends on that relatively unexamined formulation. It has become dominant in literary studies, not only in the major emphasis on work grouped by it, from James and Conrad to Beckett, but in the extension of interests and methods developed from it to most other kinds of writing. Again, to a remarkable extent, the decisive theoretical positions that are brought to this and related studies are key elements of the formulation. Formalism in literary analysis; the epistemological break that is said to distinguish Marxism; the break and innovation of psychoanalysis; the break and innovation of theoretical linguistics, from Saussure; structuralism in anthropology and sociology: these, as forms of thinking and in the cultural practice that accompanies them, compose 'modernism'. I am not offering some list of achievements or of errors. I am interested in the formation, the map. It is characteristic that each of these developments offers the terms of its own interpretation, and that it is difficult, in any particular field, to get beyond these. This is as true of modernism, as it is perceived in literature, as in any of the more evident and controversial theoretical positions. Characteristically, also, each of these developments—and early 'Cambridge English' with the rest—reaches towards dominance of much wider fields than its own. They are breaks and innovations which extend their light everywhere. The light is often real; I am not questioning that. What I have to say is different: that we need to see these developments as a specific cultural formation, which has been at once a response to and governed by an underlying and decisive unevenness of literacy and of learning: the unevenness, specifically, of a class society, at a definite and critical stage.

This would be much easier to see if the central impulses of modernism were not precisely a series of breaks from the most orthodox representations and forms of thought of an established class society. It is the reality of this series of breaks which makes it impossible to reach back beyond them to some hitherto stable position which can be offered as 'tradition' or as 'commonsense'. That impossible attempt was the decay of 'Cambridge English' in its most defining sense. For it had found its own most significant directions in modernism, abandoning much else that would have sustained a more orthodox continuity, yet at a certain stage—I am thinking especially of Leavis—it refused its further development and tried to reconstruct a common-sense tradition from its then limited materials. The underlying unevenness of literacy and of learning, to which modernism had been an innovating response, came to be accepted and rationalized as a condition of at once necessary and privileged work: as the minority carriers of a common tradition, an 'Englishness' of the literature which was made to stand for the 'Englishness' of a people.

This in turn made it more difficult to see modernism as it is. There was always that lively dead-end to point to. But in any wider perspective the issues are clear. The common factor in the different theories and practices that are grouped as modernism is an estrangement—a sense of both distance and novelty—which is related in its own terms to some large characterization of the 'modern world' but is in reality the response of a disturbed and exposed formation—writers, artists and intellectuals—to conditions which were blocking their own most significant kinds of work. The reality of estrangement began in cultures which were failing to offer conditions for serious work of these kinds: in residual traditional cultures, where dogmatic restrictions were experienced as a crippling provincialism; in affluent commercial cultures, where the art and thought that would get paid for were based on flattering misrepresentation; and in the despairs and revolts that were growing inside these societies, in their darkest, most hidden areas. There was then at once a rejecting and a rejection. Most of the early modernists broke not only from the cultural institutions but from their own practical cultures. In literature, for example, Conrad, James, Apollinaire, Joyce, Eliot, Pound, Beckett made, if in different ways, this necessary move. What was at issue in writing and also in painting was the need to find, within the practices themselves, new kinds of signification as received and local systems failed or were abandoned. That is the orthodox and, as far as it goes, still accurate account.

It is what it leaves out that now matters. For the practice was never solely technical, to be addressed in its own isolating terms. The decisive condition of the practice was the availability, within a new kind of social formation, of social relationships which eventually corresponded to the practical initiatives. These were found within the new social form of the metropolis: typically the imperial metropolis of Paris, London and eventually New York. An extraordinary number of the innovators were not so much exiles and emigrés, though that was how they started, but immigrants, which is where the conditions of their practice formed. Distanced from, though often still preoccupied by, more local cultures, they found the very materials of their work—their language, which writers had once fully shared with others; their visual signs and representations, which shared ways of life had carried—insufficient yet productive in one crucial way: that writers, artists and intellectuals could share this sense of strangeness with others doing their kind of work but who had begun from quite different familiarities. From the initial strangeness what was forged was a specific form of a possible aesthetic universality, but this would not have made its way on its own. It was the increasing dominance of metropolitan civilization, its emergence as a type of an increasingly mobile and dislocated society, which promoted the versions of artistic and intellectual universality—the reductions as well as the discoveries—which were originally the experiences of both estrangement and exposure. In the central development of both old and new cultural technologies, from book production to cinema and broadcasting—technologies which were to become central in the new culture but which a print-bound academy could scarcely recognize even when they became arts— these political and economic centres acquired a practical dominance of all cultural production and distribution, over a range from a new commercial popular culture to the now decisive groups of metropolitan intellectuals and artists. What began in isolation and exposure ended, at many levels, in an establishment: as the decisive culture of an international capitalist world, which could trade both the original and the adapted forms.

One part of this establishment, eventually, was a new way of life— in the universities—for intellectuals, though it was always less so for writers and artists. But this could not have happened, in the ways it did, if there had not been a wholly corresponding movement of sub- jects and theories and disciplines which were formed within the same decisive perspective. A new sense of the objectivity of systems, and of this objectivity as something that needed to be penetrated by new forms of analysis, taking nothing as it appeared but looking for deep forms, deep structures, with the eyes of a stranger, came through in field after field: in linguistics, in anthropology, in economics, in sociology, in aesthetics, in psychoanalysis. Deep forms and shaping forces—forms and forces without recognizable everyday agents— were powerfully and revealingly identified. Few specific histories and experiences could stand against them; none, in truth, could be substituted for them. The whole text was to be read without date and author: this was the new and necessary discipline.

By my educational history I belong to these developments, and in those terms respect them. But in my full social history I continue to look at them. in turn, with the eyes of a stranger. What I then see is not only what they have achieved but their own deep forms. I can feel the bracing cold of their inherent distances and impersonalities and yet have to go on saying that they are indeed ice-cold. I see, prac- tically and theoretically, the estranging consequences of the general assumption—as active in modernist literature as in theoretical linguistics and structuralist Marxism—that the systems of human signs are generated within the systems themselves and that to think otherwise is a humanist error. There is then a paradox: that these systems, as systematic analysis reveals them, have great explanatory power, but that the form and language of their explanations are at a quite exceptional distance from the lives and relationships they address, so that what is reaching furthest into our common life has the mode of a stranger, even the profession of a stranger.

This is clear in one area, one discipline, after another, but it is especially clear in language itself. There are few greater contradictions than those of modernist literature, and especially the contradiction now expressed as 'literary language'. People still back away from language studies until they are hastily—and misleadingly—reassured that what is being proposed is a study of the language of literature—literary language. But this has a history, not only in detail but in the concept itself. What it once meant, within Renaissance ideas of decorum, was a suitably elevated language: a conscious and conventional formality of composition. It was a decayed form of this—as mere 'literary' and 'theatrical' language—that modernism both challenged and replaced, including even in its most innovating experiments new forms of colloquial vigour and popular reference. Yet at the same time it generated— ironically repeating the development of romanticism—its own internal idea of literary language; a process of composition centred wholly in its own self-generating system of literary signs. As it became more conscious of its own processes, it separated them, in some quite new ways, from the general social processes of language which were in any case there, in their own active and problematic and innovating ways, and which at its best it was itself exemplifying, as against both the polite old literary language and the reduced theoretical accounts of language as simple rule-bound reproduction.

The deep form is again evident. The movement of deepest connection comes through both as isolated and as isolating itself. Addressing the fullest substance of our time, it finds itself—and can become content to find itself—at a greater distance from its peoples than the most shallow and adaptive forms of commercial popular art but also of inertly reproduced traditional art. In writing as in theory, what is now in substance most living and general is at a wholly paradoxical distance from the general life.

The point, of course, is to change this, but that is possible only if we begin from its origins, beyond the simple view of heroic innovation. What happened in modernism was at root defensive: an intransigent response to a general failure, in which the unevenness—the willed and dominating unevenness—of literacy and of learning was decisive. Pushed beyond the frontiers of self-confirming and containing social and cultural orders, modernism had no choice but distance but then came to a further moment of choice. The inherent contradictions of its own practice forced one or other general position, where we can see all the innovators divide. There was the majority rejection of the orthodox social and cultural order in terms of an option for the past: for what could be called its traditional culture, within the continuity of the practices, but also for its different kinds of order, its clearer authorities and privileges. Art and culture, it was said, were inherently aristocratic, and the most improbable marginal people started behaving but especially thinking like their idea of lonely proud aristocrats. The minority rejection went the other way: to ideas of absolute revolution, the new art and thought as revolutionary; the one process kin to the other, except that the kinship was more often proposed than mutually acknowledged.

So the unevenness within which modernism was formed would either be stabilized or at last overcome. From positions of even relative privilege, within an expanded cultural market and within universities, the attempted stabilization continues to make more immediate sense, in English studies as everywhere else. In all my work I have tried to be on the other side, but I say 'tried' because to succeed would be a transformation beyond the powers of any individual or small group. Yet this is why I now look beyond Cambridge English: beyond that remarkable but characteristic innovation which settled to self-definition in an important privileged institution. What I believe is beginning to happen, in English studies and in other important parts of the culture, is the first stage of a new project of transformation: taking what has been learned in necessarily difficult work on to testing encounters with all those men and women who have only ever intermittently and incompletely been addressed: going to learn as well as to teach, within a now dangerous unevenness of literacy and learning which both directly and in all its indirect consequences is radically dislocating what had been assumed, in both literature and education, to be stable norms; a dislocation that is beginning to reach, harshly but instructively, into the old privileged places.

This new work is happening mainly on the periphery of the old systems; in some of the new universities, in several polytechnics, in the Open University, and in many practical initiatives beyond the settled institutions. It is also happening, thankfully, in some Cambridge colleges. But then that was how English studies, in their earliest phase, began. The oldest walls were the last to have gates. It is tempting to suppose that this history will repeat itself, or that in any case the remarkable international development of these new kinds of work—in several countries now well ahead of us—will eventually be heard about, by someone on a visit, who will come back with the good safe news.

But neither of these possibilities is the main point. When the perspective really alters, the work can be done anywhere, accepting and confronting its difficulties with the established authorities. This is clearer if we remember that at the most important level we are not talking only about courses and syllabuses. We are talking also, and primarily—as for a while Cambridge English did—about an intense crisis of culture and society: a crisis diversely defined and diversely met but in any case much more than an academic problem.

Be practical, we are told; think of the limits of what we can do. Yet in its own ways Cambridge English, especially through Richards and Leavis, recognized the central practicality which is often now forgotten: that the object of the course is not to reproduce its instructors, by imparting the habits that made them instructors. Most of those who take it go on to very different work, in which different kinds of active knowledge and skills, new and much more severe tests of perception and value, are the real practicalities. They should never have to contrast the soundest academic instruction with a world of more pressing real choices. Still in English studies, and in its convergences with other humanities and human sciences, there is so much active knowledge, so many active skills, which are very valuable in themselves and which really can connect with a world of practice and choice and struggle. It is to that vigorous connection—disturbing and yet profoundly encouraging both inside institutions and courses and beyond them—that I now pay my respects and look forward.

5

Region and Class
in the Novel

I am not sure when certain novels, or kinds of novel, began to be called 'regional'. My estimate is that the distinction began to be significant only in the late nineteenth century, and to be confident only in the twentieth century. At first sight it seems a simple distinction; it indicates a novel 'set in' or 'about' such regions as the Lake District or South Devon or mid-Wales. But then as distinct from what? There are three possible answers, each ideologically significant. First, that certain places are 'regions', with a recognized local or provincial character, while certain other places are not. Second, that certain novels are 'regional' in the sense that they tell us primarily, or solely, about such places and the life lived in them, rather than about any more general life. Third, that one kind of novel is 'regional' because it is 'about' or 'set in' some specific social life, as distinct from novels which address broader and more permanent kinds of human experience.

We can look more closely at each of these answers. The first has direct political significance. A 'region' was once a realm or kingdom or country, in the sense of *regere* = to rule, but it was also, with the characteristic political ambiguity of such divisions of the earth, a specific part of a larger ruled area: a diocese, a district, a bounded tract, in the sense of *regere* = to direct. The latter sense became common in English from the sixteenth century in church government, though the former, more absolute, sense persisted in natural and metaphorical descriptions. It was then obviously as a function of increasingly centralized states, with a newly formalized centralization of government and administration continuously 'delegating' and 'devolving' limited kinds of authority, that 'region' came to take on its modern meaning of 'a subordinate area', a sense which is of course compatible with recognition of its now 'local'—'regional'—characteristics.

And then what is striking, in matters of cultural description, is the steady discrimination of certain regions as in this limited sense 'regional', which can only hold if certain other regions are not seen in this way. This is in its turn a function of cultural centralization; a modern form of the 'city-country' discrimination. It is closely connected with the distinction between 'metropolitan' and 'provincial' culture, which became significant from the eighteenth century. Yet this is no longer a distinction of areas and kinds of life; it is what is politely called a value-judgement but more accurately an expression of centralized cultural dominance.

One entertaining form of this cultural description is the expression 'Home Counties' derived from the assize circuit—the 'Home Circuit'—centred on London, and taking on wider significance in the nineteenth century. The point can be tested by asking whether a novel 'set in' or 'about' the Home Counties, or 'set in' or 'about' London or some district of London—Chelsea, Hampstead, or Bloomsbury—would be described as 'regional' in a way comparable to descriptions of similar novels 'set in' or 'about' the Lake District or South Devon or mid-Wales—or, shall we say, Dorset or 'Wessex'? At this level, the description is plainly ideological. The life and people of certain favoured regions are seen as essentially general, even perhaps normal, while the life and people of certain other regions, however interestingly and affectionately presented, are, well, regional.

The second possible answer is obviously, in many mouths, a mere variant of this, and because less explicit more pretentious. Experience is not, *a priori*, more general or more significant because it occurs in London or Paris or New York rather than in Gwynedd or the Carse of Gowrie or Anatolia. Yet, at a different level, there is a real point here: a distinction which, as we shall see, is important also in considerations about 'class' in fiction. For there is indeed a kind of novel which is not only set in its own place but set in it as if there were no others. As a matter of fact this is at least as likely to be true of a New York or California or Home Counties novel as of the more readily perceived type, in which what happens in, say, the Lake District (compare the novels of Constance Holm) is seen as happening, even in the twentieth century, as if this were indeed an essentially self-subsistent life, which in none of its major characteristics is influenced or determined by social relations extending beyond it and penetrating into it. To be sure, the most important cases of this kind are particular types of late-bourgeois fiction—the *rentier* novel, the corporation novel, the university novel—in which absorption in the details of an essentially local life depends, ultimately, on not seeing its relations with a more general life: the work which is at the source of the rentier income; the market and power relations which are the true substance of the corporation's internal operations and manoeuvres; the wider processes of learning and resources and access which constitute a particular kind of university.

Yet that there is a form of encapsulation which is distinctly 'regional' cannot be doubted. It is indeed a popular form. Much twentieth-century rural fiction has this fly-in-amber quality. Its essential strategy is one of showing a warm and charming, or natural and even passionate, life, internally directed by its own rhythms, as if rural Britain, even in its most remote and 'unspoiled' parts, had not been shot through and through by a dominant urban industrial economy. Or, as a variant of this, the 'region' is so established, in autonomous ways, that pressures on it can be seen as wholly external: that other life against this region.

I suppose I am particularly conscious of this because I can see that it catches up certain actual social processes; much of the pressure has indeed been that way. But the truly regional novel, in this limiting sense, has initially so isolated its region, and thus projected it as internally whole—'organic'—that it is unable to recognize the complex internal processes, including internal divisions and conflicts, which factually connect with those wider pressures. I know that I wrote *Border Country* seven times to find that alternative form in which these internal processes and divisions have their real weight, and in *The Fight for Manod* I found that form very consciously and explicitly, though it is still, deliberately, a novel about a particular region. To put the matter more generally, the fiction in which to explore and clarify the problems of 'regionalism' is, of course, preeminently Hardy's. Some metropolitan idiots still think of Hardy as a regional novelist because he wrote about Wessex—that strange, particular place—rather than about London or the Home Counties. But at a more serious level, the distinction is very clear inside Hardy's work, as between, on the one hand, *Under the Greenwood*

Tree and even *Far From the Madding Crowd*, which can be seen as regional in an encapsulating and enclosing sense, and *The Wood-landers* or *Tess of the D'Urbervilles*, which are set even more deeply in their region but which are not in any limiting sense 'regional': what happens in them, internally and externally—those two abstractions in a connected process—involves a very wide and complex, a fully extended and extensive, set of relationships.

The third answer, at its only serious level, can be connected with this point. At its trivial conventional level it is merely a late-bourgeois prejudice: that novels are not 'about' or 'set in' kinds of social life; novels are about people—individuals—living sexually, spiritually, and above all privately. The very idea of a novel which recognizes a wider social life is pushed away. Indeed it is lucky—though luck now is ambiguous—if it is not put on a different shelf as Sociology. Yet at the same time, not in those late-bourgeois terms but more generally, we do have to distinguish one reasonable sense of regionalism in fiction: a sense which indicates that a novel is indeed more about a region or a way of life than about those people in relationships who inhabit or constitute it.

It is not a matter of simple categorization. The question of people in relationships—their degree of realization, individuation, space and time for development—is of course historically and socially variable, and the only relevant distinctions are in turn historical and social. The late-bourgeois isolation of private individuals, whose lives can be closely and intimately explored as if there were no wider social life, is evidently dependent on the social existence of individuals in whom power or money has created the possibility of *practical* distancing or displacement. In other communities and classes there is no such firm distancing or displacement, but of course it can then happen that a novel so concentrates on the most general features that it is unable to recognize—a recognition involving the simultaneous existence of real pressures and some space—the individual people who inescapably embody and enact these general features. More significantly it can fail to recognize those real areas of experience and relationship which, while they must coexist with and are usually influenced or are at times determined by the most general and common situations and processses, are still not reducible to the most general and common terms: for example, sexual and spiritual experiences (to retain these conventional descriptions), which are not only or 'merely' functions of the social situation. 'Regional' is not the most obvious word for those many novels which effect such reductions, but the factor of subordination of certain kinds of experience to the most general 'way of life' is common between certain directly regional types and more recognizable 'documentary' or in a genuinely specifying sense 'sociological' novels.

It is at this point that we can make a useful transition from the concept of 'region' to the concept of 'class' in fiction. It is particularly relevant to the idea of 'the working-class novel'. There are, evidently, uses of this description which are strictly comparable with uses of the 'regional' description: assigning certain novels to a deliberately limited area; indicating their limited status by this kind of 'narrowness' or by their limiting priority of 'social' over 'general human' experience. On the other hand, yet in some overlapping ways, such novels have been valued in the labour and socialist movements, just because they declare their identity in such ways. The undoubted neglect of majority working experience, and of the majority of working-class people, within the bourgeois fictional tradition, seems to justify the simple counter-emphasis. A whole class, like whole regions, can be seen as neglected. The implication of its marginality or, as often, its inferiority of status or interest, is rejected by deliberate selection and emphasis. A programme in defence of working-class fiction is then proposed in terms which in effect accept elements of the 'regional' definition, but with some of its values transposed.

The issue has again to be considered historically. The 'working-class novel', in the broadest sense of fiction which includes substantial elements of working-class experience, has to be seen as from the beginning different in kind from the regional novel. Thus the earliest novels of this type—the English industrial novels of the 1840s—were not written from within these class regions. On the contrary they were written by visitors to them, by sympathetic observers, or by people with some special though still external mode of access. This is very unlike the regional novel, which is from the beginning characteristically written by natives. It is a major fact of nineteenth-century cultural history that the many talented working-class writers did not, with only the occasional exception, include novelists. This had primarily to do with the available *forms* of the novel, centred predominantly on problems of the inheritance of property and of propertied marriage, and beyond these on relatively exotic adventure and romance. These offered few points of entry for working-class writers, unless they left their class and pursued individual careers through conventional themes. Where most working-class writers turned, instead, was (apart from essays, pamphlets, and journalism, directly related to class causes) to autobiography and memoirs, or to popular verse.

However, one paradoxical effect of the social base of the first industrial novelists was that *class relations* were at issue from the beginning. Through all the observable ideological manoeuvres and shifts, Elizabeth Gaskell, Dickens, Kingsley, Disraeli, George Eliot and others were continuously and intensely concerned with the active relations between as well as within classes. A problem in the definition of 'class' is then especially relevant. A class can indeed be seen as a region: a social area inhabited by people of a certain kind, living in certain ways. That is indeed its ordinary descriptive sense. But a Marxist sense of class, while indeed and inevitably recognizing social regions of this kind, carries the inescapable and finally constitutive sense of class as a formation of social relationships within a whole social order, and thus of alternative and typically conflicting (in any case inevitably *relating*) formations.

Thus to see a class on its own, however closely and intimately, is subject to the same limitations as seeing a region on its own, and then to some further limitations in that certain of the crucial elements of class—that it is formed in and by certain definite relations with other classes—may then be missed altogether. We can find examples of this in the late nineteenth-century 'Cockney School' of fiction, with some precedents in Gissing, where much of the real life of the East End of London is effectively written, but characteristically in isolating—and then often in externally 'colourful' or 'melodramatic'— ways. For one of the essential constituents of East End life was the existence—pressing and exploiting but of course by definition not locally and immediately visible—of the *West End*. Without that relation, the most vigorous depiction of specific localities and characters lacks a decisive dimension.

This is relatively easy to see, theoretically, but that is not—as in structuralist analysis—the end of the matter. For what is really in question is practice, and the conditions of practice. These can be observed, in their actual and complex development, in the twentieth century.

In England there are the very different examples of Tressell and D. H. Lawrence. What is distinctive about Tressell is that *The Ragged-Trousered Philanthropists* is founded, from the beginning, on a view of class *relations*. All his observations and fictionalizations of working-class life are even determined by that, to the extent of the deliberate adoption of caricatured and rhetorical modes. In one sense this connects with the older mode of the sympathetic observer—and the link with Dickens is clear—but the observational mood has changed. This is a participating and exposed observer, seeking transformation rather than reconciliation.

Yet the element of externality persists, as can be seen by the strictly literary contrast with Lawrence, who has turned out to be typical of at least two generations of 'working-class writers' in the specific conditions of his practice. For Lawrence was *born into* at once a working-class family and a densely settled locality (in both respects, it seems, unlike Tressell/Noonan). 'Working-class life' is then from the beginning mediated by the experiences of family and locality, with their particular and powerful immediacies. Thus Lawrence is never in any danger of writing a reductive novel about working-class life, since what first materialized was not the class but family, neighbours, friends, places. Of course he eventually saw some of the true class relations, but significantly only when he was already moving away from them—as in *The Rainbow* and *Women in Love*. And by that time he was already primarily interested—from a determination in the conditions of his practice quite as much as from his personal and ideological predilections—in individuals who were moving out and away from their origins. Thus, in his later fiction, both the working-class and the general complex of class relationships are displaced: the former to childhood and adolescent experience, without significant attention to the continuing conditions of adult working-class life; the latter, almost wholly, to generalities of an ideological kind, often fictionalized by a kind of back-formation, in ideologically 'representative' figures such as Gerald Crich.

This is an analysis, not a criticism. These particular conditions of practice have continued to be powerfully determining, and especially in the matter of fictional form. Thus the direct inheritance from Lawrence is a series of fictions of escape and flight, or at best of retrospect. Yet much of this is still represented as 'working-class fiction' *tout court*.

Yet some other moves were possible, within these conditions. They are well exemplified in the Welsh industrial novel. This began with the work of Thomas Keating (see *The Flower of the Dark*, 1917), but with all the marks of the nineteenth-century difficulties. Keating was a working miner who later became a journalist. His novels include some of the finest direct descriptions of colliery work that we have, but in *The Flower of the Dark* these are inserted in, and in effect overwhelmed by, a bourgeois romance of a familiar nineteenth-century kind. It was really not until the 1930s that the best form of the 'working-class family' novel was found, in Gwyn Jones's *Times Like These* (1936). This is remarkably close and convincing, and it is free of the (largely ideological) distances between the class and the particular family which disfigure Lawrence. On the other hand, as Gwyn Jones came to recognize, the limitation to a single family has a certain effect of closure, even where the action is that under economic pressures the family is broken up and dispersed. However, that this general social action can be shown, as again and very powerfully in T. Rowland Hughes's *Chwalfa* (1946), is a significant advance on the fiction of individual (an individual writer's) escape or flight.

In the 1930s there are two Welsh examples of quite different directions, each attempting to move beyond the class as (family and locality) region. There is the work of Jack Jones, socially panoramic as in *Rhondda Roundabout* (1934), family-based but through generations and therefore through history as in *Black Parade* (1935). There is also the world of Lewis Jones, in *Cwmardy* (1937) and *We Live* (1939), again family-based but with the difference that the class element and indeed the class struggles now have explicit presence in the experience of the Miners' Federation and the Communist Party. It is significant that each of these new directions was found by an adult working-class writer, as distinct from writers who had been born in the working class but had moved out of it.

The common view of these Welsh novels as regional—indeed as doubly regional Welsh and working-class—is to a large extent simple prejudice. Yet there are still basic obstacles, even in these new forms, to any full realization of class relations. To any actual working class, within its locality, other classes are very selectively and often quite misleadingly represented. The local class enemy is usually the manager, or more broadly the local petty bourgeoisie. The dominant bourgeoisie is less visible and indeed is often, at this stage of capitalist development, physically absent. Thus class relations materialize either in very local (internal or working-class and petty-bourgeois relations) or in very general and fully ideological ways. The short-cut to full class relations via the political party, as in Lewis Jones, thus has its (in factual terms) substantial as well as local historical and political difficulties. Even with the fine perspectives of history, as in *Black Parade*, the very strength of class and locality cuts off certain moving forces in its very constitution, because they are distant and alien, in the fiction as often in the fact. It is ironic that the best historical fiction about the Welsh working class has been written (though with its own kinds of fault and limitation) by a sympathetic outside observer, who could *read* as well as experience the history: Alexander Cordell (see *The Rape of the Fair Country*, 1959). The form does much, but with still significant and weakening connections to the historical romance. The way in which the form avoids some of the local difficulties as well as some of the hardest local recognitions can be seen in a comparison with the most important novel of this whole phase, Gwyn Thomas's *All Things Betray Thee* (1949), which significantly is centrally concerned with the problems of writing—speaking, singing—this complex experience: the clear objective reality as subjectively—but by a collective subject—experienced.

Given the generations of neglect, there is more than enough room for hundreds of working-class novels which are still, in effect, regional novels: of a district, of an industry, of an enclosed class. But the central creative problem is still that of finding forms for a working-class fiction of fully developed class relations. The problem has in some ways become more objectively difficult. Further tendencies in monopoly capitalism have removed to an even greater distance the decisive individuals and functions and institutions by which most working-class life is formed. To realize such relations substantially—as distinct from the alternative modes of projection and extrapolation, as characteristically now in science fiction—is then especially difficult. Changes inside the working class, in types of community and in both general and individual mobility, provide both problems and opportunities. It is becoming virtually impossible, wherever the writer stands, to write serious enclosed fiction, except in retrospective and residual modes. Thus just as the limited 'regional' novel is passing out of serious consideration and possibility, in advanced capitalist societies (though it is still being effectively written in post-colonial and intermediate societies), so the limited 'working-class' novel shows its limits ever more clearly.

But then there is still great need for those works, rooted in region or in class, which can at once achieve that close living substance (in marked contrast to what is now happening, through etiolation, in metropolitan and international bourgeois fiction) and yet seek the substance of those finer-drawn, often occluded, relations and relationships which in their pressures and interventions at once challenge, threaten, change and yet, in the intricacies of history, contribute to the formation of that class or region in self-realization and in struggle, including especially new forms of self-realization and struggle.

The formal and technical problems, for the novelist, are very severe, but if we are looking for a direction—and not to be doing so, in the present state of fiction, is incomprehensible—this is our best road, or, more probably, our best set of connecting paths. Historically, in any case, regions and classes are only fully constituted when they fully declare themselves. There is still much for novelists to contribute to those decisive declarations.

The Ragged-Arsed
Philanthropists

We are meeting today to celebrate the writing of *The Ragged-Arsed Philanthropists*. For three reasons. First, because the composition of that quarter of a million words by a signwriter and decorator, often working up to a 56½ hour week, remains extraordinarily impressive. Second, because after its all too probable initial rejection, it made its way, first to what is often called the 'abridged' but is more properly the 'reduced' edition, and then, largely through the sustained and devoted work of Fred Ball, who I am pleased to see here today, came through very much in its original terms. And third, because we can now see it in the context of a growing body of working-class and socialist writing, which at once is a body of achievement and sets quite new problems of analysis and context.

But first, the celebration, and you will notice that I took the title which, it's a fair guess, would have been preferred if there hadn't been the restrictions which Tressell mentioned in his short preface, on what he dared to write within the conventions of the time while still giving a faithful representation of the language of working people. I have a sore point about the title because I was prevented, for many years, from reading this extraordinary book in its then reduced edition, because I took it, from knowledge of its title alone, to be one of those maudlin Victorian tracts which showed that it didn't matter how poor you were, you could always help others, and I'd assumed—I suppose I shouldn't have—that it would be a sentimental tale of people down on their luck who were helping others, which was one of the forms of evasion of social and moral questions which were standard in Victorian writing addressed to working people.

The savage irony of the title could never have been missed if the true sense of what was being talked about—'The Ragged-*Arsed*'—

was there and explicit. We shouldn't, of course, now, change what Tressell had to call it, but it is useful for a moment to think of the difference because it raises the first of the problems. One of the problems all through has been whether working people are a proper subject for fiction. You have to get some historical perspective on this, and it's comforting in one way to realize that, as late as the 1830s, middle-class people were still wondering whether they were interesting enough to have novels written about them. Still in the 1830s, the preferred material of the novel was either something wholly exotic, in the literal sense of being about adventures in other parts of the world, or about the aristocracy—the loves and romances of the aristocracy. And this, oddly, though it is the way a culture often works, was still dominant at least a century after important middle-class fiction had begun to be written. How to believe, at that time, that there was important material in the lives of people who spent much of their time in work, which was as true of that new small bourgeoisie as it was later true of the wage-earning class who were the next fictional stage—that was the question. Would *work* be interesting enough, would *shops* (as, a century later, Virgina Woolf was still wondering) be part of significant life? Eventually, of course, some of the major classics of the Victorian novel were made out of the daily substance of that kind of middle-class life, though still with older and residual preoccupations about the inheritance of property, about advantageous marriage, and so on. That new life broke through, and if we look back at what we are increasingly discovering, the number of articulate, literate, energetic, highly intelligent working men and women—all through, but we know most about them from the mid-eighteenth century—the astonishing thing is that this different area of society didn't get written about earlier, and particularly in the novel, which was then the most widely distributed popular form. In general it didn't, although we are still discovering a few isolated and largely forgotten working-class novels from the nineteenth century, just as there has been a steady discovery of what preceeded them, a large body of working-class verse from the mid-eighteenth century, and again (and these may be, in the end, almost innumerable) working-class autobiographies, direct stories of their own lives by working men and women.

We can now see that autobiography was the more accessible form, because there was a basic lack of fit between the shape of working-class lives and the inherited forms of the novel. This was true even of middle-class lives because even there, and to a much greater extent in the working-class, the inheritance plot and the marital property-settlement, which between them furnished eighty to ninety per cent of the basic plot structures of the nineteenth-century novel, were largely irrelevant. So there was a certain nervousness about the novel. If the novel had to be about things like that, then any other kind of material had, so to say, to be inserted, apologised for, transmuted in some way. The autobiography was a more directly accessible form, but itself with problems. On the one hand, there was a tradition, very available to the organised working class of the nineteenth century, of religious witness, especially in the Nonconformist churches in which somebody described his experience to justify his beliefs. This passed directly into certain kinds of political writing, the tract and the pamphlet, but also stayed at the level of autobiography as in Samuel Bamford. This is writing which depends on the tradition of witness—'I am like this because I have lived like this', and then in the description of 'living like this' comes a condition which is not only personal but that of a whole class, a whole people.

But there is another less favourable precedent for autobiography, evident in all too many nineteenth and, of course, twentieth-century examples of the story of the man who has risen out of, or through, his class, who could use the autobiography precisely to show that he was an *exceptional* person. This produced that structure which persists in a lot of working-class writing of every kind, in which working-class conditions are the early chapters—'My Life and *Early Hard Times*'—as a preparation for the climb-out to the Peerage, the Membership of Parliament, the leadership of one of the great Unions, Chairman of one of the great Companies. And these things happened.

The tone of some of the worst examples is extraordinarily odious but, on the other hand, even given what we now know about how many working people were writing, they were all likely to be—in the human sense, not in the false sense of social privilege or honour—exceptional people. They would be exceptionally stubborn and persistent. They would have exceptional energy and often exceptional gifts. And for these different reasons the form of the autobiography, for a very long time, absorbed the translation into writing of working-class experience, instead of the novel. Moreover, there

might be a further reason, in the hardest times, in the simple conviction that the truth had to be told, and truth, within a positivist
culture, seemed to belong to documents rather than to what was called 'fiction', although both, really, are matters of *writing*, and truth
is only rarely determined by those generic choices.

So, the importance of Tressell's work lies not only in the fact that
he broke through to the novel but that he broke through to it in spite
of these real difficulties. In his striking, original way, he broke with
precisely the inherited assumptions of what it was to write a novel,
and to write a good, competent novel: assumptions which were very
strong at those key points where he was engaging his own real
material.

There are three ways, when you come to think of it, of writing
about working-class lives. The dominant one throughout has been
the novel centred on the working-class *family*, for which there is
much formal precedent. For it is only a step, usually a conscious
step, from the kind of family novel through generations of middle-
class life, which was written over and over again in the nineteenth
century, to the novel of working-class life in which the family is
presented, lived with, lived through, with more general conditions
arising naturally as the circumstances of that family, or with some of
the great crises of working-class experience happening to that family,
often disrupting it. There are some major examples in Welsh
working-class writing including those in Welsh like that remarkable
novel by T. Rowland Hughes, *Chwalfa*, about the North Wales
quarrymen, or the novel about mining life like Gwyn Jones's *Times
like These* where the writing is composed around the very close family whom you get to know close up as people. Thus a familiar fictional transition happens at once, and yet this is a family living under
pressure and usually hitting crises. Again and again the crisis of this
kind of novel is the major strike, typically those of the appropriate
period, the strike of 1926.

Then there is the attempt to move beyond the controlling fictional
form of the family, in that difficult transition, even at times ambiguity, between working people and working class. For the class is a matter of consciousness, the class is a matter of organization, the class is
a social reality and yet at the same time it is not necessarily a social
reality which exists in anything like the way in which a family does.
To speak of a working-class family can be simply descriptive. To

speak of the working *class*, that is different; although there is some overlap. Because what is then being looked at is the life of people defined not only by the kinds of work they do or by the fact that they have families and the ordinary crises of life, but by the fact that they have come to see something common in their situation which they call class, which is either their explicit organization—and it's usually easier to do at those very articulate and organized moments, hence the popularity of the strike, the dispute, as ways of showing them as a class operating collectively—but which is there in another sense, yet often ambiguously or with great difficulty, often being the very question which people are asking or which some inside the class are asking other members of the class who may refuse the description which is being offered to them. No such condition is as physically available as a family. So, if we're talking about working-class crises in the strictest sense there's this new problem in fiction which didn't touch middle-class writers in the same way, since their dominant consciousness was from the beginning posited on the notion of individuals and their immediate primary relationships. What the most engaged working-class writers had to face was the new problem of showing whole, determining social relationships.

It is at this point that a lot of recent argument has gone round and round and at times got stuck. To show whole, determining social relationships requires a new perspective, and this perspective is best known in its more generalized and abstract forms. Moreover, the best known of these forms is socialism, and once you arrive at that, quite apart from the familiar difficulties, you soon get told that if it is a novel about socialism it is about something which is not manageable in fiction at all. This is the familiar doctrine of orthodox criticism, which attempts an *a priori* rejection of ideas and movements as the materials of imaginative writing (even after *War and Peace* and *The Devils*). But then the interesting thing about Tressell is that he did write about a wage-earning family; he did write about its relation to a class and to the consciousness of the class; and he did this not only positively, but also in terms of its absence, yet the absence defining it in another way, the absence of that consciousness in a sense defining the question.

The three kinds I've described—the family novel, the family novel partly extended to a class, and the novel written from a conscious class perspective—do not easily overlap or integrate, because the work is set on different bearings from the beginning according to which of those emphases the writer is most interested in. Yet if you look in Tressell's preface you see, first, 'my intention was to present in the form of an interesting story, a faithful picture of working-class life'. This indicates a realist version of extending the family novel, its extension to many working people.

Then you get: 'I designed to show the conditions resulting from poverty and unemployment and to expose the futility of the measures taken to deal with them'. He is moving rapidly now to the sense of a new perspective, and he adds: 'and to indicate the only real remedy which I take to be Socialism'. He was then worried because, in received terms, he was writing not a treatise or essay, but a novel. So he went on: 'My main object was to write a readable story full of human interest and based on the happenings of everyday life, the subject of Socialism being treated incidentally'. This is pulling back from what he had earlier said, but of course it is just where the problem is, and not only for him but for many others. It is a problem of writing, but as such, in its fullest sense, it is also a problem of social and historical consciousness. This requires some more general consideration.

If you look at the history of working-class writing, you find, as indeed you find in more directly political manifestations, that there does seem to be a problem of correlation (which some of us for theoretical reasons used to be rather unwilling to acknowledge) between working-class life in its simplest descriptive sense, that of wage-earning, primarily manual workers, and the degree of combination or concentration which is usually a factor of the nature of their labour process. And if this is so, it follows that you cannot begin to discuss the problems of working-class writers without defining—here or there—what kind of working class.

If you go back to the nineteenth-century middle-class novelists who wrote about industrial life and who included often sympathetic, sometimes distorted but very responsive material from their observation of working-class life, you will find them looking first at the textile mills, where a new form of social organization was visibly and dramatically present, so that instead of the old conditions of scattered hand-work where the workers might never be more than twos or threes, or a dozen or twenty at most, or would even still be working in homes inside the family, suddenly there was this new, vast social innovation of hundreds of workers under the same roof. This life in and around the textile mills accounts for more than three-quarters, I would say, of that early writing which acknowledged the existence of working people. They were the visible minority in what was of course, in general, the great majority of wage-earning people in the culture and society that was producing this writing.

And then if you go on, you find that there are kinds of labour process which need a certain significant kind of close, even closed, community. And you find also that it is these communities which have been most prolific over a run of time, to our own day, in producing working-class novels: the mining areas, whether the coal-mining areas or the quarries; or the tailoring sweatshops; or the shipyards or the docks: places where you are simultaneously a working man or woman, a member of a working-class family in the simple, descriptive sense, but also a member of a working-class community, often almost wholly a working-class community like a mining village or a dockside urban district or a shipbuilding area or a textile town. Moreover, these communities exist in a particular part of the country, Welsh or Geordie or Cockney or Clydeside, and because of this the whole spectrum of social relations comes at once in an integrated form. You only have to step outside in the street to be in a working class community, and then within that very intense, often one-track community, the problem of class, which would in more mixed communities be subject to much more complex interpretation, arrives enmeshed with what is also your identity as the people of that place and the people of that region, for you belong simultaneously, over the whole range.

There is then a positive correlation, of which can there be no doubt whatever, between places of that kind and the development of working-class political ideas. Still any political map of the country will show you that it is in the places where such labour processes created working-class communities of that kind that the great institutions of the labour movement were built and are still, after so many changes, most evident. Or take another example which I usually irritate my friends by mentioning. The General Strike of 1926 was a high-point of working-class self-organization and protest. It was strong in many places and indeed present and active in most. But look also at that less convenient memory of 1926: at that organization for strike-breaking against the organized working class: the

OMS, the Organisation for the Maintenance of Supplies, one of those things we've half-forgotten although we may see its like again. Look where that was recruited. It was not, as some of the books tell you, all undergraduates and their debutante friends. It really was not.

In certain parts of the country, where the problems of social self-definition, of class-consciousness in that hard, arresting, challenging form, are in fact quite different, there was significant recruiting of poor men against what was objectively their own class. For those were the mixed communities where the labour processes do not deliver with them a community which gives you a common identity from the beginning; where you can be simultaneously a local patriot, a loyal member of the working class, a good neighbour, a good member of the family; it is all one, or nearly one. Get to a mixed community, get to where people are living next door to each other but are not necessarily in the same kind of work, get to where there are radical differences of social situation and position right inside the community, and you have a different basic sense of what a community is. It is then no surprise at all that most of the positive working-class novels have been written from inside the self-conscious and confident working-class communities. What is a surprise is that the first socialist working-class novel in English was written in the other kind of place: in a community which did not, so to say, deliver class consciousness, but actually obstructed and confused it. And then of course we see what we should have seen before: that this is the key to *The Ragged-Arsed Philanthropists*. It is this that determines much of the actual strategy and tone of the book. The novel is as it is because what Tressell is writing about is a place which is not at all like those archetypal working-class communities. It is not a place where, although there are local representatives of the employing class such as the local managers, foremen and so on and sometimes, in those stages, even a few proprietors, the dominant definition of 'local people' is a working class already organized by a single or one major labour process. In those close communities it is all positive, everybody is working class. This gives a marvellous integrity to the novels, but where is anyone else? You're fighting against something which you call the system, but actualizing it inside this warm community life is often very difficult, except in arguments among yourselves. In the other sort of community—as Hastings,

Mugsborough, was and is—with a few mixed trades, with people working for the corporation, people working in the public utilities, people working on the railway and on the buses, in shops and hotels, and of course the building craftsmen, tradesmen, labourers, it feels very different. There is no common over-riding loyalty proceeding from the conditions of the mining village or dockyard street— nothing like that. There is then a problem of self-perception among working men from the beginning. And beyond that, as you can see in the character of most of the trades, you have not major production for a general market but precisely, in majority, service jobs for a mixed community in which the ultimate employers are people in a different social situation, on whom you depend -for getting any custom and trade at all. Moreover the intermediaries, typically the small employers, the local shop-owners, building-firm owners, or even the Council that Tressell so memorably shows, these are not the big capitalist employers, who by that stage of the early twentieth century in Britain as a whole were the dominant people, and against them in those other areas self-conscious movements were formed and forming, and although it was never unified, a certain collectivity was given.

What Tressell faced in Mugsborough was this very different situation, in some ways a much harder situation. People from those relatively uniform, working-class communities often speak with a quite unreasonable kind of patronage about working-class organizations in less developed or more backward parts of the society. They often fail to realize how much of their own consciousness comes wrapped in the much more available facts of neighbourhood, workplace and local loyalty. Once you get into the mixed community, and in particular one which is relying on people bringing money in from outside as tourists or residents, then the argument about trade, about wages, about whom you are dependent on, about how you should conduct yourself as a working man, where your money comes from, what the future of the country has to be, what makes common sense—that is transformed. To argue the socialist case in that kind of community is a much harder job. Yet the remarkable fact remains that this first successful working-class novel was generated in those circumstances, and not from inside the working class in the more settled and conscious communities.

Of course this has an effect on its strategies. I think we have to say two things at once about Tressell's position as a writer: two things at once (there's no way of saying it, but although I say them one after the other they are both aspects of a single statement). One, that he was writing his novel while he was a worker fully engaged in his own work. It is, in that sense, authentically a novel from inside the working class, very different from many examples before and after it. The working-class situation is entirely contemporary with the writing, not from an earlier time, a memory or a reconstruction. It is directly from a man who comes home from his job, writes, goes back to his job, writes, all under pressure. But second, *and at the same time*, he is for quite evident reasons, at some level of his mind—and it's very important to him—an outsider, a man in certain respects very conscious of *difference*. I mean not only that he comes from elsewhere, with his Liverpool and Irish connections; that he'd been in South Africa, in a much more complex, harder-fought, colonial culture; that he'd come back and eventually ended in a seaside resort where the very fact that he'd travelled that much, that he'd seen that much of the world, gave him, from the beginning, a different perspective. I mean also what it was very important to know, as the biography was eventually assembled, that this was, in many ways, a very literate man; that his command of languages was very wide; that he was a man capable of sustained reading and of assessing statistics. And then there was this double situation, that he was coming home day by day, from hard slog to earn his bread, doing his job and yet with a mind which had reached a different perspective, having read and having seen other parts of the world. So he knew that a familiar kind of deference, an acceptance of the formula that to live you have to get favour from the ones with money or custom that offer it, wasn't an immutable law of life but a specific social condition. He also knew from his reading that the arguments so proudly produced by supposedly educated people that the economic situation was inevitably like this were usually quite shallow, and that many of those who looked down on labouring men were themselves very ignorant in terms of conventional education and knowledge.

Then, from this double vision, the bitter irony of the title—Ragged-Arsed and Philanthropist—is the best way of reminding us that the book has advantages which the most positive, realist novels from inside working-class communities don't usually have. It also (inevitably because it has other things to do) has less of the sustained substance of that other fiction at its best. Actually, it is very difficult to assess the proportions of the different modes. In actual length most of the book does after all follow individuals and families, follow them through various typical crises: of death, of seduction, of betrayal; of illness and accidents; and through and beyond these the affections of family life. In the other kind of working-class novel such feelings extend outwards, from kindness to neighbours to loyalty to mates to loyalty to the union to loyalty to socialism, without too many barriers being set up, because it's much the same feeling being a neighbour and defining yourself collectively as this kind of industrial and political person. Among the ragged-arsed inhabitants of that deliberately named Mugsborough, the structure of feeling is very different, and there is a bitterness which could only have been let out in any tolerable way by a man who was also earning his bread directly as a working man.

Indeed there are parts of this book which, taken on their own—which is quite wrong to do, but analytically you can hypothesize it—have such savage things to say about so many working-class people, about the general conditions of ignorance and misunderstanding and cruelty, that there is hardly a line between them and a certain kind of reactionary rendering of the working class and working people as irredeemably incapable of improving their conditions. Tressell's awareness of this is beautifully dramatized in Barrington's encounter with the renegade, who is able to say 'You have these wonderful ideas for the future of the class and for the future of society. I know these people. I know what they're like, I know how they think, and I know you're wasting your time'. This is the kind of position which becomes a problem again in a writer like Orwell, who typically did not include in his diaries or notebooks those working-class men and women he met who were well-read, articulate, politically conscious or active in some pursuit which is conventionally not assigned to the class. If, on the other hand, he met somebody who fitted a middle-class vision of the drunken or feckless or ignorant or helpless working man, down it went. When he wrote *The Road to Wigan Pier*, he sought out the lowest doss-house in town, even though he'd arrived with introductions from leaders of the Unemployed Workers' Movement and trade unionists and had stayed with educated working-class socialists. He then 'proved' that socialism is just a middle-class idea. Working-class people are either just not interested or they've got more common sense or they're good-natured, thoughtless, rather childish and at times drunken people—what he represented in *Nineteen Eighty-Four* as the Proles.

Now, something not too far from that is often very near the edge in Tressell, precisely because the whole inner tension of the book at once an entire and, at that level, almost involuntary commitment, which comes from going back day after day to that kind of exploiting job, and a special concern which quickly becomes anger, rage even, despair often, at the fact that people will not admit their common condition, that they will accept any phoney explanation or distraction, that they will listen to their actual exploiters and believe the most self-evident rubbish rather than admit the truth of their own lives. The rarest and most invigorating quality of Tressell is that he goes head down, head up at that kind of ignominy, which could only ever be challenged effectively, could indeed only ever be represented effectively, from inside It's been done repeatedly from outside, but then it always goes sour. In Tressell it is a fresh, clean anger. Moreover it is at once put into tension with what is *nevertheless*—and that word should be emphasized—an absolute belief that conditions can be changed, that they can be changed by this class, that what is described by others as a mere ideal is perfectly available and practicable, and that it really doesn't depend on the assumption, typically complained about, that people are more unselfish, more noble than they are.

The argument is precisely challenged at that point, for socialism is not really to do with that. It is to do with understanding social relations, understanding the system. If experience alone will not teach, then experience *and teaching* will teach. That kind of confidence is decisive, although it doesn't come easily. Great care is taken to show something very different from the easy ideas of bringing the truth, bringing the message, and being gratefully received by the suffering masses. On the contrary, we see Owen being beaten up, we see things which are like the reception of the nineteenth-century Russian populists who went out and told the peasants that they were poor and ignorant and that they'd come to educate them and who were sometimes lucky to escape the village alive. This is the whole experience of coming even with the truth to people already so hard-pressed that truth is a short-term question, if it's a question at all. In Tressell this happens from inside, and is seen both ways. But not as an evasion, for he includes—it is the most radical innovation in this work, often sitting uneasily with the other writing but there it is, extraordinarily successful—the two interventions which do what, to this day, the fiction text-books tell you you can't do. I mean the two teaching chapters, 'The Oblong' and 'The Great Oration'.

In 'The Oblong' you get a figurative demonstration of an analysis of the social order which leads to certain clear conclusions about it. It is given by a man to whom we've been introduced in a rounded, fictional way, for people whom we've got to know in rather more angry ways but nevertheless whom we know as people and as names. It is just done, it is not apologetically done. It's done *as* demonstration, characteristically in the form of a visual figure—Tressell as Noonan the signwriter. 'The Great Oration' is the inclusion, with remarkable courage as a writer, not only of a long speech about the new socialist order—a speech full of some difficult socialist positions of that time, through mainly a typical early-twentieth-century form of state socialism, with the notion of the industrial army. It is the inclusion of the full speech, and at the same time of the reactions and interactions. The chairman, the interrupters and the general scene reproduce just that consciousness which is resistant to sustained serious talk, and this is not for light relief; indeed it shows both the need and the problem of that kind of serious discourse. So there is this innovation of inserting (it would now be done more often in avant-garde fiction) levels of discourse which do not cancel each other, and both teaching and the problems of teaching are there. It is done because experience alone will not teach, as, in a way, it does or is supposed to do in the positive kind of working-class novel. You've seen people suffering; you've seen them suffering undeservedly; you say people should not live like this; let them—even, at times, let us—not live like this. That is what that kind of novel typically offers. And yet, reproducing itself from generation to generation, even with marginal improvements, often of a significant kind, that *general* condition persists. What Tressell has tackled is not just the pity of it, which recommends sympathy, which passes too easily into the notion that we could all live better and differently if we'd only make up our minds to. The book gets to that position, in the end, but it halts very deliberately along the way, to see what is really involved in making up your mind about it, setting your mind to it. It looks hard at the obstacles, the barriers, which are put up not only among those who have a lot to lose but among those who have everything to gain. That is the savage sense, and that's why we have to say *The Ragged-Arsed Philanthropists*, with its much harsher edge. That is what is being said: these are people whose own conditions ought to force them into consciousness, who are nevertheless engaged in the large-scale philanthropy of subsidizing people who either do not work at all, or work much less hard and for much more reward than the journeymen and labourers.

This hard, satiric tone goes back to a different tradition from that of the realist novel. It goes back, in quite an immediate sense, to Cobbett. In the early nineteenth century, that great representative figure of the common people of England said, harshly: 'I despise a poor man who is contented'. This rejects the arguments, usually of the rich, that you can be contented even if poor, or the other kind of argument that although poor in material goods, although lacking social status or respect, nevertheless we're good people. This harsher tone from Cobbett rejects that absolutely. He says, in effect: to be poor and contented is below the quality of man. To be deprived and cheated and yet still to be contented is below the quality of a man. It is to lack self-respect.

This is then generalized from an individual to a class. If a body of people are suffering conditions they ought not to suffer, conditions which are avoidable, and yet they somehow find reasons for contentment, or even acquiescence and co-operation with what is making them like that, then no kind words. An ultimate sympathy is there but its tone is harsh. As Owen thinks in his worst moments, the real enemy, the real oppressors, are the people who soak in the daily evidence of their condition and yet remain content; who displace their dissatisfaction onto other people; who refuse with extra-ordinary complacency any talk which would try to explain their condition. In the book as a whole, the conditions for sympathy are created and then cut across by something so sharp and challenging that it could only come from that double situation of the writer. inside and outside: inside the condition of the class, outside its consciousness.

We can then go back further, to quite a different tradition, to Bunyan. As you read in Tressell the description of the Mugsborough Organized Benevolence Society and those who were present, you can hear the tradition, a popular tradition, which gets printed in Bunyan but which is much older than him. 'Mayor Alderman presiding and among those present were Sir Graball D'Encloseland, Lady D'Encloseland, Lady Slumrent, Rev. Mr Bosher, Mrs Cheeseman, Mr Builder, Mr Grocer, Mrs Dairy, Mrs Butcher, Mrs Taylor, Mrs Bacon, Mrs Starvem....' and there follows about a quarter of a column of names of other charitable persons.

That is the Bunyan tactic of attaching at once the names of social positions and the names of moral qualities or their absence. It is an assembly of the respectable who are on their way to damnation. Or at least Bunyan could have said that. The great confidence of *that* popular and radical tradition was that the wicked of the world were on their way to hell, and that the virtuous Christian could name them by the names God should have given them and would give them when it came to judgement, while Christian himself had his own pilgrimage.

For a Socialist writer in the same tradition it is not so clear. There is historical optimism but it is less close than that kind of Christian perspective. You can say that Noonan-Tressell, like the other Socialists he described, a small minority among building workers—and other workers—belongs to a vanguard. It's a very honourable, heroic thing to be in the vanguard of a great cause. It's also, of course, a standing temptation to pride, that all around you is ignorance, wilful ignorance, an inability to understand, but you hold your place, you continue the work. It is for this reason that Tressell has always appealed especially to relatively isolated militants and questioning men. Pride either way: a justified pride, or at times that angry pride that controls isolation and depression. In Tressell the full justification comes through, not only because it is done from inside but because he sees so clearly, beyond the heroics and the anger, that such men are themselves going to be crushed down. When Owen starts coughing blood, and beyond the general condition there is this suffering but still clear-sighted man, we are shown that double condition of hero and victim, neither acknowledged by others, which is a true inner history of so long and so hard a cause.

Tressell needed, if only for that reason, the figure of Barrington, the wealthy young man who takes up labouring work in a kind of benevolence, to find out the conditions of working people, to experience them directly, yet in the end can withdraw from them, use his own money for the comfort of the Christmas presents, or, as in that episode near the end, go away and come back to finance the socialist van. That kind of wealthy young sympathizer, participator, has his own crisis of confidence, as he encounters not only the conditions but the ignorance and the refusals. Yet it is less bitter than Owen who is inside it, where the bitterness is not just that they won't see the light, which is an abstract way of putting the problem, but that if they go on being this stupid, what sort of world are my children going to grow up in? That's hard. That's not just saying: wait, for the time is coming when the campaign will succeed. It's saying: is there going to be a world for my kids, if people go on being this stupid? It's a hard question and it's put hard and it should be taken hard.

There is another question, finally, which must continually have occupied Tressell. It's a problem anyway for a man of his varied history, from Liverpool and then from South Africa, coming to a smallish southern English provincial town. It is the problem of the level of working-class literacy and its relation to working-class speech. I was very interested in that chapter in Fred Ball's book, about restoring the manuscript; about the inconsistencies of spelling, the problems of grammar, the problems of abbreviations, the general problems of the representation of working-class speech.

Now first there is no finer representation, anywhere in English writing, of a certain rough-edged, mocking, give-and-take conversation between workmen and mates. This humour, this edge, is one of the most remarkable achievements. But he was interested also in something else which relates to the wider theme. It was obviously a very sore point, to a man earning his living with his hands who knew himself to be a man of substantial intelligence and mental accomplishment, that the standard response to working men who talked about socialism or how the country should be run differently, was to say that they were ignorant. So he took great care with the Brigands—the people who ran the town council, the small employers, the Forty Thieves as I heard somebody in Hastings, when I was living here, say we still ought to call them—I make no comment on that—he took great care to show the Brigands as ignorant people. He uses all the devices of what I have called the orthography of the uneducated: all that torturing of the already tortured nature of English spelling, to indicate that somebody's pronunciation is not standard, not educated. This always leads to the most extraordinary contortions, since if you believe that English sounds are represented by English spelling, so that there is a standard from which some 'dialect' divergence can be identified by a spelling divergence, then you get into this curious situation in which it is really different in a novel for somebody to say 'I love you', spelled I LOVE YOU and to say 'I love you', spelled I LUV YER. But different in what sense? We are asked to take the first seriously, or at least to wait and see how it works out. The second is marked for a different response. What sort of emotion is that? 'I luv yer.' Probably very vulgar and inadequate. You are represented as feeling or thinking through your spelling, although of course you're not spelling anyway; the writer is spelling, you're just talking in the language of your own place.

Now, Tressell uses this for the Brigands to show that, although they are puffing themselves up, they are in fact ignorant people. But he uses it also in a kind of counterpoint between people who have got some sense and people who haven't. It's a very interesting differentiation, not in class terms but as a literary technique. Compare, for example, the way Owen and his family speak to each other, usually in standard orthography, and the way the men speak to each other at work, in ways carefully indicated by the distorted spelling.

There's a marvellous example in 'The Great Oration'.

' "And there's another thing I object to," said Crass, "and that's all this here talk about hignorance. Wot about all the money that's spent every year for heducation".' The one word I would especially bring to your attention, because it's symbolic of this whole larger problem, is 'Wot': 'Wot about all the money....' W O T. 'You should rather say,' Barrington replies, 'what about all the money that's wasted every year on education?' W H A T. Now since everyone knows that somebody who is represented in the text as saying W O T is ignorant, can we invite any native English speaker to pronounce the word spelled W H A T in a way that is not W O T? I mean, try it. In fact everyone says W O T, but this is a device for distinction between someone who knows what he is talking about, and for him you spell W H A T, and somebody who doesn't know what he's talking about, and for him you spell W O T.

This kind of contrast is entwined with the challenge of the book. It is part of a textual strategy which is not necessarily entirely conscious but which is so regular that it can't be accidental. It is in one sense repeating a standard prejudice of English middle-class writing, but within a broader strategy which is the whole point of the book. For he is saying that it is terrible for people to have to live like this when they are doing useful and good work, and could do more useful and better work in different circumstances. It is terrible to live like this, to be this vulnerable to the whims of others, to be this vulnerable to the accidents of trade and the imbecilities of the system. It is terrible also, however, to be vulnerable not only to propaganda and the self-justifications of others who have an interest in perpetuating ignorance, but to an ignorance that gets built in, inside people themselves; an ignorance that becomes their commonsense. Being a prisoner can come to seem common sense, or can be made to seem what it is to be human. There is one way of responding to this, by pitying the person. As, in certain parts of the novel, Tressell does. But there is also another way, still an original and a lasting way. And that is to say: 'You *are* a prisoner, and you'll only get out of this prison if you'll admit it's a prison. And if you won't call it a prison, I will, and I'll go on calling it a prison, come what may.' This strength, this challenge, is the lasting quality of Tressell's book: Ragged-Arsed Philanthropists!

On First Looking into 'New Lines'

Oh yes of course...
Ask for your country of the mind
To be that cool and temperate.
It will be. Haven't you determined
The answer with your question?
You are that cool: other men's sweat has dried.
You are that temperate: other men have died.

I like no more than you that bibulous density
Mistaking verbal dropsy for immensity
(We catch the manner as we call the odds)
And yet the prophet's and the drunkard's song
Are not, by definition, wrong
And have not really dated.
Is it not just that you've evacuated
(Leaving aside that myth of the dark gods)
All other regions of the mind but those
That can be smiled at in a casual prose?
That is, except when you are writing verse
Which needs at least a minimal intensity:
At least on matters like communication,
Knowing which word, which face, to pull
Until defeat becomes congratulation.

'A neutral tone is nowadays preferred.'
'How dare we now be anything but numb?'
If neutral, how be anything but dumb?
If passionate, yet anxious, what's the word?

—Careful. At least you cannot be exposed.
Is it not really this that you've proposed?

But you are no group at all.
The tone you talk about does not unite,
Being a manner, not a meaning,
As some of you, in time, will recognize.
What can you do about it? Call
Attention to your own real seriousness?
This volume just a literary leaning?
I can't advise. There's never that much choice.
Only I ask you now to realize
While everyone's still learning how to write
What happens when you shrug and drop your voice.

1956

The Tenses of Imagination

Imagination has a history. There are changing and conflicting interpretations of what it is and of its value. Imagination also has a structure, at once grammatical and historical, in the tenses of past, present and future.

Commonsense appears to predicate that it is bad to lack imagination but almost as bad to have or use it too much. This follows from
the complex history of the idea. The negative senses are strong and
early in English: 'full of imagination, of dreads' (1390); 'conjecture
and ymaginacion' (1460). This is the idea of a mental conception of
something not present to the senses, but there was always uncertainty
whether this should be valued as vision or dismissed as fantasy. The
Latin root word had at first a simple physical sense, the making of
images or likenesses; it is linguistically related to the idea of 'imitating'. It developed a later sense of picturing things to oneself, and
it is there that the double judgment starts. As in English in 1576:
'they accounted his undoubted divinations madde imaginations'. Or
as in the lines of *Midsummer Night's Dream*:

> The lunatic, the lover, and the poet
> Are of imagination all compact.

One sees devils, the next sees beauty where there is none, the next
'gives to airy nothing a local habitation and a name'. This last sense
of 'creative imagination' has come through very strongly. It is now
one of the two main positive senses, the other being connected with a
capacity for sympathy and understanding in the ability to 'imagine',
to 'realize', someone's else situation. Yet in context the 'strong imagination' has 'tricks', summoning but often mistaking the objects
of joy or fear.

The ambiguous valuation has persisted, in spite of attempts on the one hand to distinguish and distance 'imagination' from mere 'fancy' and on the other hand to distinguish both from 'reality' and 'facts'. 'Fabricating images without any foundation in reality is distinguished by the name of imagination', Kames wrote in 1762. 'Imagination,' Darwin wrote in 1871, 'is one of the highest prerogatives of Man. By this faculty he unites, independently of the will, former images and ideas, and thus creates brilliant and novel results.' But 'facts and not imagination', almost everyone seemed to say, if the occasion suited.

It is not surprising that so powerful and universal a process should have been so variously interpreted. Moreover, there is no simple way of resolving the ambiguity: much that is valuable has been imagined, and much that is worthless and dangerous. Yet at a different level it may be possible to make some different distinctions. In the course of my own work I have often been struck by the varying tenses of imagination. The sense of imagination as working on the past to create some new present is familiar in Darwin's concept and more widely, over a range from associationist psychology to psychoanalysis. The apparently opposite grammatical sense, rooted in ideas of divination but also given different and more rational bases, turns imagination towards the future, towards foreseeing what will or could happen. At the same time one of the strong current positive senses is essentially involved with the present: having enough imagination to understand what it is like to be in some other contemporary condition: bereaved, unemployed, insane.

These are everyday uses and are all important. But in the processes of writing, the considerations and then the actual practices seem to me to be different, and they are different also according to whether the directive tense of the writing is past, present or future. Writers have related in varying ways to the everyday definitions: to the processes of combining images and ideas to create something brilliant and novel; to the process of imagining, down to fine detail, what could happen, given this selection of characters and cirumstances; and to the processes of empathy, to be able to write of a condition not directly experienced. All these are involved in different kinds of writing, but there is also a major conflict of ideas, in the long argument about whether imagination, in any of these kinds, produces or can produce things more real than what is ordinarily observable, or whether these are specific processes for 'realizing'—embodying in communicable form—what is already, at other levels, undoubtedly real. There is also the popular bypassing of this problem in the idea that imagination creates autonomous objects of art, which have their own rather than some other reality.

I have thought about these problems, in theory and in practice, but the problems of actual work seem to me quite different. I can give examples only from my own writing, though I think—or imagine—that I notice them also in the work of others. They would not be problems of the same kind if I could believe, like most of my contemporaries, that I am sitting here alone doing the work. I am in fact physically alone when I am writing, and I do not believe, taking it all in all, that my work has been less individual, in that defining and valuing sense, than that of others. Yet whenever I write I am aware of a society and of a language which I know are vastly larger than myself: not simply 'out there', in a world of others, but here, in what I am engaged in doing: composing and relating. And if this is so at what can be seen as one end of the process, it seems to be equally true at the other: what is usually defined as what we are 'writing about'. Many writers talk of researching their fiction, not only for historical novels but for contemporary stories and plays. Even tax inspectors will sometimes make an allowance for travel to get what they nicely call 'copy'. I can't be sure, but while I have often visited places and people and asked questions, and also looked things up, this has usually seemed quite separate from writing. Even the ideas and experiences you think you are taking to the blank page come out differently, again and again, as you go through the actual practice, which is one of intense and locally isolated concentration and yet, at the same time, as I have experienced it, a condition of active presence—assisting and resisting—of the wider forces of a language and a society.

I have tried to understand this after the work has been done. For example my 'Welsh Trilogy'—*Border Country*, *Second Generation* and *The Fight for Manod*—has a simple structure of past, present and future. This covers the actual periods of the action; a succession of fathers and sons; even the forms of transport that are among the most evident social relations. Yet I could not get *Border Country* right until it was more than the past—the period of *my* childhood. I had to make that past present in the fully independent and contemporary figure of a father: in fact, as it turned out, two fathers, to make an inherited choice of directions actual. But then this was eventually accessible because it was a lived past. For the sequence during the General Strike I could go to my father's direct memories and to the documents he had kept. Yet I had then to invent episodes which activated the sequence, as distinct from what can happen in memories—especially prepared memories, *memoirs*—when what is there is the summary product. There is then also the process—obvious but quite hard in practice—of seeing this happening to a young man rather than to the old man who is telling you about it. Yet still, while the voice is there, the past has this living connection.

It is proving very different in the trilogy I am now writing, on a vastly greater timescale, following a place and its peoples through very long changes: what I think of as historical rather than as period novel-writing. Its only living connections are the physical presence of the mountains in which and under which so many different kinds of life have been lived, and the physical inheritors of all these lives, who are however *not* historically aware of them, whose memories are recent and whose projections, beyond those memories, are usually (not through their fault; it is what has passed for education) vague and wrong. My wife and I have done long research for these novels: research in archaeology and history and in exploration. It has often proved possible to find a real and surprising base: a different physical landscape, different and yet precise kinds of work and living.

Yet what is then involved in making people move and speak on that base—people 'like ourselves' when the point is so often that they are at once very like and very unlike, and differently so as the real history of the place develops: is that imagination? I suppose it must be; it certainly feels like it, not least in its practical surprises, in what has actually got onto the page. Yet much of the time it is as if prolonged thinking about what I have called the base, especially when this is done, far away from books, on the actual ground, however altered, where it all happened, is not imagination in that inventive sense at all, though of course one is literally inventing. It feels, rather, like some kind of contact, and not irrationally so; like some authentic information, stressing every syllable of that word. Then later of course you have to check up and see if you got the discoverable facts right or at least not wrong: facts that are the condition but only the condition of these other lives that you think you have begun to feel move.

I was recently trying to compare this with what at first sight seems most different from it: the experience of writing a consciously contemporary novel, begun in Oxford on a city much like Oxford, with its places and kinds of work and kinds of people all around me. 'Kinds of people': that was where I hesitated and then took the experience across. For if you read the novel *Second Generation* back, from the finished product—and this is the normal procedure for most people who write about what they call imaginative works—you can see a fairly clear set of social relationships, positive and negative, between the car factory and the university in a single city, and these relationships as embodied in people who, however sharply individualized, are social figures of that set of relationships: liberal don and working-class graduate student; shop steward and his politically and intellectually ambitious wife; the non-political home-centred worker and his family-centred wife. I am forcing myself to describe them in these abstract ways, as a way of facing the problem that this is how they might or even should be construed when in conscious practice nothing of that kind of thinking happened at all. Of course I was strongly aware of what I have been calling the base: the strong social, economic and cultural contrasts between the people around the car factory and the people around the university. At an important level I sought to inform myself more fully about the kinds of life being lived: visiting the car factory and talking to people who worked there as well as more consciously observing the university and political circles in which I had a more connected presence. But still there, in an actual city and in an immediate present, this base was only fully relevant at an early and then at a late stage of the writing: preparation and checking, one might say, though each process is more complicated than that. Indeed it was not so very different, in that available actuality, from the later situation in a much more distant, relatively unknown past. But then how can this be so?

I can say only that what seems to happen is the emergence of a structure of feeling. This is a phrase I have used in analysing works written by others, when I know little or nothing of their making but only what has been made. It is a difficult phrase and idea, but it comes much nearer the experience than any other I know. For I remember being preoccupied, before either the car factory or the

university was there as material for writing, with that extension of
the father-son relationship which comes through as a movement of
generations. I was engaged by the experience which I once tried to
describe as having, simultaneously, a loved physical father and a
quite different 'social father', who in a time of exceptional social and
especially educational mobility was taking on many of a real father's
functions: passing on knowledge and experience and judgments and
values in this differently constituted and discontinuous social situation. Father and son, tutor and student: the relationships are in different dimensions but both, in these circumstances, are real and can
become confused.

The simpler structure of feeling of *Border Country*, within a
relatively more stable world which had nevertheless been brought to
a point of radical choice of values and ways to live, was at once connected and suddenly much more complicated, and the complication
soon settled in the figure of the mother: intellectually ambitious but
without her son's apparently defined place and role. That mother,
necessarily, invoked another mother, so that Kate and Myra were
there with Harold and Robert Lane and Arthur Dean. And then
what happened was what writers often describe, that certain
characters and situations were being strongly felt, and the base which
was there both before and after them was where they lived rather
than where they were lived from.

Perhaps that has to happen, if the people are to come through, but
I am not persuaded by some reductive accounts of the process, in
which persons, 'individuals', simply materialize, in a creative
alchemy, any more than I am persuaded by the theoretically opposite
reductive accounts, in which the writer reads the real structure of the
society and then sets figures to it: types who are then personalized.
What I have called the structure of feeling seems to me different
from either kind of account. It is strongly felt from the beginning, in
the way that important actual relationships are felt, but also it is a
structure and this, I believe, is a particular kind of response to the
real shape of a social order: not so much as it can be documented—
though it ought never, I think, to contradict the documentation—but
as it is in some integrated way apprehended, without any prior
separation of private and public or individual and social experience.

Moreover, so far as I can understand it, this process is not distil-
lation or novel association; it is a formation, an active formation,

that you feel your way into, feel informing you, so that in general and in detail it is not very like the usual idea of imagination—'imagine if...', 'imagine that...'—but seems more like a kind of recognition, a connection with something fully knowable but not yet known.

There must, all the same, be a radical difference in how this happens as it relates on the one hand to societies in which you are living and then to other societies which are at some significant difference in time. I have known this difference, in obvious ways, in trying to approach a kind of life in which, for example, the land was not known and named but was being explored, or in which very different kinds of primary relationship were decisive: the kind of hunting group or family, for example, in which people were close and loving but where the need to abandon a crippled boy or to be pressed, by custom and scarcity, to female infanticide had to be felt not only as alien and distant but as *recognized* in actual people and situations. Perhaps across such distances it is not possible, yet I have not so far found it so. I know that I am getting beyond my own life, as those structures of feeling form, but in a lesser degree that was also what was happening even when writing about contemporary life in a known place. Either past or present, in their ordinary and reasonable temporal senses, seems to have to go through this other process before, as we say, people begin to move and speak. There may be a very general idea of what one is doing, but all the active and detailed formation seems to happen somewhere else. People may call the results 'imagination', and if the connection really happens 'imaginative', but this is where the matter of tense comes in again, for something very different is involved if a writer tries to 'imagine' the future: to 'project' a future, as it is often put.

I am fascinated by the forms of 'future fiction', just as much as by that other large area of 'science fiction'—the very best of it anyway—in which what I see happening is a structure of feeling formed as some alien life and environment. Often this stands out more sharply than the structure of feeling, even a very similar structure, which in the course of writing has been saturated in known and recognizable and connecting detail: our everyday, which can seem and sometimes be the whole object, and is then so different from that distant and surprising and discontinuous 'science fiction' world. I have no direct experience of making that kind of work, though I respect its obviously 'imaginative' reach. But I have now twice—in *The Fight for Manod* and in *The Volunteers*—set novels ahead of their time of writing: in one case more as a plan, in the other case—deliberately and discontinuously—as an action.

I may be wrong but I found in these two very different cases that something much nearer the ordinary idea of imagination was directly involved. I mean that at some important stage, in work with the future tense, a writer sits and *thinks*; assembles and deploys variables; even constructs what in secular planning are called 'scenarios', in the interplay of this and that projected factor, when even the factors are only partly known—their degree of development can be variably estimated—and when their interaction—bringing this factor up, fading that down—is quite radically uncertain. It can of course be argued, and in many cases demonstrated from actual works, that the structures which are projected and realized are usually no more than reproductions of existing structures in externally altered circumstances—the trivial case of those American stories in which Planet Earth encounters aliens through a President and corporations in Washington and New York is only an example of hundreds of more serious cases. Even some of the more surprising futures, in Huxley and Orwell for example, can be shown to rest on striking *interpretations* of the present, from which countervailing or mitigating factors are simply excluded: a negative present, you might say, rather than a positive future.

But beyond reproduction and interpretation there do seem to be cases—Le Guin's *The Dispossessed* is an example—in which there is evidence both of deliberate and sustained thought about possible futures and then, probably both preceding and succeeding this, the discovery of a structure of feeling which, within the parameters of that thought, is in its turn a form of recognition. In *The Fight for Manod* I tried to include some of the relevant thinking and argument about a possible future, but without any convention of cut-off from the present. The whole point of that novel was the relation between necessary and desirable plans for the future and at once the ways in which they get distorted and frustrated and the even more complex ways in which they relate to what is already lived and known and valued. In *The Volunteers* I used a degree of cut-off from the present, to get an action in which both received and abstract values were tested without the familiar context of supporting and reliable institutions embodying them: a possible near future, I then thought, and with whatever variation of date and detail, I am not yet persuaded it was other than closely possible.

In any real future tense, then, what we call imagination seems more like the usual accounts of it than in either present or past tenses. We speculate, we project, we attempt to divine, we figure. The actual writing that goes with that dimension is in its turn distinctive: more general; more immediately accessible to ideas; often more angular and more edged; relatively low in the kind of saturation by detailed and unlooked-for experiences so common and ordinarily so valued in the other tenses. I do not want to turn a contrast of kinds into some order of merit. Each kind of writing does quite different work. But if that is a recognizable kind of imagination—over a range from the secular and political to the solidly traditional and the surprisingly private visions and divinations—there is a problem in using not just the same word but the same concept, pointing to the same general process, in the other tenses. The problem is already there, however, in the everyday range of the word. The mental concept of something not present to the senses, which corresponds to future-writing and to many kinds of fantasy, coexists in the language with the sense of empathy, of feeling our way into a situation which in a general way we know but which we can come to know as it were from the inside—a sense which I think is not far from the idea of discovering and being moved by a structure of feeling within what is already nominally and even carefully known. Yet if the word can be applied to either process, the real processess are still different, and the key difference, as it matters in writing, seems to me essentially a matter of real tense.

There are periods in a culture when what we call real knowledge seems to have to take priority over what is commonly called imagination. In our own image-conscious politics and commerce there is a proliferation of small instrumental professions which claim the sonorous titles of imagination and creativity for what are, when examined, simple and rationalized processes of reproduction and presentation. To know what is happening, in the most factual and down-to-earth ways, is indeed an urgent priority in such a world. A militant empiricism claims all; in a world of rearmament and mass unemployment seems rightly to claim all. Yet it is now the very bafflement and frustration of this militant empricism, and especially

of the best of it, that should hold our attention. It can quickly identify its enemies among the hired image-makers, the instrumental pro-
jectors of the interests of wealth and power. But now, very clearly,
there are other deeper forces at work, which perhaps only imagination, in its full processes, can touch and reach and recognize and embody. If we see this, we usually still hesitate between tenses: between
knowing in new ways the structures of feeling that have directed and
now hold us, and finding in new ways the shape of an alternative, a
future, that can be genuinely imagined and hopefully lived. There are
many other kinds of writing in society, but these now—of past and
present and future—are close and urgent, challenging many of us to
try both to understand and to attempt them.

Index